TINCAN

A History and Stories of a 20th Century Destroyer

USS FISKE

(DD/DDR 842)

&

Fiske Tales-Take Three

Third Edition

Revised August 2019

G. E. Beyer

Dedication

To all that that served aboard the USS *FISKE* from
November 1945 to June 1980, their families and
all other 'Tin Can' sailors of that era.

Initiated by
R. C. Mabe – Association Historian
USS FISKE Association
October 1999

Edited, Revised & Compiled by
G. E. Beyer – Association Historian
USS FISKE Association
August 2019

Preface

The USS *Fiske* was a Gearing Class destroyer, the last of the World War II design destroyers. She served the US Navy from November 1945 until June 1980 and was then transferred to the Turkish Navy where she served as the TCG *Piyale Pasa* (D350). The former *Fiske* was heavily damaged in 1996 when she ran aground and was scrapped in early 1999. Altogether this ship served two navies for over 54 years.

When this book was first conceived it was to be a history with first person stories blended in. Over the years it has become more of a scrapbook. A collection of personal stories with history inserted. It has been said before that if something isn't written down it may as well have never happened. It is for that reason that this work came into being. I believe that the stories contained within these pages have as much importance as the 'Big Picture' histories that are written.

History is so much more than places and dates, winners and losers. It is the stories of those that were 'there' that make our history. Their stories add texture and detail to history. They are presented as I received them. These stories are their 'stories' as they lived them. I believe every word to be the truth as it was perceived and remembered by those that wrote them.

The original subtitle of this work, 'An Incomplete History of the USS Fiske DD/DDR 842', simply meant that it probably never can be completed. Too much time has gone by, too many of those that served have passed on and too many documents lost in files and bureaucracy.

Some of the stories probably could not happen today. It was a period in time when the world was less complex. There were more black and white, less shades of gray. As one contributor said, "Different world, different Navy". I miss that world and that Navy.
G. E. Beyer

The Soul of a Ship

Now, some say that men make a ship and her fame
As she goes on her way down the sea:
That the crew which first man her will give her a name Good,
bad, or whatever may be.
Those coming after fall in line
And carry the tradition along –
If the spirit was good, it will always be fine –
If bad, it will always be wrong/
The soul of a ship is a marvelous thing.
Not made of its wood or its steel,
But fashioned of mem'ries and songs that men sing,
And fed by the passions men feel.
It's built of ambition, of jealousy, strife,
Of friendship, of love, and of fear;
It includes almost all of the makings of life;
It's nurtured on grumble – and cheer.
The soul of a ship is a molder of men –
Her spirit lives on through the years.
As she started her life, so she is in the end;
She shares each new crewmember's hopes and his fears.
And each man who joins feels the breath of her life –
As he stands up and takes heart again –
So he takes to himself the old sea as his wife,
And the ship has made a man among men.

Arthur A. Ageton
Naval Officer's Guide – 1943

Chapter I
Ship's Namesake
Rear Admiral Bradley Allen Fiske
13 June 1854 – 6 April 1942

Bradley Allen Fiske was born in Lyons, New York to the Reverend William Allen Fiske and Susan (Bradley) Fiske. He was the oldest of five children. They were Frances Eliza Holt Davis (Fiske) 12/1855 to 12/1931; Sophia Hurlburt Fiske 6/1859 to 5/1863; William Clarence Fiske 1/1861 to 8/1941; and John Brown Bradley Fiske 2/1863 to unknown. Bradley Allen's youth was spent in New York and then in Cleveland and Cincinnati, Ohio.

He received his appointment to the U. S. Naval Academy from Ohio on 24 September 1870 and graduated, commissioned as an Ensign, in June 1874.During his early service years he served onboard the Sloops-of-War *Pensacola* and *Plymouth*, both ships operating on the Pacific Station (another name for the Pacific Squadron), operating primarily between the west coast of the Americas and the Hawaiian Islands but eventually expanding to cover the entire Pacific Ocean. He also served onboard the paddle steamer *Powhatan* in the Atlantic.

During this period he received instruction in the then young field of torpedo warfare. Fiske was promoted to Master in 1881 and Lieutenant in 1887. In 1882 he married Josephine Harper, the daughter of the man that published 'Harper's Bazaar', and they had one daughter, Caroline Harper Fiske, born 29 June 1885. During that decade he had training ship duty onboard the Sloop-of-War USS *Saratoga* and the Sailing/Steam Frigate USS *Minnesota*. The *Minnesota* had been severely damaged by the Ironclad CSS *Virginia* (the former USS *Merrimack*) during the Civil War but had been rebuilt and served until 1898.

He also served in the South Atlantic Squadron onboard the steam sloop USS *Brooklyn* and was twice assigned to the Bureau of Ordinance in Washington, DC. As one of the Navy's most technologically astute officers he supervised the installation of the ordinance onboard the USS *Atlanta* between 1886 and 1888. The *Atlanta* was one first of the "A B C D Ships", the first of the Navy's steel hulled ships. *Atlanta* was followed by the *Boston, Chicago* and *Dolphin.*

OFFICERS, SECOND BATTALION BLUE JACKETS.
Lt. Fiske is fourth from left with holstered pistol at Camp Osceola

After doing that short stint of duty at Camp Osceola on Pensacola Bay, Florida in 1888 Fiske was involved in the trials of the large caliber compressed air guns onboard the USS *Vesuvius*. These guns made very little noise when fired but they were fixed so that the entire ship had to be pointed at the intended target. It was a promising experiment but it just didn't pan out.

He also was involved in the installation of electrical lighting onboard the Navy's new cruiser the USS *Philadelphia*. The *Philadelphia* was the US Navy's first ship with electric lights.

The USS *Vesuvius*

On May 1st, 1898 the American Fleet under Admiral Dewey trounced the Spanish Fleet under the command of Admiral Montojo in Manila Bay during the Spanish-American War. It was during this engagement that Fiske utilized one of his inventions, the stadimeter, to accurately direct the American fleet's naval gunnery at the Spanish fleet.

Lt. Fiske's post during this battle was 40 feet up the mast to get a clear view to better ascertain the range to the Spanish ships. Admiral Dewey decorated Fiske for "Heroic Conduct" in helping in this action. As was often the case at those times it was said Fiske was 'mentioned in dispatches'.

Breech loading large caliber gun onboard USS *Atlanta*

Fiske followed the invention of the stadimeter with the development of optical gun sights and an optical rangefinder. Fiske (and others) is credited with improving the range and accuracy of naval gunfire from 6,000 yards in 1898 to almost 20,000 yards by WW I. Fiske also was one of the first proponents of naval air power. He held a patent for the first aerial torpedo launched from an aircraft. During the years between the Spanish-American War and World War I, Fiske advanced rapidly in rank: to Lieutenant Commander in 1899, Commander in 1903, and Captain in 1907.

He held many responsible positions on shore and at sea, serving as an Inspector of Ordnance, Executive Officer of USS *Yorktown* and the battleship *Massachusetts*, Commanding Officer of the monitor *Arkansas* and cruisers *Minneapolis* and *Tennessee*, had recruiting duty, served as Captain of the Yard at the Philadelphia Navy Yard, attended the Naval War College and was a member of the Navy's General Board and the Army-Navy Joint Board, among other assignments.

Bradley Allen became a Rear Admiral in August of 1911, consecutively commanding three different divisions of the Atlantic Fleet as well as serving as the Secretary of the Navy's Aide for Inspections. In February 1913 he was appointed Aide for Operations, a post that later became that of Chief of Naval Operations. As Aide for Operations, Fiske forcefully advocated the creation of a naval general staff and the elevation of the Nation's preparedness for war. Admiral Fiske is also credited with creating the Naval Districts.

Captain Fiske with King Neptune and His court on board the USS *Tennessee* crossing the Equator

Fiske's support of naval aviation and other issues put him at odds with the newly appointed Secretary of the Navy, Josephus Daniels.

Daniels was a newspaper editor from North Carolina that was a strong supporter of President Wilson. As a Dixiecrat he was for segregation and Prohibition. Daniels served as the Secretary of the Navy from 1913 to 1921. The animosity between he and Fiske (one of their opposing views was the removal of all alcohol from naval vessels under General Order 99) lead to Admiral Fiske retiring in June 1916 after serving for 41 years.

An excellent argument could be made that Admiral Fiske should have been the first Chief of Naval Operations but for the conflicts between himself and Secretary Daniels. Fiske was an inventor of note in the field of gunnery and was a perceptive viewer of the potential held by naval airpower. Admiral Fiske was also a strong advocate of navy preparedness. He was active in naval affairs throughout the 1920's and into the '30's serving as a consultant during that period. Fiske was a prolific writer and innovator. He held numerous patents on navigational instruments, naval guns and other electrical systems.

Fiske's biography, written after the Spanish-American War, contained many stories of his days at the Naval Academy and his postings after graduation from Annapolis reveal Admiral Fiske to be a fairly normal young naval officer. In one story he tells of attending a gala in Washington, DC and, 'after many champagne cocktails', awoke lying on the steps of his host's home in his dress white uniform

Admiral Fiske died on April 6th, 1942 at the age of 87 and is buried in Arlington National Cemetery, Section 2, Site 1233 along with his wife Josephine Harper [d 10-2-1919] and his daughter Caroline [d 3-9-1967]. Based on the fact that Caroline is buried alongside her parents in Arlington National Cemetery it appears that she never married.

No record has been found of Caroline Fiske ever having attended the commissioning of either ship honoring her father.

With Caroline's passing in 1967 that branch of the Fiske family came to an end.

Rear Admiral Bridger & Fiske in Mexico in 1914

Editor's notes: Josephus Daniels may have been a thorn in Fiske's side but he did do some things of note. The aforementioned Article 99 is still in effect today. He is unconsciously remembered every time someone says, 'let's have a cup of Joe'. He also suggested to President Wilson that all federal employees should be White. This created segregation in the Federal employment system until President Truman started to end it after WWII.

He did do one very good thing. After Mexico nationalized their petroleum industry in the 1930's Daniels, as the US Ambassador to Mexico, convinced FDR not to got to war with Mexico. All the American oil companies were all for going to war, insisting they get their property back. Daniel's argument was based on the facts that 1-

We weren't prepared for a war with anybody. And 2 – He thought that we were headed towards another war in Europe in the not too distant future. He was right on both counts.

One additional note: When Daniels proposed reparations be paid by the Mexican government to the American Oil Companies for their lost property the Mexican government agreed to repay the companies based the amount declared on those companies' tax returns. Since the oil companies had been substantially under-reporting the incomes from their oil production they received only a small percentage of the true value of their lost property. As Shakespeare put it, "They were hoist on their own petard."

All in all, Daniels was definitely a man of his times. He would not be cheered for anything that he did then in today's environment but he surely left his mark in history.

A Destroyer

A destroyer is a lovely ship, probably the nicest fighting ship of all.

Battleships are a little like steel cities or great factories of destruction.

Aircraft carriers are floating flying fields.

Even cruisers are big pieces of machinery, but a destroyer is all boat.

In the beautiful clean lines of her, in her speed and roughness, in her curious gallantry, she is completely a ship, in the old sense.

John Steinbeck
1902 - 1968

Forward

Those of us that served during the last century were not the professionals we have today in the Post-9/11, no draft world. Every sailor was a volunteer but usually we were just avoiding being drafted into the Army.

The draft was still in effect. I was in Boot Camp at Great Lakes when I received my draft notice. I gave that letter to my Company Commander, AO1 Rivers, and he took it from there. I knew that I wanted to see the world but I didn't want to have to walk there.

The Navy, like all the armed forces, practices everything they do. Repeating every drill, event and exercise until doing that task becomes almost automatic. A task done without conscious thought when events call for quick action.

Many of the 'Tales' in this book involve doing what we were trained to do. These evolutions, as the Navy is fond of calling them, are often routine and boring for the non-participants. Those that are involved in these routine evolutions often find themselves, literally, in life or death situations.

As 'Tin Can' sailors we had to depend on the other crewman to do their jobs as well or better than we did ours. From the FN's on sight glass watch in the Fire Rooms to the SN's serving as lookouts on the bridge wings and every sailor and officer between we had to rely on each other to 'do our jobs'.

This was a unique environment. It was a small town where everyone had to depend on others to live every day. We may not have liked everybody in our 'hamlet' but it was our town and we were proud of being part of it.

What follows is our effort to breathe life in what has passed. We believe every word in these personal stories is the truth as the authors recall those events. I've done my best to verify the history and the 'Fiske Tales' included. We hope to provide some insights into our world and preserve some things that might be forgotten.

Chapter II
The First Fiske (DE 143)
August 1943 – August 1944
Call Letter: NQDA

The first *Fiske*, an Edsall-class destroyer escort, was laid down on 4 January 1943 by the Consolidated Steel Corporation of Orange, Texas. She was launched on 14 March 1943 and commissioned on 25 August 1943. *FISKE* was sponsored by Mrs. H. G. Chalkley and her first Commanding Officer was Lt. Commander R. P. Walker.

She began service as a convoy escort with a voyage from Norfolk to Coco Solo, C. Z. to New York between 12 and 25 November 1943. On 3 December *Fiske* cleared Norfolk and the first of three assignments from Norfolk to New York to Casablanca.

During the third of these, on 20 April 1944, her convoy came under attack by German torpedo bombers in the western Mediterranean but none came within range of *Fiske*.

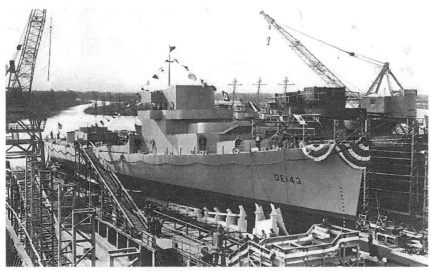

Launching of the DE 143 at Port Orange, Texas

Completing her Casablanca runs with her return to New York on 21 May 1944 *Fiske* joined the hunter-killer group Task Group 22.6 formed around USS *Wake Island* (CVE 65) at Norfolk on 10 June 1944. Five days later her group sailed to patrol across the Atlantic, putting into Casablanca to replenish in late July.

Fiske (DE 143) & *Douglas Howard* (DE 138) shortly before the torpedo strike on *Fiske*

On 2 August, during a special hunt for submarines known to be transmitting weather information from a station in the central Atlantic, *Fiske* and USS *Douglas L. Howard* (DE 138) were detached to investigate a visual contact both had made. The contact – north of the Azores – was the surfaced U 804, which quickly dove, but the two escorts picked it up on sonar and began their attack approach. Suddenly, *Fiske* was torpedoed on her starboard side amidships and within 10 minutes she broke in two and had to be abandoned. All crewmen that survived the explosion were rescued by the USS *Farquhar* (DE 139).

Of the 214 total compliment onboard that day there was 1 Officer and 32 Enlisted killed. There were 64 Enlisted and 1 Officer wounded in the attack. Two of the enlisted wounded later died of their injuries and are included in the total that died that day. All of the wounded and other survivors were taken onboard the *Farquhar*. Also included in the total that died are Warren Walden, F1/c and Charles Vasslowski, MoM1/c. Both men apparently went down with the ship.

Fiske just before she broke in half

One of the wounded survivor's, PhM2/c Horace E Cornell was transferred (among others) to the Naval Hospital in Chelsa, MA. The children and grandchildren of Horace E. Cornell Jr., only recently learned that he was onboard the *Fiske* at that time. They learned of the history of his naval service after he died in January 2014. Cornell was in the hospital until 29 August 1944.

Recently located records confirm that PhM2c Cornell was awarded the Purple Heart for the injuries he received that day onboard *Fiske*. He was buried with full military honors.

The stern of the *Fiske* slips beneath the waves

A recently discovered story in the *Charlotte Sun* newspaper of Port Charlotte, FL told the story of Ted Schultz, MoM3. Schultz was in the Engine Room when the torpedo struck and he along with the rest of the survivors in that space escaped out a hatch on the fantail.

When the order to 'Abandon Ship' was given the more severely wounded were put in the liferafts and the other survivors hung onto the rafts. The *Farquhar* picked them up after 3 to 4 hours in the water.

Both Cornell and Schultz went on to serve on other ships and were honorably discharged after the war. Horace E. Cornell had a long teaching career in the Mid-West after the war.

Ted Schultz ended up in Erie, PA where he and his wife purchased a beer distributorship. They ran that business for the next twentyfive years before retirng to Port Charlotte, FL in 1979.

The _Fiske_'s rescue ship, the destroyer escort USS _Farquhar_ (DE-139), is shown here approaching an escort carrier in October, 1944. After the _Fiske_ was torpedoed on August 2, 1944, the _Farquhar_ (Lt. Cdr. D. E. Walter, USNR) first conducted a sonar search of the area and then began rescuing survivors. In the next 2-1/2 hours the _Farquhar_ remained dead in the water while she picked up 182 survivors and 4 bodies. Two of the survivors died on board from their wounds, and many others were seriously injured. All survivors were weak and chilled. About half of them had to be bodily hauled aboard. (U.S. Navy Photograph.)

Chapter III

(DD 842)

November 1945 – April 1952

Call Sign NBBU

Motto: "Detect and Destroy"

In keeping with time-honored naval tradition Hull 262 at the Bath Iron Works, Bath, Maine became *Fiske* to honor a ship lost in wartime. *Fiske* was sponsored by Mrs. Archie Ribbentrop. The second *Fiske* was christened and launched on 8 September 1945. Mrs. Ribbentrop was the mother of MoM3 Walter Ribbentrop who was onboard the first *Fiske*. One might question how out of the 33 that died that day the mother of possibly the youngest crewmember to die on August 2 1944 was selected. An inquiry was made to the Society of Sponsors of the US Navy with that question. The following answer was received. Mrs. Linda Winter, Society President, offered the following explanation, "It is possible that Mrs. Ribbentrop was selected simply because she lived in Freeport, Maine (where Walter was raised) and was close to Bath." This theory can easily be given credence for a couple of reasons. The launching occurred just less that a month after VJ Day (August 14th) and the Navy were already making plans to halt ships under construction that hadn't reached that level of completion. *Fiske* was commissioned at Boston Naval Shipyard on 28 November 1945 with CDR C. H. Smith commanding.

USS *Fiske* painted for WWII

[As a short aside - of the over 100 destroyers and destroyer escorts built by Bath Iron Works between 1939 and 1945 only seven were lost due to enemy action. Ships built by BIW became known as 'lucky ships' throughout the Navy]

Copies of the first day's Ship's Log listing all members of the commissioning crew are shown below. It is interesting to find that an injury to a crewmember is mentioned during the very first entry on the Ship's Log. This injury to S2c H. Pressley occurred during an 'unauthorized' demonstration of the ready service rack in Mount 52.

PAGE 3

NAVPERS-LR (REV. 1-44)

DECK LOG—REMARKS SHEET

UNITED STATES SHIP _____ FISKE _____ DD842

Wednesday 28, November , 19 45

The U.S.S. Fiske (DD642) was built at Bath, Maine by the Bath Iron Works Corporation, and was launched on 8 September 1945. The U.S.S. Fiske is named in honor of the late Rear Admiral Bradley Allen Fiske, U.S. Navy and is the second vessel to bear his name. The ship is moored port side to Pier #2, U.S. Navy Yard, Charlestown, Massachusetts, receiving all services from the pier.

At 1430 the crew and officers went on board and were paraded aft for the Commissioning Ceremony. At 1505 Captain P. M. Rhea, U.S. Navy came on board. He read his orders, and at 1515 the band played the National Anthem, the Colors and Commissioning Pennant were hoisted and the ship was placed in full commission. At 1516 Commander Charles H. Smith read his orders (BuPers dispatch of 8 July 1945) and assumed command of the ship. At 1517 the first watch was set and Lieutenant O. F. Ames, U.S.N.R. assumed the duties of Officer of the Deck.

The following named officers and enlisted men are attached to and serving on board:

NAME	FILE NUMBER	RANK	NAME	FILE NUMBER	RANK
Smith, C. H.	71332	Comdr.	Young, J. P.	413840	Ens.
Sharer, Jr. D. M.	85676	Lt. Comdr.	Waters, J. P.	440473	Ens.
Sell, L. H.	165625	Lieut.	Kelsey, C. B.	309757	Lt. (jg)
Ames, O. F.	244715	Lieut.	Lesch, H. T.	341078	Lt. (jg)
Kerr, R. B.	332891	Lt. (jg)	Rusche, J. P.	448886	Ens.
Leamcks, W. H.	200125	Ens.	Niemeyer, R. T.	161481	Lieut.
Severin, A. G.	431948	Ens.	Sutton, R. M.	269272	Lt. (jg)
Moorman, Jr. A. J.	185661	Lieut.	Warrick, J. W.	326832	Lt. (jg)
Whitehouse, Jr. N. A.	184972	Lieut.	Ukropina, J. R.	432047	Ens.
Coburn, J. F.	441799	Ens.	Wagner, L. H.	441855	Ens.
Foster, D. G.	439346	Ens.			

NAME	SERVICE NUMBER	RATE	NAME	SERVICE NUMBER	RATE
Adcock, Orson N.	783 67 63	S1c	Coughlin, Donald J.	807 32 39	WT3c
Agricola, Otto J.	509 75 84	Y1c	Crawford, Carrington	935 87 64	S2c
Allen, S. E.	201 50 81	CTT	Creban, Paul J.	244 75 16	Y2c
Baggett, James J.	645 06 04	S1c	Crows, James H.	266 64 12	Ck2c
Bainbridge, James Leo	368 49 89	CQM	Cross, Richard E.	570 64 28	S2c (I)
Baird, James T.	910 90 40	S2c (RdMO)	Culbertson, Jesse E.	635 29 31	WT3c
Bales, William F.	845 66 19	MM2c	Dail, Percy W.	936 91 26	S1c (SC)
Barbatelli, A. L.	907 32 07	F1c	Davanzo, Paul A.	814 59 90	F1c
Bartlett, John E., Jr.	748 86 90	S2c (RdN)	Davis, Clayton B.	932 18 44	S1c
Baucom, Reache J.	264 68 62	S2c	Davis, Ephram G.	265 75 90	BM1c
Beattie, Robert Jr.	313 73 79	S1c	Demichele, Nolm	949 62 41	QM3c
Beatty, Charles L., Jr.	753 64 96	S1c (GM)	Donahoe, Daniel G.	892 18 00	EM3c
Belch, Shirley R.	385 98 82	M1c	Dosch, William A.	811 38 70	QM3c
Bamboos, Marcus F.	951 48 56	S1c (FC)	Dougherty, Robert D.	709 60 03	CM2c
Bieber, Jerome S.	715 44 24	S2c	Dulen, Henry L.	868 74 40	RM2c
Bittner, Tillian S.	975 58 40	S2c (FC)	Dunnigan, Robert A.	713 65 34	S1c (GM)
Bjelke, John G.	715 43 04	S2c	Elvin, Franklin J.	611 94 49	WT3c
Bletter, Murray	910 70 04	S2c	Endlich, George F.	715 65 63	S2c
Blossom, Ernest L.	765 13 50	S2c	Erath, A. E.	275 10 68	S1c
Bogdanski, Henry J.	715 51 94	F2c	Estepp, Talmadge O.	930 79 71	F2c
Bouzou, John Leo	301 50 14	CEM	Farrell, Harold G.	804 72 52	S1c (FC)
Bowmcu, John H.	922 97 00	S1c	Fast, Frank J.	627 94 06	BM2c
Boyd, Norman J.	338 44 37	F1c	Field, Robert H.	362 74 09	TM2c
Brendelson, Donald	306 22 66	MM2c	Fields, Robert E.	850 99 07	SC2c
Brewar, Foster W.	922 78 25	S1c	Fishack, Eugene F.	759 16 34	S2c
Butler, William J.	835 48 95	SM2c	Fleming, Robert J.	609 79 45	F1c
Calvin, Virgil L.	337 31 40	GM2c	Formica, Frank H.	382 74 09	EM2c
Callicoat, Paul E.	266 30 49	MM3c	Freeman, Roy L.	311 61 89	FM2c
Campbell, Arthur J.	262 50 39	SC1c	French, Richard M.	247 49 66	S2c
Campbell, George R.	252 64 38	F2c	Fray, Richard C.	247 29 22	S2c
Campbell, Sheldon L.	932 94 87	F2c	Fusco, Caesar R.	910 91 83	S2c
Carter, James	575 40 44	ST3c	Garcia, Catalino	557 70 23	StM2c
Gersosimo, Leonard	252 33 48	S2c	Gates, William R.	247 37 74	S2c
Cochran, William	376 93 57	GM2c	Gettys, William P.	252 22 31	S2c
Coffman, Joseph A.	339 21 62	S2c	Giffi, Costanzo J.	205 33 72	MM2c
Cohen, Abraham N.	202 82 75	S1c	Gillette, Robert S.	976 22 78	S2c
Colburn, Clint R.	982 67 26	S2c	Gordon, Edward	810 15 23	EM3c
Gollman, Howard L.	947 12 43	RT1c	Greten, Charles L.	283 77 24	SoM2c
Conaway, Robert R.	247 31 77	S2c	Hall, Boyd A.	283 67 79	MM3c
Cone, Bernard R.	360 23 55	BM1c	Hall, Mathew J.	378 94 74	S1c (GM)

APPROVED:

C. H. SMITH, Comdr., U.S.N. COMMANDING

EXAMINED:

W. A. Whitehouse U.S.N. NAVIGATOR

TO BE FORWARDED DIRECT TO THE BUREAU OF NAVAL PERSONNEL AT THE END OF EACH MONTH

26

NAVPERS-134 (REV. 1-44)

DECK LOG—REMARKS SHEET

PAGE 5

UNITED STATES SHIP FISKE DD842

Wednesday 28, November , 19 45.
(Day) (Date) (Month)

(Con't)

NAME	SERVICE NUMBER	RATE	NAME	SERVICE NUMBER	RATE
Hall, James H.	266 28 58	MM3c	Miante, James B.	834 81 89	QM1c
Haltigen, Emmet A.	714 32 83	S1c (FC)	Miller, Walter B.	819 21 50	SoM3c
Hamby, William H., Jr.	294 92 93	Wt1c	Mixon, Lonnie J.	269 03 18	MM2c
Harris, Earnest	971 27 35	StM2c	Mook, Carl N.	252 25 93	S2c
Harris, J. J.	936 11 15	StM1c	Morgan, Matthew	714 62 30	S2c (SM
Harris, Russel	982 05 75	S1c	Morrison, Archie O.	557 60 00	S2c
Heberlein, D. M., Sr.	959 26 00	TM3c	Moyer, George N.	245 52 52	F2c
Helton, Robert D.	756 33 09	S2c	Muenze, Robert J.	896 39 62	MM3c
Hendricks, George H.	690 87 77	S2c	Mulkey, James A.	575 72m34	S2c
Hess, Jerome	826 78 31	RM3c	Myers, John H.	759 28 90	F2c
Hickson, Thomas	711 16 56	GM3c	Newhall, Everett W.	212 79 90	WT2c
Hilden, Veldo E.	209 06 79	SoM3c	Nobae, Les	873 29 77	F1c
Hodulik, George T.	712 23 68	WT3c	Newell, Malcolm C.	601 10 93	MM3c
Howard, Green H.	261 49 32	CCM	O'Rourke, Lawrence E.	202 21 50	MM1c
Howell, Jack D.	252 63 86	S2c	Padgett, Eulitt M.	556 97 31	S1c
Huenfield, Marion C.	372 14 64	CRM	Panatone, Donald J.	385 90 72	MM2c
Hunter, A. C.	817 78 15	StM1c	Paulovich, Pete	252 33 12	S2c (Rd
Hurt, Venon D.	671 43 59	SF3c	Peifer, Robert B.	248 63 14	F2c
Hutchins, Hubert C.	238 80 33	RM1c	Pickel, Edward H.	266 68 40	FC3c
Iorio, Hohn H.	817 58 33	MM3c	Piercey, William H.	295 65 53	EM1c
Jars, William C.	715 81 43	S2c (RdM)	Posinak, Eli	857 77 05	S1c
Jasiek, John J.	875 67 19	RKr3c	Powell, Sam H.	266 64 33	SC2c
Jeffrey, Billie O	266 43 77	Ma3c	Prey, Edward F.	212 78 81	EM3c
Jordan, Alfred	560 84 54	MM3c	Pressley, Harrington	970 66 92	S2c
Kahn, Lawrence	715 64 47	S2c (RdM)	Prince, Thomas H.	715 53 01	S2c
Kaja, Chester L.	306 01 09	GM3c	Quance, Earl S.	751 18 57	S2c (rd
Katusz, Joseph T.	248 59 28	S2c	Reed, Henry E.	872 87 59	SM2c
Kasimir, James J.	910 05 62	S2c	Ricker, William E.	970 69 28	S2c
Kelly, Francis, E.	250 59 36	MM1c	Rigg, Rex E.	945 19 53	F1c
King, Henry R.	909 20 13	F2c	Roach, Raymond L.	943 51 30	F1c
Kline, Loring	258 29 86	Wt1c	Rooth, John L.	706 48 34	F1c
Knight, Wilner B.	560 89 41	S1c	Rothman, Robert F.	372 21 60	GCX
Kidd, James A.	875 37 42	Cox	Rudnicki, Gus J.	873 30 56	F1c
Kohan, William	252 22 32	S2c	Ruth, Russel B.	706 17 95	MM1c
Kovacs, Steve E.	909 96 41	S2c	Ryan, John C.	782 98 43	S2c
Krause, H. F.	848 73 08	FC1c	Salassi, Peter A.	357 17 02	RdM2c
Krohak, Stanley M.	983 73 33	S2c	Sanches, Hilary E.	889 66 25	SC3c
Krots, T. S.	611 67 50	B2c	Saryur, Arthur B.	561 11 56	S2c
Lacey, William O.	952 01 97	S1c	Scamihorn, Charles	291 54 45	CRMA
Laird, Raymort	357 62 60	GM2c	Scarborough, Charlie	934 90 08	S2c
Largent, M. D.	550 32 34	S1c (RT)	Schaub, Arthur E.	984 34 22	S1c
Le Blanc, Joseph L.	667 24 10	GM3c	Schroeder, Erwin J. R.	338 47 65	F1c
Lewis, Robert J.	871 75 72	GM2c	Schuck, John H.	245 31 15	F2c
Lewis, William F.	375 95 14	CHM	Sehr, John J.	626 73 57	MM2c
Lindsey, Roy O.	982 38 16	S2c (RdM)	Simpson, James	247 09 84	S2c
Lindstrom, Harold, Jr.	321 85 59	S1c	Skettingland, K. R.	553 17 27	SF2c
Linn, Leonard R.	970 76 96	S2c	Smith, Arvel E.	932 72 35	F2c
Lipinski, Edward P.	899 39 37	F2c (EM)	Snyder, Maurice	783 17 27	S2c
Little, Charles A.	751 06 17	S2c (RdM)	Snyder, Robert T.	983 57 83	S2c
Long, Earl A.	343 01 29	S1c	Spainer, Franklin J.	715 71 98	F2c
Lyman, G. A.	321 03 26	CMM	Spates, David J.	256 42 82	EM3C
Martin, Everett	236 64 97	MM1c	Speight, Edward J.	970 93 89	STM2c
Martin, James D.	871 47 48	F1c	Spondike, Nicholas J.	286 25 08	F2c
Martin, John E.	934 97 90	S2c	Steinfurth, Willias L	246 01 91	Rm3c
Marty, Shelton E.	976 87 28	S2c	Stevenson, Donald E.	251 99 71	S2c
Matecki, John E.	894 86 19	S1c	Stokes, John C.	245 90 88	RM3c
McClintic, Robert D.	627 79 86	WoM41c	Sundin, Robert L.	756 34 47	S1c (RM)
Mc Cown, James I.	669 16 84	RM1c	Sutton, Billy	641 70 01	SK3c
Mc Donald, Curtis J.	275 35 03	F2c	Sweeney, Robert F.	928 04 61	S2c
Mc Elaney, William G.	402 30 74	RM3c	Talarico, Lawrence J.	905 99 22	S1c (FC)
Mc Govern, Robert W.	691 44 47	F1c	Talley, Edward W. Jr.	782 98 42	S2c
Mc Greehan, M. J., Jr.	608 73 04	GM2c	Thomas, Dennis M.	756 38 36	S2c
Mc Hugh, Francis J.	651 92 45	F1c (MoM)	Thomas, Francis E.	557 55 49	S2c
Mc Que, Joseph H.	818 31 88	MaM3c	Templeton, William O.	722 11 99	F1c
Meny, Lawrence J.	864 02 23	SSML3c	Tower, Harold J.	807 67 04	S1c (SM
Mezick, Newton C.	759 09 53	S2c	Twiss, Howard B.	981 51 67	F1c

APPROVED:

C. E. SMITH, Comdr., U S N COMMANDING

EXAMINED:

W. W. Whitehouse, U S N NAVIGATOR

TO BE FORWARDED DIRECT TO THE BUREAU OF NAVAL PERSONNEL AT THE END OF EACH MONTH

U S GOVERNMENT PRINTING OFFICE

NAVPERS-154 (REV. 1-44)

DECK LOG—REMARKS SHEET

UNITED STATES SHIP _____ FISKE _____ DD 842 _____ Wednesday 28 November, 19 45
(Day) (Date) (Month)

(Con't.)

NAME	SERVICE NUMBER	RATE
Vann, Roy M.	272 98 69	FCO3c
Varner, James A.	252 27 79	F2c
Varney, Ernest R.	579 91 11	S2c
Walker, Richard A.	942 04 76	F2c
Wallitsch, Louis A.	205 60 49	F1c
Walton, Howard D.	560 80 62	S1c
Ware, A. R.	272 95 90	FC2c
Watson, H. W.	664 57 79	FC1c
Weidner, Marvin C.	759 14 32	S2c
Weissenborn, Stuart	682 97 54	PhM3c
Weltzin, H. C. Jr.	329 19 21	WT1c
Westbrook, Raymond C.	957 75 05	F1c(EM)
Wetzstoon, George G.	554 94 50	S2c
Wewiorski, J.	400 14 10	CWT
Whetzel, William J.	753 82 66	F2c
Whitefield, William A.	351 06 32	WT2c
Wilhelm, Henry J.	570 67 46	S1c(Y)
Williams, Kenneth W.	557 63 78	S2c
Willis, S. J.	934 36 83	RT2c
Willis, William C.	248 80 59	F2c
Wilson, Raymond L.	269 46 35	S2c
Wilson, Robert L.	256 55 40	WM3c
Wolfe, John M.	264 66 16	S2c
Wood, Lawrence R.	970 66 81	S2c
Wright, Roscoe P.	804 22 20	S2c
Wright, W. F.	611 96 46	FC2c
York, Leslie S.	951 95 87	S1c
Young, John H.	925 82 32	F2c
Zarcone, Joseph C.	205 30 86	WT3c

W. A. WHITEHOUSE, Jr.,
Lieut., USN

1515-1600. Moored port side to pier # 2, U.S.Navy Yard, Charlestown, Mass. Receiving all
services from the pier. Ships present are various units of U.S.Fleet. SOPA is Fleet Administration
Officer. 1550 Pressley, H., 970 66 92, S2c, USNR, while making an unauthorized demonstration
of equipment caught his left wrist in the rotating ready service rack of upper handling room,
5"/.38 cal. mount #2. Rotation of ready service rack stopped upon proper functioning of
interlocks and prevented serious injury. Man suffered cracked wrist bone and was treated
at the yard dispensary and returned on board.

O. F. Ames
O. F. AMES,
Lieut., USNR

16-20. Moored as before.

W. H. LEMACKS,
Ens., USN

20-24 Moored as before.

R. W. Niemeyer
R. W. NIEMEYER,
Lieut., USNR

APPROVED:

C. H. SMITH, Comdr., U. S. N. COMMANDING

EXAMINED:

W. A. Whitehouse Lieut. U. S. N. NAVIGATOR

TO BE FORWARDED DIRECT TO THE BUREAU OF NAVAL PERSONNEL AT THE END OF EACH MONTH

U. S. GOVERNMENT PRINTING OFFICE: 1944 O- 578941

When commissioned in November 1945 *Fiske* carried the then standard armament package of three dual 5"/38 gun mounts; three 40mm quadruple mount AA guns; two 40mm twin mount AA guns; five 20mm twin mount AA guns; one quintuple 21" torpedo tubes; six 'hedgehog' mounts; and, two depth charge racks. The additional 40mm and 20mm AA guns were added to all destroyers shortly after Japan started using kamikaze attacks against our fleets. All of this armament was packed onto the decks of a ship that was 390'6" long and 41'1" at her widest point.

With this much armament onboard the Gunnery Department was a large percentage of the crew. A look at the commissioning day roster reveals several rated Gunner's Mates and Specialist ratings that can be assumed to be involved in effectively employing that firepower. One of those crewmen was GM2 Robert J. Lewis. His family submitted the story below.

The 'Gun Boss'

While we were in the Charleston Naval Yard for final outfitting the Gunnery Officer invited some of us to his home in Boston. It was a very nice place and he was a very nice guy. We were served drinks by a Butler. I can't remember his name but I do remember that the address on his house had only one number!

Robert J. Lewis, GM2 1945-46

A check of the ship's roster indicates that the 'Gun Boss' was probably Lt. Oliver F. Ames who had served as Assistant Gunnery Officer onboard the USS *Little* (DD803). The *Little* was sunk by kamikazes on 3 May 1945 with a loss of 62 lives and 27 wounded out of a crew of 200. Lt. Ames received a Bronze Star for his actions onboard the *USS Little*.

Lt. Ames was a descendent of Oliver Ames, founder of the Ames Shovel Shop in 1774. The Ames shovels were used in every conflict since the Revolutionary War. During both World Wars the Ames shovels were standard issue to the Army just as they were in the Civil War by the Union forces.

After the war Ames served in politics and rose to become a State Senator in Massachusetts from 1962 to 1970. When he was redistricted out of office in 1970 he continued his civic works. He was active in Greater Boston Community Development, now Community Builders, and was president of Easton Community Corporation for almost 30 years. He died in November 2007.

The 'One Eyed Indian'

I was sent with a group of people to Maine [Bath Iron Works] around the 8th of November 1945 to get the ship ready for commissioning. The Fire Rooms and the Engine Rooms weren't ready yet to put in service. We actually had to finish building the ship. We had to make sure all the equipment was in the Fire Rooms was ready.

We never had to dress up. We were allowed liberty in our dungarees. The tides up there were 28 feet. When we were drunk we had a hell [of a time] getting back to the ship.

We were christened in Maine and once we were ready we were underway to Charlestown, MA. When we got to Boston Naval Shipyard for commissioning and final outfitting we never ate onboard ship. We ate at the Mess Hall on the Naval Yard.

My mom and my brother came went up there for the commissioning. Our families were actually allowed on the ship for the ceremony. After the families' visit was over the ship was sent to the Caribbean for a Shakedown cruise to ensure it was fit for use. That took a few months.

When we were on liberty in Havana, Cuba we drank 'Hatuey' [pronounced 'Ha – toowe] beer. After you drank 4 of those beers the picture on the label would be looking back at you. We also used to drink rum and coke. There was a popular song, a rumba, about that.

After the shakedown we went to Rhode Island and I was discharged from the Navy.
George Hodulik BT2 1945-1946

Hatuey -The 'One Eyed Indian'

After her 'shakedown' cruise *Fiske* joined the Atlantic Fleet and served as the Engineering School ship for the Destroyer Force, Atlantic Fleet and was home ported in Portland, Maine. In February 1946 *Fiske* assumed operational duties and her homeport was changed to Newport,

RI. She made the first of her three Mediterranean cruises out of Newport in mid-1946 and was awarded the Navy Occupation (Europe) medal for service in Italian waters helping to clear mines in the Adriatic Sea left over from WWII. *Fiske* was credited with the destruction of seven mines in one day during these operations.

Fiske was assigned to escort and assist another destroyer in its return to the Brooklyn Naval Yard after that ship sustained damage to its stern from an exploding mine.

USS *Fiske* in early 1946

G. Zero, SM1C

In October 1946 a new member of Fiske's crew came aboard. While new to being on destroyers – having previously served only on shore duty – SM1C Zero quickly adapted to shipboard life. Zero's attitude and demeanor quickly established him as a valued member of crew. Although it took some adjustment Zero rapidly got his sea legs and got accustomed to shipboard chow. Yes, there were some missteps

some might say 'accidents' but Zero soon became an integral part of the crew. The only serious mishap was when Zero broke a leg and had to have it placed in a cast for a few weeks. That cast did not affect Zero's contributions to the Fiske's mission or operations. SM1c G. Zero was a dog. The SM1c was the designator for 'Ship's Mascot First Class'. Medical records clearly show that Zero was healthy and well-nourished. He served on Fiske until October 1947 when he was transferred to permanent shore duty in Brooklyn, NY.
Ray Fisher TM2 1945-47

SM1c 'Zero'

According to information received from the family of TM2 Fisher 'Zero' went to permanent shore duty in Brooklyn, NY with John G. Bjelke, S1FC in October of 1947. The photo shown below shows Zero ashore with V. Bryan BM2 (date unknown). A search of Navy records indicates that S1FC Bjelke was transferred to the USS Damato (DD 871) in late 1947 and died in 2001 in southern California. The life story of Zero after leaving the *Fiske* is unknown but he left a lasting impression on those he served with.

Zero and BM2 Bryan

'Shore Party in Greece'

Sometime in late spring or early summer the Fiske was called upon to go into Greece and pick up some aircraft parts for the Philippine Sea (CV 47). At that time Greece was having some problems with Communists rebels attacking the government forces. The Fiske mustered up a shore party made up of a couple of officers and several sailors. The sailors were armed with carbines and M-1s and the officers had .45s. They gave us a truck and we headed for the airport where the parts had been flown in.

A few days previously the Communists had attacked one of the Greek navy's patrol craft and killed several of the men onboard so things were a little tense. We arrived at the airport, picked up the parts for the Philippine Sea and headed back to the port. We had no incidents either way.

Several days later Fiske was again called upon to make a parts pick up at the airport. We again got a truck but this time we weren't issued any weapons. Again we had no incidents either way but I don't know which of those trips was the tenser.

Another thing we did was to clear some mines around Italy that cruise. We didn't have any problems but one ship did get a little too close to one of the mines and suffered hull damage. We escorted her home to the Brooklyn Naval Shipyard where I was transferred to the USS Rich (DDE 820) in August of 1946. I finished out my enlistment on the Rich and left the Rich as an RDM1 in 1951.
William Chandler, RDM1
Jan 1946-August 1947

The *Fiske*'s next trip to the Med in 1947 was much of the same. She spent the Christmas and New Year's holidays in Venice in both 1946 and 1947.

'Throttleman'

When I reported as a Fireman Apprentice to the Engine room, someone asked me what job I knew, or could do. I had never had any training in the first three years of service, and I believed I would not get any training on this ship either.

I said I could do anything in the engine room. With a smile, he said "can you operate the throttle?", and I said "yes!" He didn't ask if I had done it before, and I didn't tell him I had - but — I had watched others do it!

A week later we got underway; the throttle was set up for in port and not for cruising, so I changed from port to cruising without changing the R.P.M. They watched me for part of my shift and then vanished. For a year I relieved a MM 1/c, and a MM 2/c relieved me.

Once, a high-ranking officer on a tour saw the throttle board with all the gauges and stepped between me and the board. I stepped back a long way and folded my arms because when someone steps in front of me that outranks me, he takes over. I said, "I'm the lowest rank on board ship - if you don't know how to operate the throttle, you better move" – and he did!"

USS Fiske, Malta

Harvey "Luke" Lucas FN Dec 1947 – Dec 1948

The late '40's brought the onset of the 'Cold War' with Communist insurgencies in Greece and other places. Anecdotal evidence appears to indicate that during *Fiske*'s 1948 Mediterranean cruise she participated in gunfire support operations along the coast of Greece against communist insurgents. This cannot be substantiated in official records but US Navy operations did occur during the period that *Fiske* was in the area.

It was in Venice during December 1947 that then LT Cyrus H. Butt reported onboard. LT Butt reported onboard as Weapons Officer and by late 1948 or early 1949 became the Executive Officer. He had

Fiske as configured in 1947

graduated from the Naval Academy in 1944 and was first assigned to the USS *Davis* (DD 395) and sent to the Torpedo Control Officer School from 5 May to 29 June. He became the Torpedo Control Officer upon his return. While Ens. Butt was at school the *Davis* struck a mine, on 21 June 1944, heavily damaging her Port Quarter. In September Butt he was appointed Acting Lt(jg). The *Davis* returned to Charleston, SC for repairs and was decommissioned in October 1945.

Lt Butt was transferred off the *Fiske* in July 1949 prior to her deployment to Korea and there is proof (below) that he was XO before he left. Cyrus H. Butt III will again appear and be a part of *Fiske* history.

During the 1948 Med cruise *Fiske* made port calls in Gibraltar, Sfax, Tunisia, Argostolion, Patras and Suda Bay (Crete), Greece as well as Toulon, France, Tripoli, Libya, Naples and Syracuse (Sicily) Italy. Upon her return *Fiske* participated in an Atlantic Fleet exercise to evaluate radar fire control developments. This exercise took the *Fiske* from the Florida Keys to Davis Inlet, Newfoundland.

PLAN OF THE DAY   SATURDAY   9 APRIL 1949

```
0300  Anchor detail on deck.
0415  Call MAA and messmen.
0430  Reveille.
0440  Morning Coffee.
0500  Special Sea detail.
0530  Moor berth 16, Brooklyn Navy Yard – On deck Section 3 import watch.
0545  Turn to, clean ship.
0615  Mess gear.
0630  Breakfast.
0800  Quarters for Muster.
0810  Turn to.
1045  Inspection of Messmen.
1130  Knock off Ship's work.  Liberty to expire for Section 2 at 1000 Sunday Sections
      1 & 3 at 0530 Monday.
1145  Mess gear.
12000 Dinner.
1300  Holiday routine.
1400  Pipe sweepers.
1645  Mess gear.
1700  Supper.
XXXXXXXXXXXX
1910  Muster PALs and restricted men.
1915  Muster eight o'clock reports.
2000  Movies
2200  Muster PALs and restricted men.
----  Taps lights out.

                        IT CAN BE BOUGHT
Yes, you CAN buy Peace of mind—if you buy Savings Bonds regularly through
automatic Payroll Savings.

                                    C. E. NUTT,
                                    Lt., USN,
                                    Executive Officer.
```

David Stone joined the Merchant Marine in 1945 when he couldn't join the Navy as he was underage. When he turned eighteen he left the Merchant Marine and joined the Navy and became the leading Seaman in First Division onboard the *Fiske* based on his experience in the Merchant Marine.

'Butter and Egg Man'

I was onboard the Fiske from October 1947 until I was discharged on December 20, 1951 – just 7 days before my 22nd birthday. During my time onboard I was a deckhand, Gig Bowhook, Gig Coxswain and, for my last 3 months, Keeper of Boatswain's Stores.

In port overseas I sold cigarettes for $28 and $34 a carton. They cost $0.60 on board ship. When we got back to Newport I had over $1000 back pay on the books.

Some shipmates called me the 'Butter & Egg Man' [In the 1930's that was a small town big money man]. I even had a car when not many did.
David F. Stone SN1/c 1947-1951

David F. Stone SN1/c

In her first five years of service *Fiske* earned the Battle Efficiency 'E' in 1948, 1949 and 1950. Additionally she won the Marjorie Sterett Battleship Prize in 1949 (the monies from this prize allowed *Fiske* to become the first destroyer to have a TV set) and the DESLANT Basketball Championship. With *Fiske*'s string of 'E's she was given some desirable tasks and liberty ports of call.

'Cuban Shore Patrol'

"When we visited Santiago, Cuba I was put on Shore Patrol duty. The Shore Patrol Officer assigned me and one other SP to a place called Marie's Bar. In actuality Marie's was a whorehouse with a bar downstairs. Our assignment was to break up any fights that started over the girls. Never figured I'd be acting as a bouncer in a whorehouse but it was interesting.

As we were getting ready to leave Santiago a crowd of Cuban policemen and a very irate civilian came down the pier. It seems that someone onboard had bought a saddle from the civilian and given him a roll of money that contained some less than valuable currency. The tradesman had accepted as U.S. currency some script from the Coney Island Amusement Park. I don't believe that the culprit was ever identified."

Paul Shipe, TM3 1948-1949

Fiske in Santiago, Cuba 1949

With the commencement of hostilities on the Korean Peninsula *Fiske* sailed from Newport on January 3rd 1951, transited the Panama Canal and arrived in Sasebo, Japan on February 12th. Along the way *Fiske* experienced some severe shaft vibration problems and made stops in Naval Shipyards in Norfolk, Charleston and Guantanamo Bay, Cuba.

Transiting the Panama Canal January 1951

It should be mentioned that *Fiske* had a long history of shaft problems throughout her life. *Fiske* transited the Panama Canal and the Pacific unaccompanied with fueling stops in Hawaii, Midway and Sasebo.

After reporting to the Seventh Fleet *Fiske* became part of Task Force 77, operating on the East coast the Korean peninsula. She became the flagship for Group, Sonjin-Chomjin Area.

Recently declassified 'War Diary' documents for that period yield a clearer picture of that deployment. As an example Task Element, Korean East Coast Blockading and Patrol: at 0807 on February 7th, while enroute to the war zone, *Fiske* went to GQ (General Quarters-battle stations) and over the course of the next two hours expended 31 rounds of 40 mm HEI; 24 rounds of 40 mm HEIT; and, 144 rounds of 20 mm HET. It was called, "Blowing holes in the ocean." But when you are headed into a war zone it does seem prudent to check your weapons. Over the next few days *Fiske* repeated this exercise many times.

On February 13th *Fiske* rendezvoused with other units of TF 77 comprised of USS *Philippine Sea* (CV47), USS *Valley Forge* (CV45), USS *Juneau* (CLAA119), USS *W.R. Rush* (DD714), USS *Frank Knox* (DDR742), USS *Hollister* (DD788), USS *Alfred A. Cunningham* (DD 752), USS *Frank E. Evans* (DD754), USS *Blue* (DD744), USS *Walke* (DD723). TF77 patrolled the east coast of Korea in accordance with CTF OpOrder 1-51.

On February 15th the USS *Missouri* (BB63) and the USS *Bole* (DD 755) joined TF 77 and stayed with the formation for several days. At 0945 USS *Philippine Sea* sighted a floating mine close aboard. *Fiske* slowed to 10 knots to locate mine and located same at 1000. Mine was identified as a Russian Mk 26, fairly old and covered with barnacles, and was sunk at 1016. This sinking was accomplished with the expenditure of 111 rounds of 40 mm HEIT, 5 rounds 40 mm APT, 4 rounds of 40 mm HEI, and 365 rounds of 20 mm HET.

'Cold-cold-cold'

While I was onboard the FISKE, we got orders to join Task Force 77. It was a bad time out there!

As I stood watch on a 40MM mount it was cold-cold-cold! I had never been that cold before, and I've never been that cold since, but I made it.

I was first loader on the forward mount. We knocked out a train as it came out of a mountain – blowing it up with the forward 5" mount.*

*Fiske did receive credit for disabling a train in June.

Tommie Green, SD3 1950-1951

These War Diary reports indicate that floating mines were a consistent and constant hazard. On February 19th at 1850 local time *Fiske* sighted an object dead ahead and maneuvered radically to clear the object visually identified as a mine. This mine passed down the starboard side at a distance of approximately 20 feet.

Heavy weather between February 27th and 29th caused a short circuit at frame 68-70 that started a small electrical fire at 2154 on the 27th. That electrical circuit was isolated and fire put out. Fuse had failed due to improper installation of retaining clip. At 1510 on the 28th heavy seas stove in the gun shield on Mount 44 and crushed four rounds of 40 mm. These shells were disposed of by being jettisoned overboard. This same sea carried away the provisions for life raft no. 6 and bent a retaining bar on the port side 'K' gun stowage rack. The depth charges were secured with line to prevent movement. At approximately 1550 another large wave bent frame 131, port side of the after deck house, inward about two inches.

It appears due to the gaps in War Diary reports that *Fiske* spent much of March either in Sasebo or another port for upkeep and repairs.

During April and May of 1951 *Fiske* performed 'Flycatcher' patrols in the Songjin area. These patrols were designed to intercept North Korean coastal shipping, escort shipping from Japan to Korea, and provide gunfire support. *Fiske* was credited with sinking one North Korean junk and damaging several others, as well as the destruction of numerous floating mines (primarily of Soviet manufacture). USS *Burlington* and the HMCS *Nootka* also conducted interdiction fire at assigned Songjin area targets.

Also in May *Fiske* participated in pre-D-Day shore bombardment in support of ROK (Republic of Korea) units in the Kosong and Kansong areas. It was reported by the shore fire patrol party that this support prevented the annihilation of those ROK units.

At 0942 on May 30th Commanding Officer of *Fiske* relieved Commanding Officer of USS *Stickell* (DD 888) as Commander Task Element 95.22. Task Element 95.22 consisted of *Fiske*, USS *Burlington* (PF 51) and HMCS *Nootka*. [Editor's note: The Canadian ship *Nootka* participated in the Cuban Missile Crisis and patrolled off the north coast of Cuba over 10 years later.]

On that same day, at approximately 1600 hours local time, *Fiske* fired 18 rounds of 5" AAC at two railroad bridges, gun emplacements and a highway junction. One hit dropped the north span of the railroad bridge at Lat. 40° 36' 24" N, Long. 125° 10' 12" E. This bridge was considered a priority target since it could not be bypassed and rendered rail traffic impossible when this bridge was destroyed.

With the change of command between *Stickell* and *Fiske* the *Stickell* transferred Ltjg. Y. S. Sin, of the ROK Navy and 14 ROK enlisted men aboard *Fiske*. *Stickell* detached and headed for Sasebo, Japan. Ltjg Sin and his team were to act as reconnaissance personnel along the Korean coast.

On the same day at 1820 USS *Burlington* reported a man overboard. After an extensive search of the area by all units with negative results the Northern Patrol was cancelled and HMCS *Nootka* was detached from TE 95.22 and headed to Wonsan.

On the evening of June 1st USS *Thompson* (DD 627), USS *Burlington* (PF 551) and *Fiske*, lying to off Chunronjin (south of Chongjin), commenced shore bombardment on interdiction targets. At 0136 with night firing completed *Fiske* had expended 60 rounds of 5" ACC at a railroad bridge, a railroad crossing, a highway bridge approach and a tunnel entrance. One large explosion and one secondary explosion were observed at the intersection of a highway and railroad line. *Thompson* expended 90 rounds at similar targets without visible results being observed. The *Burlington* expended 85 rounds of 3" ACC at similar targets in the Songjin area with no results reported.

By mid-morning on the 1st the haze and slight fog had cleared revealing that the bridges at Lat. 40° 38' 45" N., Long. 129° 38' 00" E., and Lat. 40° 36' 45", N. Long. 129°10' 12" E had been repaired using wooden cribs. *Fiske* and *Thompson* were assigned the latter bridge as a direct fire target and rendered the bridge unusable. At 1443 *Fiske* came under fire by machine guns located near the vicinity of the bridge previously targeted. *Fiske* commenced counter-battery fire and silenced those guns. There were neither casualties nor damage to the *Fiske*.

On June 2nd the *Fiske* and the *Thompson* laid to off Chunronjon, North Korea while the ROK team conducted a landing. The purpose of this landing by the ROK team was to gather intelligence data and capture prisoners for interrogation.

At 2255 the ROK Recon Team was deployed to the coast of North Korea. The team was taken ashore on a small sampan towed by the ship's whaleboat (MWB). A machine gun was mounted on the motor whaleboat for protection.

As the ROK Team was being picked at the end of their mission the whaleboat came under fire from North Korean machine guns. These guns were quickly silenced by the fire of 40mm's from the *Fiske* before any injuries or damage was sustained. According to the *Fiske*'s War Diaries there was significant 'information about troop disposition and military traffic was obtained' and two North Korean prisoners were also taken aboard. These prisoners were subsequently transferred on June 3rd to the USS *Burlington* (PF 51) for interrogation at Wonson.

The ROK team had returned onboard *Fiske* at 0312 with these two prisoners. The prisoners were placed in the *Fiske*'s brig, under guard, by order of CDR John E. Pond. Anecdotal information received indicates that there was an incident involving the ROK officer and one of his men but there is no mention of it in the Deck Logs or the War Diaries for that period

'Korean Justice'

I was on the fantail when the ROK Landing Party returned from their foray into North Korea. They returned with 2 prisoners and some intelligence as they were directed. It seems that one of the ROK party lost his weapon either when leaving the shore or in re-boarding the Fiske.

The reaction of the ROK officer in charge was to draw his sidearm, shoot the offender in the head and kick the body overboard right there in front of CDR Pond and the rest of us on the fantail.

CDR Pond screamed, "God Damn it! You can't do that on my ship!" but the ROK officer paid no attention to him. The prisoners were taken down to the ship's brig by order of CDR Pond and shortly

thereafter they were transferred to the USS Burlington (PF 51) for further 'interrogation'.
Joseph Kufel QM1 1947-1952

    The *Fiske* departed the Seventh Fleet in late June 1951. During her service in Korea waters *Fiske* was awarded the Korean Service medal with two Battle Stars. *Fiske* steamed westward from Korea and arrived in Newport, RI on August 8th 1951, thus completing her first 'Around the World' cruise and first verifiable combat duty.

Crossing the Equator on the way back to the States

'Korea – Enroute, There & Back'

Fiske went to Korea because the ship originally ordered for that deployment couldn't make the trip. We had 3 weeks to get ready. That was hectic to say the least. As busy as we were I found out later I had time to make my beautiful wife pregnant. [Some of my friends later told me the old Navy saying, "You have to be there for the laying of the keel but not for the launching." But I digress.

Our Division left Newport on January 3, 1951. Captain Von Kleek was Commodore of DesRon 8 and CDR J. Pond Jr was CO of the Fiske. I was aboard Fiske as Division Medical Officer. I can't recall exactly when but we developed a vibration which was thought to be one of the screws. We left the Division and went to Guantanamo, Cuba for service. I can't give the details but we also went to Charleston, SC. While there someone realized that the rest of the Division did not have a Medical Officer. I got orders to catch up to them somewhere. My bag was packed and I was ready to leave the ship when it was decided the Fiske could proceed to Korea. I unpacked and stayed aboard.

The Fiske went from the Panama Canal directly to Hawaii. Our speed was 11 knots so our fuel would last otherwise we would have gone to San Diego for refueling. However the time was spent preparing for combat. All kinds of drills for the crew and deep sixing all gear that could be a hazard. We took on all kinds of supplies in Pearl Harbor and then to Midway Island for refueling and arriving in Yokosuka, Japan near Tokyo. Sasebo later became her port.

I would go from ship to ship by high-line as I was needed while underway and was onboard the J. P. Kennedy Jr when our Commodore who was senior ended up in charge of east coast something or other [Editor's note: Task Element, Korean East Coast Blockading and Patrol Group, Sonjin-Chomjin Area] and pressed all his staff including the Chaplain and myself into extra duty. I became a logistics officer. Somehow we ended up in the northern port of Keelung, Formosa (Taiwan) where a large supply and repair ship [Destroyer Tender] was stationed to service our destroyers. The Commodore transferred his Staff to the Tender. The destroyers would come in for services and then go to Hong Kong for R & R.

Because a tender was always in port the crews decided to open an Enlisted Men & Officers Club; first floor Enlisted Men, second floor Officers. The Chinese beverages were bad – in fact hardly passable – so the Navy men knew something had to be done. They started using the destroyers going to Hong Kong as Rum Runners. Now back to the Fiske. I had a tough time convincing Captain Von Kleek allowing me to go with Fiske to Hong Kong for R & R but I did. Lt J. Juncker, my roommate on the Fiske, was the Supply Officer and a friend. House of Lords gin and Canadian Club whiskey Imperial quarts were ten dollars ($10) a case. I repeat a case! We loaded up with all the supplies for the clubs. While at it I loaded 5 cases into Medical Stores to be removed at some future date. [Eventually off loaded to my house in Newport – it lasted for years!]

While there [Hong Kong] for a week a gal named Shanghai Lil made a deal for her people to paint the sides of the ship for our garbage. A shoemaker came aboard and sold everyone shoes and sea boots (half Wellingtons). The crew had a great liberty.

Later Captain Von Kleek ordered [that] sea boots were not uniform. Later I had to go to the Kennedy by highline. We did not have a chair type but the type where your legs hung down and pants riding high. I put on my sea boots and went across boots flying. The crew loved it, the Captain walked off the bridge.

I remember our times on Fiske along the North Korean coast as well as time in Wonson harbor doing coast bombardment. We did intermittent fire with our 5" guns around the clock. One particular area was troublesome and the USS Missouri and rocket launching ships came in and neutralized the area. It was a real show. The Fiske also ran with aircraft carriers as escort – refueled at sea – etc. My roommate, Lt James Juncker, and I played a lot of cribbage and I think that I lost about a million dollars. Of course I didn't pay. We had a lot

*of fun in Kowloon when we were taken to a fancy restaurant and
supplied with pretty girls because Jim was the ship's supply officer.
Why I was included I have no idea.*

*We finally got orders to head for home and we did via
Singapore, Colombo Ceylon [now Sri Lanka], Bahrain in the Persian
Gulf then through the Red Sea where she went through a sand storm
and was covered with fine dust. Port Said, Egypt and into the Med and
to Naples, Italy. Half the crew had liberty in Naples. Unfortunately five
members of the crew developed polio which negated going to
Marseilles, France. I turned the after Chief's Quarters into a
quarantine area and we headed for Gibraltar where these five men
were transferred to shore for further disposition. The only patient that
had residual effects that I know of was a young Coast Guard Ensign
who had a slight limp.*

*Also on the way back we crossed the Equator and there was
hazing of those crossing for the first time. No one was spared,
including me. I went first so I would be available for any problems. We
now crossed the Atlantic only stopping on a calm day so we could paint
the sides of the ship so we would look good coming
into Newport. Our wives and friends were waiting with open arms. My
wife Ellen had changed – now 8+ months pregnant.*

*After Thoughts – The Chief's getting coke syrup in Honolulu so
we could make cola using life vest CO_2 cartridges.*

*I remember Father Fay the Chaplain. He was always first off
the ship when we hit port. I gave him Med Store whiskey if he had a
cold and he gave me altar wine.*

*Captain Pond calling me to the bridge and telling me not to
fraternize with the enlisted guys. He caught me in the forward CPO
Quarters playing cards.*

*When I went to BuMed after duty at the Philadelphia Navy
Hospital an officer told me if I wanted to be in the real Navy a
tour of duty on a destroyer was the best for my resume. Somehow Ellen*

did not agree. I'm glad I did. I think I did.
Bernard H. Cobetto, Lt, M C 1950-1951

U.S.S. FISKE (DD 842)

12 June 1951

Dear

As our tour of duty in the Far East heads into its final week, I thought I'd drop you a line to let you know what the FISKE has been doing. Until recently, we had been part of the destroyer screen for the fast carriers of Task Force 77 and later a participant in the patrol between Formosa and the China coast. Last week, however, we had our first opportunity to do any direct damage to the enemy when we became part of Task Force 95.

We were sent to the East coast of Korea in the vicinity of Songjin and also Chongjin some 50 miles up the road. As you know, a war can't be run efficiently or successfully without a dependable steady line of supply. Task Force 95's main function has been to keep enemy supplies from reaching their troops at the front. There are five supply routes available to them as I've sketched on the back. Our force, Task Force 77, and the Fifth Air Force have practically eliminated all of them.

While at Songjin and Chongjin the FISKE continually fired its 5-inch (t railroads, bridges, and highway junctions. This 24 hour a day fire made it tough on our sleep but I'm sure it was tougher for those on the receiving end. The Navy calls it interdiction fire, but to me it means being a pest and a nuisance by never letting up on the enemy. I'm sure it's no fun for the Reds to know that a shell is on the way every few minutes.

It's really a United Nations effort too. In addition to our battleships, cruisers, destroyers, and minesweepers, there are British, Canadian, Australian, Dutch and South Korean Naval units participating in the bombardment and blockade. For example, a few days ago we came to the West Coast of Korea to operate with a British aircraft carrier and two of her destroyers. We've found that there is little difference between working alongside the British and with our own ships.

I hope this may make clear what we are doing here. Although we are filling a definite need we all realize that there is no place like home. I'm looking forward to being back on familiar ground or at least in friendly waters very shortly. Until then my best to all.

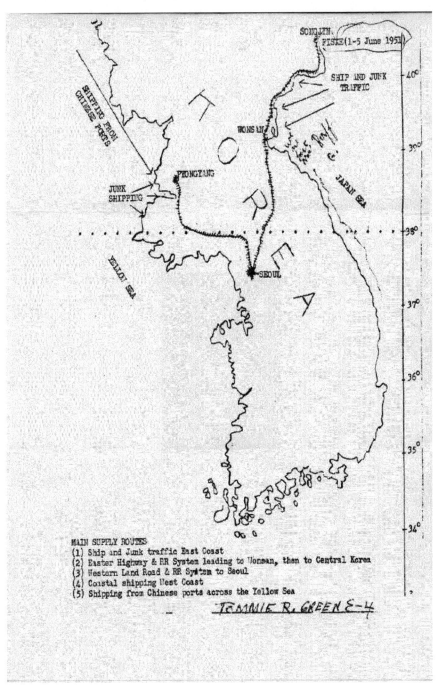

Map on reverse of letter

The recent unearthing of a letter given to all crew members in June of 1951 is included above. This letter was probably produced by the ship's Yeomen at the direction of and composed by the Executive Officer. It was meant to explain the *Fiske*'s contribution to the war effort and let all family members that all was well with the crew.

This particular copy was given to the Fiske Association by Tommie Green, SD3.

On her way home to Newport, RI *Fiske* was scheduled to make a port visit to Marseilles, France but the French authorities refused to let her enter port. The reason for was that *Fiske* had 12-14 crewmen that exhibited symptoms of polio. A high speed run to Gibraltar was made and those crewmen were medically evacuated.

This incident has been verified by Deck Logs provided by SOSN Wesley Walker. There has been further verification of this event provided by Dr. Bernard H. Cobetto, who was Division Medical Officer during that deployment. Dr. Cobetto reported that to the best of his knowledge only one crewman failed to completely recover.

The *Fiske* operations with the Atlantic Fleet continued until she entered the Boston Naval Shipyard on April 1st 1952 for decommissioning and conversion to a DDR.

'String Beans & Johnny Walker'

When we were in the MED in late 1949 we spent the Christmas/New Year's holidays in Naples, Italy. A shipmate, YN3 Jim Bryson, and I went on liberty. We ran into a young girl that was selling individual cigarettes on the street. It was a cold and windy day and Jim and I were cold in our blues and peacoats and this girl was only wearing a light dress with no coat or jacket. We gave her what monies we had and told her to go home and get warm. She insisted that we come with her. She told her story to all the relatives that were at the house and they profusely thanked us. We returned to the ship and pretty much forgot about it.

On our way back to the States from Korea we had transited the Suez Canal and made a stop in Naples. Somebody in the Naples port area must have seen the Fiske come in because shortly after we tied up a couple of men came to the brow and asked for Jim and me.

They remembered us and insisted that we come home with them. We were asked what they could do repay our kindness to the young girl. We finally came up with really having missed fresh vegetables for the past several weeks. Especially, fresh string beans. So it was decided, they would feed us a home cooked meal of fresh vegetables.

While the meal was being prepared the two guys rode us all over Naples on their motor scooters. When we returned to the house we were treated to string beans, bread and Johnny Walker Red Label.

They insisted that we drink so that 'granmama' could have a drink too. Neither one of us remembers returning to the ship that night. The OOD told us that two 'Mafia' types carried us onboard, refused to let go of us until we had been tucked into our bunks with our wallets, watches and money safely tucked in our shoes. We were told that we should have woke up dead.

The CO, CDR Pond, said that he wasn't going to punish us because he figured that the gunfire exercise we were going to conduct shortly after leaving port would be punishment enough."
Millard Wagnon, FTSN 1949-1951

ComDesRon 8 Change of Command

After returning to Newport, RI from Korea there was a change of command ceremony. Captain E. S. Von Kleeck Jr. was relieved by Captain J. J. Laffan as Commodore of Destroyer Squadron Eight.

Included in the picture above (from right to left) are the crews of the USS Joseph P. Kennedy (DD 850), USS William R. Rush (DD 714), USS Fiske (DD 842), and USS Hawkins (DD 873). Much of the remainder of 1951 and early 1952 was spent in routine operations out of Newport, RI and preparing for the decommissioning of *Fiske* (DD 842) to be converted into the RADAR Picket Destroyer DDR 842.

Chapter IV

(DDR 842)

April 1952 to April 1964
Call Letters - NBBU
Motto: Watchdog of the Fleet"

When *Fiske* entered Boston Naval Shipyard in April 1952 to be decommissioned as a DD and converted to a DDR she underwent a dramatic change not only of mission but also of silhouette. All of the 40mm and 20mm gun emplacements were removed. As were the 21" torpedo tubes. The 3" mounts remained on the 01 level. In place of the single stick forward mast forward she received the tripod mast to hold the much larger 'Bed Spring' antenna of an Air-Search Radar and an improved Surface-Search Radar as well as the UHF antennas needed to communicate with aircraft under her control.

Fiske also underwent a significant shift in the composition of her crew. With the removal of most of her gun emplacements there was less need for Gunnery Department personnel. With the addition of additional Radar and communications equipment system the Operations Department became bigger. Engineering and SupplyDepartments were largely unaffected.

OFFICERS OF THE USS FISKE (DDR-842)

CDR POWELL P. VAIL, Jr., USN .... Commanding Officer

LCDR JOHN A. REITZ, USNR .... Executive Officer

LT JAMES I. HEMPHILL, USN .... Operations Officer

LT JAMES C. EDMONDS, USNR .... Engineering Officer

LT PHILIP D. NEISWENDER, USNR .... Gunnery Officer

LTJG JOHN F. LEYERLE, USN .... Communications Officer

LTJG JOSEPH FENIER, USN .... Electronics Officer

LTJG ROBERT McL. SMITH, Jr., USN .... First Lieutenant

LTJG VADEN M. LACKEY, USN .... CIC Officer

LTJG ARTHUR L. PLEASANTS, III, USN .... Damage Control Asst.

ENS JOHN F. DISORBO, USN .... Main Propulsion Assistant

ENS NEWTON S. BURLEY, (SC), USN .... Supply Officer

ENS WILLIAM G. STEWART, USNR .... ASW Officer

ENS STEWART J. CARLSON, USN .... Assistant CIC Officer

ENS WILLIAM J. LAUX, Jr., USN .... 2nd Division Officer

ENS ROBERT RIBA, USN .... Assistant Gunnery Officer

ENS FRANK A. RILEY, USNR .... 1st Division Officer

CHIEF PETTY OFFICERS OF
U. S. S. FISKE (DDR-842)

★

PAUL AYERS
Chief Yeoman

DOUGLAS R. BRAKEN
Chief Hospital Corpsman

OLIVER M. CHARLES
Chief Radioman

EUGENE L. COBUZZI
Chief Machinist's Mate

FREDERICK I. HAMMOND
Chief Radarman

CECIL W. HENDERSON
Chief Electrician's Mate

WILLIAM N. KINNEY
Chief Gunner's Mate

ERNEST G. MARTIN
Chief Fire Controlman

CHARLES P. MILLER
Chief Machinist's Mate

RALPH E. MOORE
Chief Machinist's Mate

ROBERT A. NICKERSON
Chief Boatswain's Mate

ARTHUR B. ROBINSON
Chief Quartermaster

CHARLES E. SMITH
Chief I. C. Electrician

WILBUR L. SPROUL
Chief Commissaryman

JOHN C. SULLIVAN
Chief Electronics Technician

ROBERT D. VANDENBERGE
Chief Boilerman

★

U. S. S. FISKE (DDR-842) CREW

ADAMS, Wright H. SA
AHEARN, James W. MMFA
ALLEN, Thomas C. RDSA
ANDERSON, Oliver TN
ANTHONY, Landus BM1
ANTHOPULOS, James B. BT1
ARCHER, Doyle R. SN
ASHBY, Darrell R. EN3

BAILEY, Ronald C. SN
BAKER, Robert C. FN
BAPTISTA, Antonio SD2
BARBER, Elwood BTG2
BARBY, Donald GMMSN
BARNETT, Gary B. FN
BARTUSIANCIUS, Vido E. SN
BEARD, William J. FN
BEAVERS, Jack V. SN
BECKMAN, Donald R. GMM3
BERNERT, Ramon J. PN3
BIBEAU, Joseph F. MMLFA
BILODEAU, Gilbert L. ETSN
BITTELL, Robert J. QMSA
BLICHARZ, Edward P. SN
BOLAND, William P. BM3
BOMA, Charles W. SN
BOYD, George D. FT3
BRADLEY, John W. RD1
BRECKENRIDGE, Lonnis L. SD1
BRENEMAN, Robert G. RDSA
BROWN, Charles D. SA
BROWN, John M. SA
BROWN, Robert TN
BUCKLES, Ernest D. BT3
BUFORD, Leslie B. BM3
BURNS, George F. MM2(T)
BYBEE, Herbert E. FN

CAIN, John W. ET3
CAMERON, James A. RD2(T)
CAMPBELL, John R. SN
CARDER, James R. BTFA
CASALETTI, Joseph RD3
CATERINO, Carmen J. SN
CAULK, Elden E. SN
CAUTHEN, Guy C. SA
CHANDLER, John A. SA

CHAPMAN, William W. FT3
CHILDERS, David O. DC2(T)
CHUDY, Marion J. BMGSN
CIZEWSKI, Edward J. CS3
CLEMMONS, Edward D. FN
COBB, Billy C. YNSN
COHEN, Harold, SA
CONNER, Clyde F. SN
COPELAND, Hardie L. SD1
CROFOOT, Howard SA
CROSS, Gerald E. RDSA
CURTIS, Norman A. SOG2

DAGGETT, Marvin G. SA
DAILEY, Edward J., Jr. MM1
DAVIS, Jack W. FN
DAVIS, James E. FT2
DAVIS, Melvin D. SA
DEANE, Gerald B. FN
DEMARS, William S. SN
DENAMUR, Harry U., Jr. SK1
DENLEY, William J. FN
DEVOUS, William L. FN
DOLAN, Joseph L. SN
DOUGLAS, George BTGFA
DOWN, Walter FN
DOWNS, Harrison "F" RD2
DUFFIELD, Robert H. SN
DUMEL, Louis SA
DUNCAN, Wadus R. DK2
DUNN, Joe E. SOG3
DUREE, Gerald G. GM1
DUTCHER, Robert E. RD2

ENGEL, Harold E. SN
ENGEL, Paul J. RDSA
EUBANK, William H. SA
EVANS, John J. SA
EVANS, John T. FN
EVANS, Richard W., Jr. RMSN

FAITH, William F. GM3
FIELD, Joseph C. FA
FINACCHIARO, Ronald J. FA
FISHER, Felix B. SN
FLACK, Malcolm D. SN

FLAMMANG, Adolph J. ME1
FLYNN, Thomas M. SA
FOREMAN, Charles E. TN
FRANK, Lawren R. MMFA

GABLONWITZ, Joseph H. BM3
GAGE, James V. SA
GARABRANDT, Richard D. SN
GARRETT, George H. RDSN
GARVEY, Robert P. SN
GILBERT, Bernard W. RD3
GILLILAND, Junior D. FN
GILREATH, Elmer "T" FP1(T)
GOLEC, Ernest A. MML3
GORE, Carrol W. DC3
GRAHAM, Robert E. SA
GRIGONIS, Stanley J. MM3

HAGAN, James O. BT1
HALL, Robert L. FN
HAMILTON, James E. SN
HANCOCK, Calvin D. FN
HANESWORTH, Robert A. FA
HANNERS, Loren B. SN
HARDIN, Billie R. MM2
HARNER, Harold B. SN
HARRISON, William A. SN
HAY, Richard L. EMFN
HAYES, John C. MM3
HEIBEL, Robert T. SN
HEIMEL, George H. GM1
HELTON, Raymond A. SK3
HENINGER, Wiley O. EM3
HENRICH, Richard G. MM3
HENSLEY, Patrick FN
HIMMLER, William H. SN
HOBERT, Walter E. FN
HOCHHIEM, Harold EM1
HOLLYFIELD, Thomas G. FN
HOWIE, John W. GMSN
HUGHES, William A. MMFA
HUNEKE, Albert H., Jr. SA
HUNTSMAN, Frederick FCS2

JACKSON, George B. EN1
JACOBS, Louis A. J. MMFA
JOHNSON, Allan B. SKSA

JOHNSON, Harold L. EM2(T)
JOHNSON, Harry L. SOG3
JOHNSON, Leroy O. SHSN
JONES, Andy SN
JORGENSON, Arlo V. BM3

KEETLEY, Lawrence J. FN
KENTUCK, James BM2
KIENERT, Richard W. DCFN
KING, Jackie R. SA
KING, Roger F. SN
KIRK, Donald L. FN
KNAPP, William H., Jr. SN
KROTH, Ronald J. FA
KUHN, William A. GM2(T)

LACLAIR, Leigh M. FT3
LAGOR, Lawrence J. SN
LAKEBERG, Kenneth SA
LAMADORE, Frank J. SN
LARSON, Jack W. SN
LATOURETTE, Frank BM3
LEACH, Earl R. ET2
LEWANDOWSKI, Frank J. SN
LILEY, Emerson E., Jr. HM3
LINTON, Vurnis R. SA
LOPOPOLO, Dominic BT3
LUKER, Robert E. RD3
LUNGSTROM, Norman C. SN
LYONS, Carl R. TE3

MACDONALD, Robert E. FMMSN
MACSHARA, Calvin H. CSSA
MAGGIANO, Angelo V. SA
MAHALIK, John Jr. MML1
MANGIONE, Givanni SN
MARIANI, Robert Z. SN ,
MARSHALL, Torney D. SA
MARTEL, Leon J. SKSN
MARTIN, Houston D. FN
MATHEWS, Dan W. Jr. BMSN
MATTOX, Jimmy J. SN
MAY, Scottie D. SN
MAYES, Emmett E., Jr. PN3
MAYNARD, Dale R. SN
McDANIEL, Ivan K. CSSN
McGUIRE, Robert W. RM3

McPHERSON, Lemuel L. Jr. MM1
MEADOR, Arthur T. RNN3
MILLER, Paige B. SA
MITCHELL, John N. ET2
MOSELEY, Howard D. SK2
MOTT, Lester M. RD3
MULLIS, Thomas D. FN
MUNGIN, Louis J. QM3
MYERS, Clifford J. BT2

NESTLE, Melburn A. SN
NEVERS, Edward D. FN
NODDEN, Neill C. GMSA
NOLAN, Thomas V. SN
NORMAND, Robert H. QM2(T)
NORTON, David A. SN

O'BRIEN, Robert F. BT3
O'DONNELL, Arthur J. SN
ORNELAS, Hector J. GMM1

PACHECO, James SN
PARETCHANAN, Ernest RMSN
PARNELL, Jack M. SA
PUAL, James T. FN
PELO, Ralph A. BTGFA
PENDLETON, Donald E. RMN2
PERDUE, Joseph V. PNSN
PETERSON, Stanley F. MMFA
PNEUMAN, Gerald W. SOSN
PULASKI, Stanley H. YN2

RAINS, Roy G. SA
RANAGAN, Warren F., Jr. MMFA
RAUSCH, Lewis S. SN
REGAN, Thomas P. Jr. SA
RIOUX, Lee R. SN
RODIN, Samuel SA
ROGERS, Charles C. QMS3
ROOT, Donald D. SA
ROSS, John L. SA
ROTH, Irwin D. SN
ROYKO, Matthew SN

SCHAEUBLIN, Ernest P. SN
SCHERR, Robert B. EN2
SCHUH, Walter J. MM2
SCOTT, Howard E. SN
SHORE, Herman SH1
SIMS, Harold D. FN

SLEDZ, Charles E. FA
SLINGERLAND, M. L. Jr. MM3C
SNELLINGS, Donald N. SN
SNIZEK, Charles L. SA
SPAULDING, Rex K. GMSA
SPECHT, Benjamin L. SN
SPIVEY, Riley SN
SPRAY, Alden C. SN
STEERE, Billy C. BM3
STEIN, Albert C. SN
STEINFELDT, Lawrence R. BM3
STEINMETZ, Robert FN
ST. GEORGE, Samuel T. FT3
STIERS, James H. CS2
STIGER, Bryan E. SN
STUMP, James C. CSSN
STUSTMAN, Stanely P. SN
SUMNER, John A. SA
SWENSON, Elwood T. QM3

TAYLOR, Alfred GM2
TEGINS, John M. IC3
THOMAS, Homer L. BM2
THOMPSON, LeBurn A. SO1
TRACY, Warren W. Jr. SH2
TRANT, Kenneth A. RMSA

VELLIA, Eugene J. FA
VOGEL, Richard E. MMLFA

WAGNER, Edward W SOSN
WAGONER, Robert W. RD2
WARD, Hubert QM1
WATHEN, Gerald F. QMSA
WEADOCK, Bernard L. SN
WEISS, Leo J. QM3
WEST, Elmer L. MM3
WHETSONE, Norman L. SN
WHITE, Eugene G. S N
WICKERSHEIM, A. W. Jr. BM3
WIGGETT, Alvin J. SN
WILLIS, John Jr. TN
WIMBUSH, Tommy L. BM3
WOOD, James W. CSSN
WOOD, Robert M. SN
WRUBLE, Harry E. SN

YATES, James W. BT3

After being re-commissioned on 25 November 1952 *Fiske* returned to Newport, RI. *Fiske* became part of DesRon 14 and spent the holidays there. On 2 February 1953 *Fiske* departed for Fleet Refresher Training at Guantanamo Bay, Cuba and a 'shakedown cruise' After a period of normal Gitmo activities *Fiske* returned to Newport on 17 May 1953 after a liberty port call in San Juan, PR. *Fiske* departed Newport for the North Atlantic on 16 September 1953 for the North Atlantic and 'Operation Mariner'. That operation took the *Fiske* north of the Arctic Circle and conveyed '*Bluenose*' status on all crewmembers. *Fiske* spent 1-4 October in Plymouth, England and returned to Newport on 18 October.

The Fiske began her first Mediterranean Cruise after recommissioning in January 1954 and visited thirteen ports prior to returning to Newport, RI on 26 May.

'Courier Duty'

In December 1954, my ship, USS FISKE (DDR 842), was in the last month of a three-month long overhaul at the Boston Naval Shipyard. I had just completed the course of instruction at the DesLant Gunnery School in Newport, Rhode Island having been probably the most junior officer to attend that course. The ship's new Gunnery Officer, (and my new boss) Lt George Eidsness, had reported aboard during my absence, and he and the Captain had arranged some further training for me, the ship's most junior officer. I was to report to the Fleet Training Group at Guantanamo Bay, Cuba (better known as "Gitmo" from the Navy abbreviation for its name: GTMO).

Transportation had been arranged for me via Navy aircraft, and traveling under orders I reported to the Naval Air Station, Quonset Point, Rhode Island, for the first leg of the trip south. In short order I was aboard a Navy transport plane which took me to Pawtuxet River Naval Air Station, Maryland (better known as NAS PAXRIVER), where I was to catch another aircraft which was to take me the rest of the way.

I reported to the BOQ for what was supposed to be a two-night stay. About mid-afternoon the following day I was paged and told to report to another building. I soon found out that, as the lowest ranking commissioned officer on the plane, I had been selected to assure the proper delivery of some highly classified equipment to Gitmo. I was shown a truck laden with cases, each bearing a seal and a number, and was handed a list of these numbers, and told to inventory them. Having done this, and having assured myself they were all there, I signed a document acknowledging receipt thereof. I also received a .38 caliber Smith & Wesson revolver, four rounds of ammunition, and a shoulder holster.

After donning the holster, loading the weapon, and placing it in the holster under my blue uniform coat, I rode the truck with the mysterious cases to a hanger. There the cases were loaded aboard a locked compartment in the belly of a Lockheed "Constellation" cargo plane, and I was given the key to the compartment. An armed guard was then stationed under the plane, to guard that precious cargo until we took off, and I went back to the BOQ.

The big revolver in its holster made a rather prominent bulge on the left side of my uniform coat, and when I met my fellow passengers at dinner that evening it didn't take the more experienced officers among them long to figure out what had transpired. Naturally, I took a little good natured ribbing about my new duties. The fun part came later, when I returned to my room and wanted to take a shower before turning in for the night. There were no private showers in the BOQ, not for junior officers anyway, just a big shower room at the end of the hallway with perhaps a dozen shower heads spaced around the walls. Since almost any steward could come into my room, I wasn't about to leave that pistol behind. So, with a towel around my hips and the weapon in its holster under my left arm, I strode down the corridor to the shower. Arriving there, I hung it on the handle of a nearby shower where I could keep an eye on it, and took my bath. Then, back to my room, well-armed all the way!

Since losing that pistol would be nearly as bad as losing the classified equipment, I slept with it under my pillow that night, having first removed the cartridges from the cylinder as a safety precaution. The next morning, unfortunately, we were informed shortly after breakfast that, due to mechanical problems, our flight was going to be delayed for at least a day. Not wanting to carry that pistol around any more than I had to, I tried to return it. They refused to take it back, however, since I had acknowledged receipt of the weapon on the same form as the cases of equipment, and they didn't want to redo all that paperwork! I was stuck with it! I went down to the hanger to check on the armed guard under the airplane, after assuring myself that he was present and properly instructed in his duties, returned to the BOQ. It was a cold day in early December, there was snow on the ground, NAS PAXRIVER was out in the boondocks, and none of us were particularly interested in going anywhere except south. So, we hung around the BOQ and the Officer's Club for the plane to be repaired.

One of my fellow passengers was a middle-aged LCDR, a Reservist who had applied for a regular Navy commission. He had served throughout WWII, stayed in the reserves after the war, and had been called up for service in the Korean conflict. Now, with almost ten years of active duty behind him, he wanted to finish his twenty years and retire, but was afraid the Navy would decide they didn't need him anymore, and send him back to civilian life. We had time on our hands, and spent most of it talking, exchanging "sea stories", and I learned something about the value of my _regular_ Navy commission. After going thru the "well armed to the shower" bit, and being able to feel that gun under my pillow again that night, I can remember his greeting as I came into the dining room for breakfast the next morning, "Hi George, still got your gun?" I just smiled, and patted that big bulge under my left arm.

Fully two and a half days after signing my life away for the classified cargo and the pistol, our flight finally left PAXRIVER. We flew first to Norfolk, Virginia, to pick up more passengers and freight.

As per my orders, I requested an armed guard as soon as we landed, and waited under the aircraft until he arrived, then headed for the terminal building while the plane was being loaded. This was a cargo plane, and we passengers rode in temporary seats erected just inside the cargo doors, the freight being carried forward, over the wing. The seats were taken down while additional cargo was placed aboard and the load adjusted to relocate the center of gravity. The inside of the plane was unheated, and it was cold in Norfolk that afternoon.

We soon took off again and landed after dark at Naval Air Station, Jacksonville, Florida. It was snowing, and I nearly froze waiting under the airplane for the armed guard to show up. When he finally arrived, I headed to the terminal building to warm up and get a bite to eat. A couple of civilians were traveling with us, and I encountered them in the men's room. As I was removing my bridge coat,[1] one of them asked me rather timorously, "Are you <u>really</u> wearing a gun?" I replied "Yes, sir" just as I removed my uniform blouse, baring the butt in the process. The poor man turned white, and for a moment I thought he was going to faint dead away!

Perhaps two hours later we were in the air again, next stop Gitmo. It was bitterly cold in that plane after they finally closed that big cargo door, and due to the relatively high altitude at which we were flying as we approached Cuba, it certainly didn't get any warmer. If I have ever been colder in my life, I can't remember when, and to this day can't understand why I didn't come down with pneumonia! Then again, after all those shots the Navy had given me over the previous six years, perhaps no germs could survive in my bloodstream!

The plane finally landed in Cuba at about four o'clock in the morning. We taxied in, the engines were shut down, the big cargo door opened, and we were hit with a blast of hot, humid air, as the heat of the tropics displaced the frigid air we had carried with us from Florida. A young officer came aboard with a sheaf of papers, and I heard my name called, "Ensign Post?" I responded, "Here, Sir!" and found that he was ready and eager to relieve me of the cargo in the locked compartment, and the pistol that had never left my side for nearly four days. In short order I was sweating under that heavy winter uniform as we completed the paperwork, and he inventoried the cases as they were removed from the plane. Having assured himself that all was in order, and having checked the serial number of the pistol as well, he signed a form acknowledging receipt of it all, handed it to me, and I was free to go on my way.

Having slept very little aboard that cold airplane, I checked in at the BOQ at about five o'clock. I nearly fell into bed, having arranged a wake-up call for six o'clock. The desk called right on time, and I arose, showered and shaved, ate a good breakfast, and then walked over the headquarters of the Fleet Training Group. I arrived a little after eight o'clock, and promptly received a rather severe tongue lashing form a Lieutenant whose name I don't recall. The Fleet Training Group started work, I was informed, at 0700, and I how could I possibly have come in so late. I tried to explain when the plane arrived, to no avail. He threatened to put me on report, but finally, after verbally extracting at least a "pound of flesh" from my backside, relented and signed me in. He was right, of course, I should have determined the time they started work and arrived on time. After all, this was not a civilian job! However, I still don't think he was being very reasonable!

More than likely he was most angry over my coming there in the first place. Because of the delay at PAXRIVER, it was now getting close to the middle of December, and since was the peacetime Navy, FTG, Gitmo did not work during the holidays. My stay ashore would be a short one. The very next day I was ordered aboard a destroyer that was in the final stages of its "refresher training".[2] Conveniently, they found a billet for me, and I was assigned a battle station at one of the small auxiliary gun directors that controlled part of the ship's anti-aircraft gun battery of 40 millimeter guns. There I participated in gunnery drills and the ship's "Operational Readiness Inspection", *equivalent to a final exam. Having completed her training, the ship then sailed for her homeport of Newport, Rhode Island.*

On the long cruise from Guantanamo to Newport, the other junior officers onboard didn't mind my being on board in the least. I was simply integrated into their underway watch list, meaning that they had one less watch to stand on each rotation, and I gained some further valuable experience. On arrival in Newport, just before Christmas of 1954, I retrieved my automobile, which I had placed in storage about three weeks before , and drove to Boston to rejoin FISKE.

Footnotes: An officer's Bridge Coat is a very heavy overcoat, long enough to reach below the knees, Navy Blue with brass buttons, and fitted with loops on the shoulders to hold the markings of rank, commonly referred to as "shoulder boards". At that time only regular Navy officers were required to own them, reserve officers wearing the black raincoat instead.

Refresher Training was a period of underway training designed to work out any 'bugs' the ship might have developed as a result of a yard overhaul, and to integrate new personal into the team. A new ship, fresh from the builder's yards, was subjected to a similar training period called a 'shakedown'.

George W. Post Ens/Lt(jg) 1954-1956

U.S.S. FISKE   DDR 842

PORTS OF CALL

25 November 1952	Recommissioned, Boston Naval Shipyard
2 February 1953	Departed for GTMO BAY, San Juan, Puerto Rico, Virgin Islands
7 May 1953	Returned to Boston, Mass.
16 September	Began Operation Mariner (1-4 Oct. Plymouth, England)

18 October	Returned to Newport, R.I.	3 - 10 March	Genoa, Italy
4 January 1954	Enroute Mediterranean Area	17 - 22 March	Marseilles, France
14 - 18 January	Gibraltar, B.C.C.	23 - 26 March	Naples, Italy
19 - 25 January	Lisbon, Portugal	6 - 13 April	Tarragona, Spain
28 Jan - 1 Feb.	Palermo, Sicily	21 - 24 April	Cannes, France
1 Feb. - 5 Feb.	Augusta Bay, Sicily	24 - 29 April	St. Raphael, France
13 - 18 February	Salonika, Greece	6 - 12 May	Naples, Italy
19 - 24 February	Phaleron Bay, Greece (Athens)	26 May	Arrived Newport, Rhode Island

Combination of Shakedown & first Mediterranean cruises

4 January 1954 saw *Fiske* underway for her first duty with the Sixth Fleet in the Mediterranean as a DDR . During the next five months *Fiske* operated with units of other NATO nations and units of the Sixth Fleet. Ports of Call included Gibraltar; Palermo and Augusta Bay, Sicily; Salonika and Piraeus, Greece: Naples and Genoa, Italy; Marseilles, Cannes and St. Raphael, France; Tarragona, Spain; and, Lisbon, Portugal. The *Fiske* hosted a ship's party during the visit to Genoa. She returned to Newport on May 26th.

Fiske coming alongside a Fleet Oiler circa 1955

'The Message – Sub Launched'

During the time I served as a Radioman onboard the Fiske radiotelegraph was the most important communications system used because of it speed in transmitting messages to, from and among ships. Incoming messages could be interesting but also somewhat boring. Such as sitting [there] hour after hour copying encoded messages. As

*received these [encoded] messages made no sense until [they were]
decoded.*

*At times messages were received under the most trying
conditions [which] causing interferences that would disrupt the
frequency cycle. The most common interference was due to excessive
static from winds and storms, deafening blasts from the ship's gunfire
and when near shore Ham Operators cutting into our frequency from
overloaded antennas.*

*However, the topic of this story deals with the telegrams
received by the Fiske to and from shipmates. There were telegrams to
crew members from wives and sweethearts. These could get rather
personal. Had they known that their telegrams would be read by every
Radioman on the same circuit they might have self-censored them
before sending.*

*A lot of the telegrams were to the ship from crew members on
leave requesting one or two more days extension. Every excuse
imaginable was given from a sick grandmother to a sister getting
married. To these requests the Captain would reply with a message,
"Request denied, must have Red Cross verification."*

*While on the Fiske there were two telegrams that I consider the
best of any we had ever received. Because of their uniqueness I still
remember them word. One of them was from a crewmember sending
the message, "Request two days extension, having one hell of a time".
Captain Sweeny. Commenting on the sailor's honesty sent the following
message, "Request granted". The other was from a crew member's
wife announcing, "sub launched at 0400, has periscope".*

*All the Radiomen found this message so amusing they routed it,
per message board, so the ship's officers could share in the humor of
such a short, straight to the point, well-worded message.*
Merle Wagner RM3 1954 – 1956

There is little official information available of what operations
occurred between the end of her first Mediterranean cruise as a DDR in

1954 and her entry into the yards in mid-1957 for the extensive electronics upgrades necessary for her mission.

USS *Fiske* & *Harold J Ellison* moored quay side Naples

Anecdotal information received from shipmates indicate that after that first Med cruise *Fiske* spent much of the late summer of 1954 operating out of Newport conducting ASW Ops with the carrier USS *Antietam* and several other Newport based destroyers.

'The Coxswain'

I had reported aboard USS Fiske (DDR-842) in July 1954, and was promptly assigned the billet of Second Division Officer. The Second Division was one of the two "Deck" divisions, responsible for the ground tackle, ship's boat, and much of the topside area of the ship. Much of the work consisted of manual labor, jobs that required, for the most part more brawn than brains, and these divisions became a repository for the people that the other divisions could not use.

The Second Division was responsible for the after half of the ship and the ship's boat, a twenty-six foot motor whaleboat that served as the Captain's Gig. I soon found out that the boat's coxswain had been sentenced to thirty days in the brig. He was off the ship serving his sentence at the brig at the Naval Station, Newport, Rhode Island, and his billet was being filled by the standby coxswain.

A couple of weeks later, his sentence served, he returned to the ship. His name was Collins, and on his sleeve he wore the stripes of a Seaman Apprentice, the second lowest enlisted rank, he wore four "hashmarks", indicating sixteen years (or more) of naval service. All of his front teeth were missing, and he was one of the ugliest human beings I had ever seen. Collins was a typical rowdy, street-brawling sailor. And he wasted no time telling his shipmates how nice it was in the brig, and how badly he wanted to get back there. I didn't know it at the time, but he had chosen me, a brand new, very regulation young Ensign, as the means to that end.

One day the Captain summoned me and gave me some very explicit instructions about some improvements he wanted made on the gig. I gave him a snappy "Aye, Aye, Sir!" and went off looking for my leading petty officer, a Boatswain's Mate First Class named Homer Thomas. It was just before the end of lunch hour, so I checked the first class petty officer's quarters, but Thomas was not there. I tried a few other places too, but couldn't find him, so I decided to try the after crew's berthing space, which housed my division. (We were not allowed to page a person o the "1MC", the ship's loudspeaker system, except in an emergency which this definitely was not!)

Descending the ladder into the berthing compartment, I encountered Collins at the foot of the ladder. I quickly gave him the instructions concerning the boat. When I finished, instead of responding with the "Aye, Aye, Sir!" that I expected, Collins said simply "Fuck you!" What happened next probably took only a few seconds, much less than it takes to tell.

I am sure that I stood there, for a moment, at least, dumbfounded, with my mouth hanging open! I had backed myself into a corner by bypassing the chain of command, giving my orders directly to Collins instead of the division petty officer, as I should have done. What was going through my mind at the time included "What the heck do I do now?" and "He can't talk to me that way, I'm an officer!" Neither thought was spoken aloud, however, because I was really on the spot! The whole division, about twenty men, was looking on, and I had little doubt that Collins had told them that he was going to pull something like this in an effort to get himself back in the brig!

At Annapolis, we had always been taught to have a quick and ready reply when spoken to, even if it was only a snappy "Aye, Aye, Sir!" Plebes were always expected to address upperclassman as "Sir" or "Mister", and if they did not, the usual response from the upperclassman was "Put a 'Sir' on that!" And that is exactly what I told Collins!

He did. "Fuck you, Sir!" came back the prompt reply. Fortunately, at this point, it struck me as very funny, and I started laughing, and pretty soon the whole division was laughing with me. Everybody but Collins, that is. He was standing there waiting for me to put him on report. "You've got your orders, get busy!" and quickly dashed up the ladder before he had a chance to reply. Then I went looking for Thomas, again, and gave him the instructions, as I should have done in the first place.

I am not about to claim that my handling of the situation was indicative of any high degree of intelligence on my part. In fact, it was stupid of me to put myself in that predicament by failing to follow the proper chain of command. My quick response was solely the result of the years of excellent training I had received at Annapolis. I never did put Collins on report for the incident. Although I didn't think of it that way at the time, putting him on report for insubordination would simply have rewarded him by sending him back to the brig where he wanted to be, and at the same time deprived the ship of its best coxswain. In addition, we would have had to go the through the bother of a Captain's Mast and probably a special court martial.

As it turned out, I probably benefitted from the incident. My men found out that, contrary to popular opinion, I did have a small sense of humor. And, Collins never gave me any more trouble, or at least, nothing serious. I remember one incident the following year, after I left Second Division, when he tried me a bit. I was walking forward on the port side, main deck, when I encountered Collins and several others chipping paint on the superstructure bulkhead. Stopping to watch for a moment, I observed that, at the rate Collins was working the job would never get done. I made a good natured, if slightly sarcastic, comment on his efforts, and he responded by thrusting his paint scrapper at me with a challenge, "Let's see you do any better!" Well, if there was anything I had learned from my third class midshipman cruise, it was how to prepare a metal surface for painting, including the proper use of a paint scrapper. I took the scrapper, and in one quick swipe removed more paint than Collins had in the previous half hour. I handed him his scrapper back and walked off.

Some people doubt the value of men like Collins to the Navy, but I always contended that, with competent and intelligent leadership, the best in them could be brought out, and they could be made useful members of the service. Despite his faults, Collins was a very competent coxswain, and he took considerable pride in making the boat look good. Indeed, if I ever had to make a difficult journey in a small boat, I wouldn't mind having someone like Collins at the tiller. I remember one wintery morning on Narragansett Bay when the gig had been sent in to pick up the Captain. The temperature was well below freezing and it was windy. When the boat returned to the ship it was coated with ice. The passengers and the other two members of the boat crew were fairly dry, most having found shelter under the canvas canopy. Collins, however, in his exposed position at the stern, was coated with ice from spray that had frozen on his clothing. I can still remember the set of that ugly, toothless lower jaw of his as that boat

approached the ship, defying the worst that nature could throw his way.
George Post Ens/Lt(jg) 1954-1956

USS *Hawkins, Charles R Ware & Fiske* in Genoa 1954

Apparently Fiske was at sea when Hurricane '*Carol*' went through New England in August and anchored at a mooring buoy with 2 other destroyers when Hurricane '*Edna*' came through the Newport, RI in early September. Both of '*Carol*' and '*Edna*' caused extensive damage and numerous deaths along the Eastern seaboard. The *Fiske* did not receive any reported damage from either of these storms.

In the fall of '54 *Fiske* entered Boston Naval Shipyard for an overhaul that lasted until mid-December. During that period a new Target Designation System (TDS) was installed in CIC. Two pneumatically operated torpedo launchers were mounted on the main deck, port & starboard sides, just forward of amidships. They were designed to 'flip' an acoustic homing torpedo over the side to seek out and destroy a submarine. They weighed approximately 800 pounds each and had to be manhandled onto the launcher from a cart as no hoisting equipment was provided.

In early January *Fiske* was deployed to Guantanamo Bay, Cuba for 'refresher training'. Upon completion of 'RefTra' *Fiske* made a liberty call to Santiago, Cuba and returned to Newport and participated in an 'Operation Springboard' exercise that took her to Tampico, Mexico accompanying the battleship Wisconsin. Anecdotal reports have *Fiske* acting as a 'water taxi' conveying Mexican dignitaries from the shore out to the Wisconsin in March of 1955. *Fiske* returned to Newport and got ready to deploy to the Mediterranean. *Fiske* departed for the Med in May 1955 and made several port visits including Livorno, Italy. She returned to Newport in August.

'Mind Over Matter'

This is about an experience I had one night while the Fiske was headed to Mexico. The Radioman's sleeping compartment was directly below the Mess hall which had a steel cabinet in one corner for storing the crew's food trays.

I had just finished a stressful 8 hour watch in Radio Central and went to bed falling into a restless sleep. Around 2400 hours I was semi-consciously awakened by a loud crashing sound. My sub-conscious mind led me to think that the Fiske had struck some submerged object which might have torn a hole in its side. In the silence I dreamed that we had lost power in the Engine Rooms leaving us dead in the water.

I was going to waste no time in getting topside in case abandon ship was ordered. When I jumped out of my top rack two other radiomen were awakened also. One was a Colored 1ˢᵗ Class Radioman and the other was a Radioman striker. The 1ˢᵗ Class and I reached the ladder simultaneously, neither wanting to give way to the other. You could just see the fear in his eyes as he was uttering, "Oh Oh, the last time I heard a noise like that my ship was going down." By the time we reached the top of the ladder I was fully awake and my conscious mind had resumed control. One look into the Mess Deck reveled what had

actually taken place. After the evening meal that night when the mess cook had put the trays into the cabinet he did not fully secure the cabinet doors. Evidently during the night the Fiske ran into a swell which caused the ship to tilt slightly to port. This was just enough to fling open the cabinet doors letting 200 + steel trays to go crashing to the Mess Hall deck.
We had a good laugh and went back to bed. I was just glad that dreams seldom come true. The result of this experience was a case of mind over matter.
Merle Wagner RM3 1954 – 1956

The remainder of 1955 was spent in local operations with the *Fiske* and several other DesRon 14 destroyers being moored out at the refueling piers in Tiverton for the holidays of Thanksgiving and Christmas.

'Training Films'

As a newly minted ensign my first assignment was to the Fiske, a sleek destroyer swinging around an anchor buoy in Newport harbor, but my heart was in Boston. As newlyweds (11 months) Marilyn and I had an apartment in Boston overlooking the public gardens. As often as possible I would drive up to be with my bride.
One such opportunity occurred when the ship needed to take on a supply of classified training films, in preparation for deployment. This required an officer to go to the "Fargo" building in Boston, sign for the films and bring them safely back to the Fiske on Monday morning. It allowed me to leave Newport early Thursday morning to get the films checked out before the issuing office closed down for the weekend. All went well, and I left with a cardboard box full of training films Monday morning bright and early I kissed my bride and set out for Newport with a cardboard box filled with top secret training films. Pulling into Newport it started to rain. I got the films down to fleet landing and passed the box to the launch's coxswain. He set the box down on a

(wet) seat in the rear of the launch. We got out to the Fiske and the coxswain picks up the cardboard box of films to hand them to a sailor on watch at the gang plank, and as he does....... the bottom falls out of the box and some 30 classified films (that I signed for) slide into the mud at the bottom of Newport harbor.

After days of report writing and re-writes it was decided that I should contact and arrange with the "Yosemite" (a destroyer tender, swinging at anchor nearby) to provide a launch crew with divers to retrieve the films. To my surprise the Yosemite was happy to assist in my mission.

On a frigid December morning I climbed onboard the Yosemite's' launch and we set of to retrieve the films.... upon arrival at the spot that I remembered as the area where they went down, we put out an anchor, and the divers began getting into their hard- hat diving gear.

One of the divers lit of the portable air compressor that would provide air to the divers after a few minutes he noticed that air pressure wasn't registering ......so he tapped the gauge with his finger. then he yelled "she's going to blow".......and sure enough it did, the compressor storage tank blew a 2 foot hole in the bottom of the launch....the compressor had been left out in the launch overnight and the pressure gauge had frozen at the "0" pressure mark. Luckily, the divers had not donned the hard diving helmets; they could have been seriously hurt if they had.

Being the senior officer onboard I assumed command .... I yelled "get going and head for that destroyer over there", pointing to the USS Rush anchored nearby. And we did just that, the diver nearest the throttle cracked it wide open and off we went dragging anchor.............. With a waterspout amidships shooting 5 feet into the air, and over the side.

We got alongside and I called for lines. The deck watch must have been observing our dilemma and had lines ready. We quickly tied up fore and aft to the Rush's gangplank...... which was just enough to keep the launch from going under.

The Yosemite retrieved the crew and their launch, patched up the damage and made sure thereafter to keep all gauges warm. The films are still resting on the bottom and somewhere in the official Navy archives are the many reports I generated as a result of my first command.

Errol Terrell, Ens/Lt(jg) USN 1955-1957

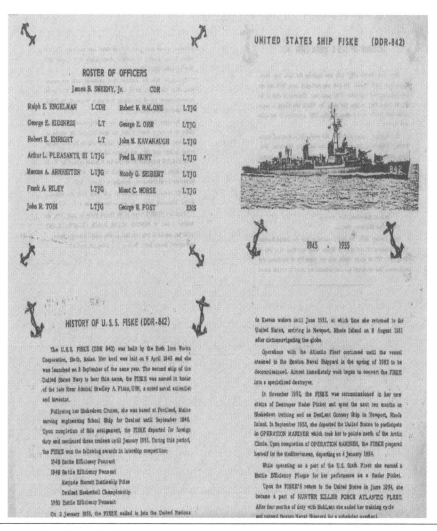

In March of 1956 while *Fiske, Myles C. Fox, Newman K. Perry* and the *Coolbaugh* were moored at the newly opened Pier One notice was made that a storm was coming into the Newport area. The storm had 12 foot waves and hurricane force winds. Preparations and precautions were made but the entire group of nested destroyers were torn loose from the pier and drifted into Coddington Cove. *Fiske* managed to drop an anchor but was unable to set the pelican hook and the entire length of chain was paid out across the cove. The *Newman K. Perry* found itself about to go aground so she broke the nest and got underway. *Fiske* ended up aground on Gould Island.

'A Nightmare for the USS Fiske'

Our whole Division of Destroyers was tied up to a pier in Newport for the weekend of 17 March 1956. Most of the crew, especially from the Fiske, had received liberty. The Captain also left the ship as his home was in Newport. If memory serves me correctly, the order in which the ships were moored was the USS Hawkins first, the USS Rush was moored next to Hawkins, then the USS Myles C. Fox was moored to Rush, and then the Fiske was moored to the Fox.

I had the watch that day and we were receiving many routine weather messages from NOA Weather Station. It was a cold, snowy day with increasing winds and blowing snow. With the weather becoming worse, I started receiving priority weather messages about every five minutes. It was all the messenger could do to keep getting the messages to the officers who had stayed on board and having to sign the messages.

Now the wind speed increased to around 80MPH with blinding snow making it one of the worst blizzards I'd ever been in. At that moment I started receiving emergency weather messages continuously. The strong winds caused the USS Hawkins' mooring lines to break and all four ships were blown helplessly from the pier. We chopped our lines loose from the USS Fox to try and control the ship and ride out the storm, but with our boilers down we were unable to get steam up fast enough to get control of the ship. All of a sudden there was a tremendous jolt knocking us off our feet. The mighty Fiske was aground with her screws stuck in the mud. We sat on an island all night until the next morning when the tide came in so a tugboat could free us and get us back a float.

The Captain, who made it down to the pier just as all four ships were blown from the pier, was left helpless on the dock. He was brought onboard the next morning. We set out for sea trials to assess any damage to the ship. We had lost our SONAR dome and there was a terrible vibration throughout the ship. That sent us down to Charlestown Naval Shipyard in Boston for repair.

The most enlightening moment that night was receiving a message from Admiral Burke saying to keep our chin up, only destroyermen could come through this catastrophe. Once repaired, the mighty Fiske set sail again.
Merle G. Wagner RM3 1954-1956

A newspaper report from the following day said, "In the Newport area storm six vessels of the destroyer fleet broke their moorings in Coddington Cove. Three were beached in mud by the raging winds. They were the RADAR Picket boats *M.C. Fox* and the *Fiske* and the destroyer escort *Coolbaugh*. All were refloated at high tide this noon."

In May *Fiske* departed for the Med and returned to Newport in late September or early October. During that cruise *Fiske* had the privilege of visiting Monaco and berthing in the inner harbor.

'Shore Patrol Duty'
In June of 1956, FISKE was assigned a two week period for repairs alongside a destroyer tender moored in the harbor of Izmir, Turkey. I was sent ashore for one of those weeks for temporary duty as Assistant Shore Patrol Officer. Thousands of years ago, Izmir was known as Smyrna, and was one of the many ancient cities visited by the

Apostles, as they spread the Gospel throughout the world. There were ancient ruins within the city limits, and I made the most of the free time I had seeing as much as possible of this fascinating corner of the world. I don't remember our exact duty schedule, but we did work some pretty long hours, and our reward was an occasional full day off, I was able to join a tour going out to the city of Bergama, site of the ancient city of Pergamus.

We boarded a bus in Izmir early in the morning. If I remember correctly, all of the people onboard were American Navy personnel. We headed off down the road, which was unpaved, and if you looked away from the road, the setting was something the apostles might have seen. We passed camel caravans, and people riding along on donkeys. Off in the distance you could see flocks of sheep and goats, tended by shepherds who looked just as we imagined they might have in biblical times. It seemed as if we had been transported back many centuries in time.

Even the little Turk driving the bus looked like he had come from another age. Clad in turban and baggy trousers, he was no more than four and one-half feet tall. The bus was a Mercedes, built in Germany, and from the radio speaker came weird-sounding oriental music, which seemed to have no real melody, just a strange squealing sound. Imagine our surprise when the oriental music stopped suddenly, and "The Yellow Rose of Texas" blared forth from the speaker. In moments we were all singing along with the radio. When the song ended, the squeaky oriental music began again, and we realized the irony of it all: Americans, riding in a German bus driven by a guy straight out of the 'Arabian Nights', watching camel caravans go by while singing about Texas in a country where most of the people didn't know where 'Texas' was!

Our day had only just begun, however! We arrived at Bergama about noon, and after lunch of native food in a local restaurant, we climbed a mountain to view the ruins of the ancient city. Very little of it was still standing, earthquakes and vandals having pretty well knocked *the place down. Judging by the remnants of the huge columns littering the ground, there must have been some very magnificent buildings there at one time. Like many ancient cities, it was built on top of a mountain, and had a wall around it at one time, to protect it from attack. Most of the smaller stones had been carried by the more recent inhabitants of the area to use in building their own homes, but the larger blocks, some of which must have weighed tons, were still there.*

After viewing the ruins, we were taken to an ancient Roman amphitheater, where we were the guests of honor for a performance which could have taken place centuries ago. First we were treated to an ancient Greek drama, all done in the local language, but still fascinating to watch. Then a group of young boys, perhaps ten to twelve years old, took to the stage and performed a series of dances. Accompanied by more of that strange music, some of the dances consisted of pairs of boys fighting each other with some pretty wicked looking swords, in almost perfect unison.

The performance lasted for a couple of hours. When it began, the amphitheater was packed, standing room only, and not much of that. We, being the guests of honor, were right down front, and those seats were made of solid stone! The locals had come prepared, with cushions to sit on, but none to spare, and so we sat, not wanting to offend our hosts, while our backsides begged for mercy! Most of the Americans, like me, were pretty lean, without much of a natural seat cushion, but I didn't see a single Navy get up and leave, even though a lot of local people did, well before the show ended.

It was dusk when we left the amphitheater, and in fact, some of my pictures didn't come out very well, because the sun was so low in the sky that much of the action was in heavy shade. We had supper at local restaurants and then boarded the Mercedes bus for the long ride back to Izmir. Most of the Americans went back to their ships, but not me. I was living in a hotel ashore.

I don't think that it was exactly Izmir's best hotel. It looked fairly modern and seemed clean enough. When you turned off the lights and went to bed, however, you started to get the feeling you weren't alone! The noises weren't very loud, but there was definitely something moving around. I soon got up and turned on the lights, and was treated to a sight of dozens of cockroaches scrambling for cover! If you are tired enough, you can sleep through almost anything, and I soon got used to my little friends. They never seemed to do any harm, so what the heck!

My tour ashore was during our second week in Izmir. Aboard ship during the first week, I had heard tales of at least one sailor coming back aboard from liberty in Izmir with his hands badly cut up, and something about "the compound". As a Shore Patrol Officer, I soon found out that "the compound" was one of the places we stationed our SP's in an effort to keep sailors out! Prostitution is frowned upon in Moslem countries, and it seems that any woman found selling herself in that area was thrown into "the compound", which was nothing but a large brothel. It was surrounded by a high stone wall with jagged shards of glass set into the top of it, and it was while attempting to scale that wall that our young sailor cut his hands to ribbons! One day I rode the Navy van that carried an oncoming shift of Shore Patrolmen to their posts, and picked up they had relieved. As we approached, a big steel gate swung open, and we drove through. Inside the wall were several buildings, and as we passed, I saw a few of the 'ladies' who inhabited the place. Only one I saw could be called attractive by even the lowest of standards, and the rest were just plain ugly! One pass through was enough for me, and I came out convinced that if they took the sailors through there on the bus when they had just came ashore and were still sober, few of them would want to scale that wall even when they were drunk!

Shore Patrol Headquarters was right down on the waterfront, near the landing where the boats from the ship came in. Like the hotel, the building looked pretty good from the outside, but there were surprises inside! One of the first things one had to locate if one was going to stay around for long was the men's room, of course. Someone pointed it out to me, and I entered a neatly tiled room that at first glance appeared empty. Upon closer examination, however, one observed a hole in the floor, more a less in the center of the room. The hole was perhaps eight inches in diameter, and beside it were two tile footprints. It seemed that one placed one's feet in those footprints and squatted, one was in position to do what one went to the men's room to do! Looking down through the hole, you could see the waters of the harbor below! Toilet tissue? You've got to be kidding! And, no place to wash your hands either! I soon got in the habit of taking care of such matters before I left my hotel room, since it was equipped with a real honest-to-goodness flush toilet.

We had a list of places that were 'off limits' to U. S. Navy personnel. Inevitably, those seemed to be the places that a few sailors most interesting! Occasionally, the owner of one of these establishments, not wanting to get in trouble with the law, would call the police or Shore Patrol Headquarters to report a sailor in his place, and accompanied by a member of the local constabulary and an enlisted SP, I would go off to remove him. I vividly remember going into one of them, and finding a dance floor with a balcony on the second floor overlooking the dance floor below. The balcony was made up of a series of curtained booths, apparently these were utilized by some of the "ladies of the evening" to ply their trade. We were shown to one of the booths and found two young sailors and two young girls sitting at a table enjoying a drink. Since merely entering one of the off limits was an offense, I informed the two sailors that their liberty had expired, picked up their liberty cards, and told them to return to their ship immediately. Their liberty cards would follow with a report chit. The sailors complied without a word of protest, both of them fortunately still being reasonably sober. As for the girls, however, that was a different story. They were civilians, and didn't have to take orders form a Naval Officer, and one of them promptly threw her arms around my neck and kissed me! Yuck! I went back to headquarters via my hotel room, where I thoroughly washed my face and brushed my *teeth! The enlisted SP who witnessed the incident naturally got a big laugh out of it, and made no secret of had happened to LTJG Post that night!*

One place put on a party for the visiting sailors, and naturally the Shore Patrol was in attendance as well. One of the attractions was a 'belly dancer', and as she performed, one of the sailors who apparently too many drinks jumped on the stage with her and started putting on a little act of his own. Actually he was doing a pretty good imitation of a belly dancer, and I wasn't all that bothered by it at first, but quickly realized that one of the American women that had staged the party was not at all happy with his unscheduled act. We quickly hauled him out, picked up his liberty card, and sent him back to his ship, again without incident. I have to admit having felt like something of a 'party pooper' at the time!

For the most part, our men behave pretty well over there, and we had no serious incidents during the week I spent ashore. Even when intoxicated, they didn't cause any real problems, except for a bit of noise now and then. I had a lot less trouble with them than I had with rowdy Annapolis classmates when I was assigned Shore Patrol duty in Gitmo during a midshipman cruise. When my week's duty was over, I reported back aboard FISKE, and we sailed to another exotic port of call.

George W. Post Ens/Lt(jg) 1954-1956

'R' Division. USS *Fiske*, 1957

'Monaco 1957'

I was a young twenty-five year old Ensign on the Fiske in 1957. After fleet operations in the Western Med, and the task force commander had detached Fiske, commanded by CDR C. Griffin, we were proceeding to our liberty port-of-call for liberty and port visit. I was the CIC Officer, Air Controller and lots of very interesting, entirely collateral duties onboard during my 18 months aboard her, including Ship's Legal Officer, Courts Martial Prosecutor, Voting Officer, Education Officer, Law Office, Tour Officer and Wardroom Mess Treasurer!

As we approaching our liberty port, Monaco, I heard the following on the Ship's Intercom, "Ensign Peloquin, report to the Commanding Officer on the bridge." I said to myself, "What have I done now?" I proceeded to the bridge, greeted by the Skipper, who informed me that Fiske was directed to proceed into the inner harbor of Monaco, that soon we would be slowing down and pick up a harbor pilot and there was a problem – the French harbor pilot did not speak English.

The Skipper, knowing of my French-Canadian heritage and that I was skilled in the French language, directed me to welcome the French pilot aboard our vessel, escort him to the bridge, get to know him and upon his 'taking control' of the Fiske and as he issued commands to the helmsman and the Engine Order Telegraph in French, my job was to translate his French commands into English and get our ship into its berth in the inner harbor.

Thanks to my French-Canadian heritage, studying French at St. Ann School, Woonsocket with the Presentation of Mary Nuns, my days at the Mount St. Charles Academy, my fluency in French served the Fiske well.

I was released from active duty in 11/1959, returning to my elementary school teaching position in the North Smithfield, RI school system. My recollection of my French translation duties aboard Fiske in Monaco are etched in my heart and mind.

Eugene Peloquin Ens/Ltjg 1957-1959

Ensign Peloquin joined the Naval Reserve immediately after being released from active duty. He became a member of Navy Reserve Unit 1-43 in Woonsocket, RI and retired in 1982 as a Captain.

In mid-1957 *Fiske* returned to Boston Naval Shipyard for a general overhaul and the addition of more electronic equipment. This additional electronic equipment (TACAN) necessitated the addition of another mast just forward of the aft stack and was also a tripod type. This mast and the large radome that it carried, plus the ECM radomes, were to become the signature silhouette of DDR's throughout the fleet.

Upon completion of the overhaul in Boston *Fiske* took on ammunition and sailed to Newport via the Cape Cod Canal. January 1958 was spent operating out of Newport. Due to a lack of berthing space at Pier One most of the in port time was spent moored at the 'Mike' buoys and taking the motor whaleboat or a water taxi to Fleet Landing. *Fiske* was also berthed at the State Piers in Fall River and New Bedford, MA.

UNREP with (l to r) *Fiske*, *Allagash* and *Essex* in April 1958

In early February she departed on a 'shakedown' cruise to Guantanamo Bay, Cuba. Enroute to Cuba liberty port calls were made to Charleston, SC and Miami, FL. Interspaced with the normal shakedown activities of drills and shore gunfire practice at Culebra, PR liberty port calls were made to Santiago, Cuba and San Juan, PR.

Fiske returned to Newport in March and departed for the Med in April for duty with the Sixth Fleet. During the next several months she made port visits to Barcelona and Valencia, Spain; Taranto and Rappolo, Italy; Salonika and Piraeus, Greece; and Lisbon, Portugal. She returned to Newport in August.

Late in this deployment with the Sixth Fleet Lebanon found itself at odds with the UAR – made up of Egypt and Syria – and many of Lebanon's own people. The Christian President of Lebanon requested military assistance from the United States. President Eisenhower authorized 'Operation Blue Bat' and ComSixthFlt sent the aircraft carriers *Saratoga*, *Essex*, and *Wasp,* cruisers *Des Moines* and *Boston* and two squadrons of destroyers. The operation involved approximately 14,000 men, including 8,509 United States Army personnel, a contingent from the 1st Airborne Battle Group, 187th Infantry from the 24th Infantry Division (based in West Germany) and 5,670 officers and men of the United States Marine Corps (the 2nd Provisional Marine Force, of Battalion Landing Teams 1/8 and 2/2). They were supported by a fleet of 70 ships and 40,000 sailors.

Operation Blue Bat lasted 102 days from July 15 to Oct. 25. Given the time frame and the number of ships involved it is extremely likely that *Fiske* participated in 'Operation Blue Bat'. Naval units that did participate in this operation were awarded the Navy Expeditionary Medal but no record of *Fiske* receiving that award for that period can be found.

In early September 1958 departed Newport to participate in a NATO Exercise in the North Atlantic. While enroute *Fiske* refueled off the USS *Wisconsin* (BB 64) in heavy seas. The *Fiske* lost power with the fuel lines connected. The in-haul lines and hoses parted, fouling the side of the *Fiske* with NSFO (Navy Standard Fuel Oil), but no injuries were sustained.

MWB with canvas top

CDR Cyril Griffin Change of Command 9-22-1958

This exercise took the *Fiske* north of the Arctic Circle off the Lofoten Islands of Norway. On September 7th at 9 degrees, 17 minutes longitude *Fiske* again entered the 'Realm of the Arctic Circle' and 'Bluenose' certificates were awarded to all crewmembers. On September 22, 1958 CDR Cyril Griffin was relieved by CDR John Hough as Commanding Officer.

The San Remo Swim

I'm the one who successfully swam back to the Fiske in San Remo. I climbed aboard the ship from the fantail, went forward opposite the Officer's Deck [Quarterdeck ?] and had just finished showering down in full dress (needed to get the salt out of the uniform) when Bill (Wolverton) came down the ladder to our "bunk area". I heard him coming so I greeted him at the bottom of the ladder.

Bill was astonished that I had not only beat him back to the ship but that I had not drowned. He had turned me in to the Officer of the Day and they had Fiske's whale boats out looking for me someplace between the shore and the ship. It was a very long distance and Bill was sure that in my "drunken state" I must have drowned and would never make it back to the boat. Bill said to me in mixed reaction, "Pettingill, I've turned you in to the OD and they are out looking for you in the whale boats . . . I thought you'd drowned." His reaction was mixed because he was happy I was alive but concerned because he had turned in his buddy.

Fortunately/luckily I had to stand Captain's Mast and was sentenced to X number of days on board. The expiration of the term was the day of arrival at our next port so there was really no penalty and no record because the Captain liked us both (Bill was a DK3 at the time and I was a recent graduate of the DK school in Newport and so Bill was my 'boss').

I served on the Fiske from 3/55 to 7/57 and then got shore duty in New England where I served out my four-year term. Bill was reasonably tall, good looking and always with a friendly smile on his face. As you can imagine, being from West Virginia, he had to take a good ribbing from us boys from the north and when we were kind to him we called him "Wolf"."
Richard Pettingill DK3 March 1955 to July 1957

DKSN Richard Pettingill

DK3 Bill 'Wolf' Wolverton

Upon completion of the exercise *Fiske* made two ports of call. She docked at the British Naval Dockyard in the Firth of Forth and tied up next to the USS *Albany* (CL 123) in the Firth of Clyde, Scotland. She arrived back in Newport in October.

In January 1959 *Fiske* again departed for the Med. Ports of call were made at Gibraltar; Naples, Italy; Valencia and Barcelona, Spain; Antibes and Nice, France. A ship's party was held at Palma de Majorca, Spain. *Fiske* was 'outchopped' from Valencia, Spain and was headed for Newport when the Lebanon Crisis had her re-routed to Suda Bay, Crete. *Fiske*, along with most of the US Navy's Sixth Fleet, spent several weeks there until the crisis was resolved. *Fiske* returned to Newport in August.

'Peanut Butter Ransom'

In the winter of 1959 the Fiske was in the Med. We were high lining stores aboard; I was in charge of checking in everything that came in at my station. About an hour or so after we had completed our replenishment the word was passed that a few cases of peanut butter

*was missing. The following day a letter was posted on the Ships Office
door which read in part " that if the peanut butter was returned at the
Ships Office door there would be nothing said or done" [I just want to
mention here that the crew did not have peanut butter on the mess deck
at this time.] The day after that someone posted a note saying "that if
the crew got peanut butter on our Mess Deck the peanut butter would
be returned." The crew won.*
Mike Petro SK3 1958-1960

USS Sierra, Myles C Fox, Fiske, Lowry & Gearing
Souda Bay, Crete 1959

'The Juice Caper'

*[Winter of 1959, location Mediterranean] We had just finished
high lining stores. I was at work in the midship's storeroom when two
Fireman came down the ladder with cases of juice. They asked me if
they could hide the juice in the storeroom. I said that I didn't want
anything to do with it.*

After a while I gave in. There was a wooden trunk that belonged to Mr. Curry, our previous Supply Officer. We put the juice in the trunk and locked it. I kept the key in my pocket.

Shortly after this the word was passed that the juice was missing and the ship would be searched. About an hour later an officer and the Chief Master at Arms came down the ladder. I was asked if I had seen any juice. I said no. The officer asked me what was in the trunk. I said I didn't know because that was an officer's trunk. The officer told the chief to get the cutters to cut the lock. I motioned to the chief that the juice was in the trunk, he shook his head that he understood.

He got the officer somehow to leave the storeroom for a few minutes. While they were gone we moved the juice the juice to another spot and relocked the trunk. The officer and chief came back and cut the lock, no juice and left. The chief saved my bacon.
Mike Petro SK3 1958-1960

November 1958 found *Fiske* again headed to Boston Naval Shipyard for an electronics upgrade. The AN/SPS-6C Air-Search Radar was removed and the more powerful AN/SPS-29 was installed. To make room for a new deckhouse on the 01 level to house the new Radar's electronics both forward twin 3"/50 gun mounts were removed. This left *Fiske* with only Mount 33 and her 3 dual 5"/38 mounts as her offensive/defensive armaments. The 'bedspring' antenna of the AN/SPS-29 Radar, combined with the TACAN dome, became the distinguishing features of the *Fiske* until FRAM conversion back to a DD in 1964.

'Shots'

Right after the peanut butter incident, the word was passed over the 1MC for all hands to report to sick bay for "shots". I said to my SKSN Richard Karcher, what the "H" are they talking about? We had all of our shots before we left for the Med. I went down to sick bay. I asked the chief 'What was going on?' He brought out a bottle of whiskey. He asked me if I wanted a 'shot'. I said sure. I had one and then he asked me, 'If I wanted another one?' I said yes. After about five 'shots' I said I had enough. I asked him why he was giving shots out. He said that he could only keep the whiskey for a certain period of time, and then he had to get rid of it. It was an unusual Happy Hour. Mike Petro SK3 1958-1960

In May 1960 *Fiske*'s homeport was changed to Mayport, FL where she became part of DesRon 8 and frequently carried the flag of DesDiv 82 and, occasionally, the flag of DesRon 8.

'Entertainment'

As you can see it appears that I was working very hard reading an official Navy Manual on the SPS-10 Surface Search Radar Maintenance. Actually, it was a girlie magazine. I was probably 20 years old at the time and enjoying a free Cruise in the Mediterranean, complete with 3 meals a day (plus Mid-Rats) and entertainment.

The entertainment consisted of climbing the mast while underway to repair a radar antenna. The view was great from way up there while the Fiske was rocking and rolling. We had a great group of ET's! I really enjoyed working with all of them, and would do it again in a minute. After the Turks ran the Fiske aground back in the late 1990's and scrapped her, I suspect she was turned into Toyota pickup trucks and refrigerators. Great ship, great crew, but the Turks were never known for being great sailors! They smoke terrible tobacco and drink awful liquor. Long live the USS Fiske and all that served aboard her. Lou Nigro ETR2 1956-1960

Fiske departed the shipyard in February 1959 and after a brief stay in Newport departed for Guantanamo Bay, Cuba in March. While in route she made a port call to Jacksonville, FL. After there was an 'incident' ashore in Jacksonville Fiske was 'requested' by local authorities to re-berth at the Mayport Naval Station.

Upon completion of Refresher Training at Gitmo Fiske returned to Newport. In October 1959 she again returned to the Med. While anchored off Cannes, France during a storm on Christmas Eve Fiske had her anchor drag and ended up on the rocks near the beach. She sustained damage to one of her screws and had to limp into drydock in Malta for repairs. Fiske returned to Newport in early 1960.

CDR John B. Hough was relieved in July 1960 by CDR Clifford E. Hunter. It appears that CDR Hough's tour was shortened by approximately three months. It is difficult to draw a direct correlation to the grounding and his being relieved but it is a safe bet that the OOD on duty that night had his career track effected.

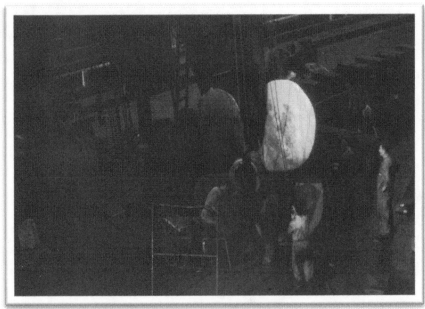

Drydock in Malta 1959

'On the rocks on the Riviera'

    We were at port and starboard liberty and I had the watch, such as it was in port for a Sonarman. Doug Gunderson, another Sonarman, had the quarterdeck watch and about 2000 hours he came down and told me that it seemed to him the lights on land were getting closer. I went topside to look. It was a windy night and, yes, it did seem we were a bit closer than we had been a few hours ago. Doug said he had told the Officer of the Deck, but he didn't believe him. The captain, the exec and most of the officers were ashore, so there was no one else to tell.

    An hour later, Doug came down again and said we were really close now and still the OOD would not do anything. Soon after that I heard a scraping noise from the hull and felt the ship bump and tilt a few degrees. I ran topside and sure enough we had dragged our anchor and drifted onto the rocks. I could almost throw a stone to the beach it was so close.

There we stayed for a day or more as the damage was assessed. Only one of the screws had been damaged so we limped to Malta and went into dry dock for several days while they replaced the damaged screw.

Valletta was a nice liberty port, and the crew enjoyed the respite, but I doubt the captain's naval career went far after that.
Jeff Kovite SOG3 1959-1963

'Flying Fish'

I'm hoping you'll include this amusing story in the history of the Fiske. One night back in 1960 I had the mid-watch in one of the engine rooms and needed a pack of cigarettes so I climbed out the outboard hatch and took a few steps. Lying at my feet was a dead flying fish and I thought maybe I could shake the after steering watch up. I slowly opened the overhead hatch and spotted the guy sound asleep with his headset still on so I dropped the fish at his feet and closed the hatch.

Next morning I looked the poor guy up and said I hear you had an exciting night. He shocked me when he said he saw the fish and panicked and called the bridge real quick and reported we were flooding back there. I don't know who all came running but after seeing it was a false alarm and the dead fish they chewed him out and warned him about sleeping on watch, which he did not admit. I guess the bridge had a good laugh over it. I never admitted it and I wonder if anyone else can recall who this guy from 1st Division was.
Leyland East EN3 1959-1962

'The Prankster'

'The Roll" – Three takes'

Okay guys, this incident stands out in my memory. I may get some flak about it but here goes......Med cruise, 1959-60, sometime after Barcelona, we are out at sea in a very heavy storm. The Fiske and other ships are listing heavily. Suddenly, the Captain (I think) announces that we took a particularly heavy roll, (to starboard, again I think). For some reason I remember 70 degrees being mentioned. The Fiske leaned on its side for an undetermined amount of time until she finally righted herself. When I related that story to others, they said it was impossible. But......why do I seem to remember 70 degrees and why did the Captain (?) inform us of that particular roll? That type of announcement had never made prior to that roll. Scuttlebut had it that we were going to return to Barcelona. Didn't we wish? Care to enlighten me?

John Degnan Jr. SOG3 1959-1961

I recall that roll vividly. I believe we were off Barcelona and were in this storm for three days- we had to sleep holding on to the railing around the bunk.

I was sitting on the deck in the compartment putting a button on a shirt. Our compartment was on the port side, just outside the Sonar Shack. We rolled to starboard and we seemed to just keep on going. I slid over toward the other compartment and was only stopped by the midship ladder going up to the mess deck. The ship just seemed to hang there for a long time, although it was probably only 30 seconds or so, then it slowwwwly came back. I don't recall the captain making an announcement, but the number 42 has always stuck in my mind as the degree of roll. It is my understanding that at 70 degrees we would not have come back.

Jeff Kovite SOG3 1959-1961

I remember that. I had just come in from the fantail where we were sent by the bridge to check the depth charge rack as there was some concern that there was a problem there. I went with Jean Marcel. We had just got inside when we started that roll and I was coming

down the ladder to our bunk area and I was walking just about
sideways to stand up. I don't recall the degree of roll but I remember
looking at everybody's face and saying to myself (Oh shit).
Frank Nicastro SOGSN 1959-1961

Editor's note: Information recently obtained from Navy sources
appears to support the premise that the *Fiske* could not comeback from
a roll greater than approximately 50 degrees. There are numerous
variables such as fuel load and percentage of stores on board but the
consensus appears to be that a roll greater than 50 degrees by a
destroyer configured like the *Fiske* would have caused her to capsize.

In September and October *Fiske* made a North Atlantic cruise
with a port call to Hamburg, Germany after transiting the Kiel Canal
and Elbe River.
While the Fiske was in Hamburg reports were heard that there
was a 'hot' new club on the Reeperbahn called 'The Top Ten Club' and
that had a band named 'The Jets' that played American style music.

Top Ten Club, St Pauli District, Hamburg

The Jets Meet the Fiske

I was the Leader of 'The Jets'-the first rock band to play in Germany-at the Top Ten Club, 136 Reeperbahn, Hamburg. The (Fiske) DDR 842 was visiting. around 1960 or 61.and members of the crew visited us many times, They were dumbfounded as we played all Gene Vincent, Elvis, Jerry Lee Lewis, Eddie Cochrane stuff for them. They couldn't believe we were not Americans. I think, perhaps the nickname of one guy who became a pal was Smithy? Ring a bell?

Anyway, all the crew visited in shifts according to duty schedules. One day Tony and myself were invited aboard - fantastic!

We met the Captain on bridge, invited for chow.-.T Bone, - can still taste it. Schlitz & Budweiser LONG before it was available here, we were given a T Shirt and dozens of packs of Pall Mall - again long before available in UK!

The Jets – (l to r) Iain Hines, Tony Sheridan & Colin Milander

Next day Tony and I went down to brunch at the Seamen's' Mission wearing DDR Ts. I noticed a couple of angry guys following us. Then additional ones till there were ten or so. We walked quicker. They did too.

They caught up, started to swing punches. Pointed at my T. and said "Deutsche Democratic Republic!" I said, 'Nein, DDR Fiske - Schiffe.' The punches – none had landed - stopped. I took them down to harbor, pointed her out. Aaaagh - much laughter.

They came down to Top Ten Club that night and I introduced them to my fantastic temporary shipmates! Much beer was consumed, Wurzburger Hofbrau.
Iain Hines, Gosport, Hampshire, UK

There was a story told throughout the ship that a junior officer missed the departure of *Fiske* from Hamburg and was seen making his approach to the ship on a small craft standing on the bow yelling, 'Schnell, schnell!' while waving what appeared to be a brandy bottle.

Many of the sea detail personnel were cheering him on but the CO, CDR C. E. Hunter, to quote Queen Victoria, "was not amused." The ship stopped to pick him up and then proceeded on her way. I believe that the phrase is "being in hack" for several days after that slight misstep.

Fiske in Hamburg, Germany 1960

During this cruise *Fiske* again crossed the Arctic Circle and the entire crew was given 'Blue Nose' certificates. She returned to Mayport in late October after encountering some very heavy weather off Cape Hatteras and losing some life rafts and all the Deck Department's staging that had been secured between the stacks on the 01 level. The top of forward davit of the MWB was twisted almost 70°. The MWB was lost

As one pier side observer stated, "She looked like she'd gone to war and lost." The shot below was taken from the USS *Shangri-La* (CVA 38) during that transit from Hamburg to Mayport. Reportedly the carrier had 'green water' on the flight deck and often could not see the *Fiske* a quarter of a mile astern.

Photo of Fiske taken from the Shangri-La 10/59

'Top Secret'

In July of 1960 the Fiske was on a Mid Shipmen cruise to Bermuda and New York City. One night on our way to Bermuda I had the midnight to 0400 Crypto watch in the Comm. Center. I didn't have to stand my watch there, I was on call. I was asleep in my rack, it was about 0200 when the messenger woke me up and told me that I had a message to break. I got up and headed up to the Comm. Center. I set up the decoder which was located in a very small room, enough room for one person and it had a sliding door. I closed the door and started to break the message, the first two words that came out were "Top Secret". I thought to myself, "why me." I broke the message and it was from President Eisenhower. Simply the message said that the Russians were trying to cause collisions with their ships and ours and trying to make it look like it was our fault.

I had to re-type the message on a form for the Captain; the type writer was located in the radio compartment. I got up and tried to open the sliding door. I heard someone laughing on the other side of the door. I told him to open the door and he kept on laughing. I told him again, open the door, he didn't. I grabbed the door and tore it off. I came out and told him, "You SOB, don't you ever lock the door on me again." I went over to the type writer and started to type the message for the Captain. While I was typing the radioman was looking over my shoulder, I told him to get the hell away from me this was top secret.

The next morning the Comm. Officer was walking down the main deck. He stopped me and asked me if I ripped the door off the Crypto room? I said yes and he wanted to know why? I told him that his radioman locked me in the Crypto room and that he wouldn't open it and that I had a top secret message for the Captain. He said okay and that was the end of it.

To answer your question on how I got the Crypto position, I was drafted. Our division officer was supposed to have that duty, he didn't want to take it so, he elected me. I didn't want it either but, what

can you do when you are out ranked? I never had the clearance for that position, that's what you call real security, ha!
Mike Petro SK3 1958 – 1960

'Plane Down'

It happened in the middle of the Atlantic on our way to a seven month Med cruise in late 1960. We were plane guarding for, I believe, the Shangri-La. In the early evening, a plane landing on the carrier came in too low, hit the stern and fell into the water.

It sank immediately, but that wasn't the end of it. Shortly after the incident, the carrier heard some sort of transmission on the frequency that had been reserved for the downed pilot. It did not seem possible that he was still alive and transmitting under water, but it had to be checked out. We received instructions from the carrier to begin search operations.

All nine of the Sonarmen were crowded into the narrow compartment, listening and watching the screen of our SQS-4 consol. There were ships all around and several other destroyers were also searching for the downed pilot, so the scope was full of contacts.

Then we found it, a small blip with a hard, almost tinny sound. It had no Doppler and so was not moving; the SQR-8 told us it was about 100 feet below the surface, although I didn't have a whole lot of confidence in that particular piece of gear. But could this be what we were looking for? We had visions of this pilot still in the cockpit, sending signals that he was alive and trying desperately to get out, but knowing that he never would.

We reported the contact to the bridge and continued watching the contact for about 20 minutes until we were told that the other tin cans had also picked up the same contact and had classified it as a "knuckle" – the whirlpool in the water that sometimes occurs when a ship makes a sharp turn. In a calm sea a knuckle can stay for hours and on sonar screen might be mistaken for a small ship until it either

*disappears or the return signal becomes so mushy that it becomes
obvious it is not a ship.*

*We broke off the search and went back to plane guarding, but
we could not help wonder if what we had seen was not a knuckle after
all, but the metal tomb of a young man whose trip to the sunny, fun
filled Mediterranean had ended before it began.*
Jeff Kovite SOG2 1959-1961

February 1961 found the *Fiske* headed back to the Med under
the command of CDR C. E. Hunter. During that cruise *Fiske* made
stops in Cannes (twice) and Golfe Juan, France; Naples (four times),
LaSpezia, Savonna and Gaeta, Italy; and Monaco. During the stop in
Gaeta about 50 crewmen volunteered for a working party to help paint
a local orphanage.

By all reports it was a lot of fun and took all day. This working
party was not 'on liberty'. It was made up of people that were on duty
and managed to get off the ship for a few hours. It wasn't often that the
duty section got to do something besides standing watches or cleaning
spaces on the ship.

The stop in Tripoli, Libya early on in the cruise was memorable.
The *Fiske* was the first Navy warship to visit in several years. The only
'recommended' liberty place was Wheelus AFB outside the city. The
liberty party was told that they could not be on the streets after dark.
The BX stores and clubs on Wheelus were the best things to be seen in
Tripoli.

'The Golden Hedgehog'

*During the 1961 Med cruise we put a small dummy hedgehog
on the conning tower of a sub. They surfaced and we sent the Motor
Whale Boat over to it to get the hedgehog back. I think there is a
picture in the 1961 cruise book. I can't tell for sure but if you look at
the picture closely I think you can see our Motor Whale Boat alongside
of it. Frank Nicastro SOG3 1959 -1961*

The MWB returning our 'Golden Hedgehog' from the USS *Corporal* (SS 346) to the *Fiske*

'ET or BT – That is the Question'

Sometime in 1961 Ens. J. Richard Jordan, Fiske's EMO (Electronics Material Officer), decided that I didn't have the proper appreciation of the exalted position we ET's held. Acting on this opinion he decided to 'teach me a lesson' and transferred me to 'B' Division as a 'non-designated striker'. Now the watch section to which I was assigned was headed up by BT2 James Conley. Conley was a legend onboard Fiske. He had come onboard as a BTFA quite a few years back and now was the senior BT2 in 'B' Division. He was big, black and was an 'Old School' leader. Conley was not reluctant to take an under preforming subordinate and 'school' him behind the boilers. The phrase 'Attitude Adjustment' was created by Conley and he did it well.

Within the first two days Conley had me on Top Watch reading the sight glasses on the boilers. It was a boring but a critical job. Four hours of tracking the tendencies on the water levels in those tubes was hard to concentrate on. If the trend was downward more water had to be put into the boilers. If upward less water was added in. The most frightening words that could be uttered by the Top Watch were, "Water out of sight!" That meant we had no idea if we needed less or more water in the boiler. Either condition was potentially catastrophic to the boilers and the ship. Conley impressed upon me the importance of this mundane task and I took it to heart.

When not on watch we had routine chores to do under less than ideal conditions. Any Snipe can tell you that Boiler Rooms are hot, smelly and above all noisy but I adjusted because I learned one very important lesson. If you did your job as best you could no one – especially BT2 Conley – messed with you. He understood the necessity of team work from the top to the bottom and made sure that everyone understood that fact.

I quickly feel into the routine – 4 on, 8 off except that if you caught the 0400 to 0800 you also caught the 1600 to 1800 First Dog Watch which did make for a long day. I did my job, stood my watches and aside from the noise and heat was happy. When you were off watch nobody called you into CIC or the Radio Room to fix things that were broken. Time flew by and before I knew it two weeks had passed. I was approached by Ens. Jordan while I was cleaning burner tips and he said, "OK Beyer, I guess you've learned lesson by now. Let's go." I asked, "Go where Sir?" He responded with something like back to the ET Gang where you belong.

Well, I'm sorry but the big lesson that I learned was that I was comfortable working with this watch section and BT2 Conley was a tough but fair boss. So I declined his invitation to return to the ET Gang. This lead to Ens. Jordan going to Ltjg McKenna, the MPA (Main Propulsion Assistant), and telling him to direct BT2 Conley to release me back to OI Division. BT2 Conley told Ltjg McKenna that he was impressed by my work ethic and attitude and had in fact recommended me to take the test for BT3. Now I've said that Conley was the senior Second Class but he was also the longest serving BT on board. He was respected for that. McKenna told Lt Merritt, the Engineering Officer, of Conley's recommendation and Lieutenant Merritt told Ens. Jordan that if he wanted me back in OI he needed to match Conley's recommendation and let me take the ETR3 test the next time advancement exams were given.

I took the Advancement Test and made ETR3 in November. To this day I thank BT2 Conley, Ltjg McKenna and Lt Merritt for backing Conley. My relations with Ens. Jordan never did improve and I'm still not sure if he learned a lesson similar to mine. I'm not sure if this is related to this incident but Ens. Jordan was transferred off the ship shortly after I returned to the ET Gang. He did not complete a normal tour onboard.

My time with BT2 Conley and the rest of the BT's are some longest-lived memories. We worked hard, stood our watches and did our jobs. We even re-bricked the firebox of Number One Boiler and cleaned the Mud Drum while we were steaming on Number Two. That, my friends, is something you never forget.
Gil Beyer ETR3 1960 – 1963

FA Bobby Waltz & Me

While in Monaco *Fiske* was anchored in the inner harbor during the Monacan Gran Prix. Some crewmen went ashore and rented space on rooftops to watch the race. Since we were on Port & Starboard status at least half the crew was on board all the time. Even if you were not on duty not everyone could afford to go into Monaco on Navy pay.

Fiske in Monaco's inner harbor May 1961

1961 Med Cruise Ship's band (l to r) ETN3 Ondo, SOG3 Ray, ETN3 Schmeiske, RD2 Still, MM2 Beal & SOGSN Nicastro

Those that stayed aboard used every pair of binoculars they could find from whatever vantage point they had access to and watched Sterling Moss wend his way through the hay bales to victory in his British Racing Green Lotus.

Upon her return to Mayport in July 1961 *Fiske* spent much of the remainder of the year conducting 'Daily Ops'. These were short daily exercises (out early in the morning and back in late afternoon) in the Norfolk and Jacksonville Ops Areas. Routine TAV's (Tender Availability) were interspaced with these at sea periods.

In January 1962 *Fiske* went to Charleston, SC for a yard overhaul. As part of the overhaul *Fiske* was to enter dry-dock to have the condition of the sacrificial anodes near the shafts and rudders checked out.

As the last of the water was leaving the dry dock a crunching sound could be heard. The blocks were too short and *Fiske* was sitting on her SONAR dome. This slight error extended her stay in Charleston by almost a month. No information has been found as to whether this incident had any bearing on the somewhat precipitous Change-of-Command held when CDR Cyrus H Butt III relieved CDR Clifford E. Hunter on April 23rd 1962.

'Landing Party Training'

I went aboard the Fiske in February of 62, 18 years old and right out of San Diego boot camp. About two months later, I and about 25 others were sent to Parris Island, Marine Corps boot camp to learn how to take part in a landing party expedition. As we left the ship they gave everyone a weapon. To my surprise they gave me a Thompson submachine gun. To a kid who grew up in Brooklyn I thought I died and went to heaven. We stayed at P.I. for 2 weeks being trained by drill instructors on how to survive during combat. We had to do the obstacle course, and the rifle range and we slept in tents one night.

We also had to have a mock bayonet fight with an opponent from another ship that was there doing the same thing we were. The name of the other ship was Pandemus (I think). As we lined up I was hoping I would be paired up with someone I could put on a good show with. I was the tallest guy from my ship, and as luck would have it I was about to mock fight the shortest guy from the other ship. I had on a hockey helmet, hockey gloves, elbow pads and other safety items which made moving very difficult. We stood facing each other holding a mock rifle with safety pads on both ends of the stick so we really couldn't get hurt, waiting for the drill instructor to blow the whistle to start the fight.

He blew the whistle, and my opponent quickly knocked the stick out of my hands. As I struggled to try and pick it up, this little guy whaled the living hell out of me. To stop the fight the D.I. had to blow the whistle again. I'm yelling, 'Blow the whistle!', but the D.I. was laughing so hard he couldn't, or wouldn't. I guess I did put on quite a show. The only other guy I remember from that group is Bill Vallencourt who I still keep in touch with......end of story.

William Loening BMSN 1962-1965

Upon completion of the overhaul *Fiske* returned to Mayport in late April or early May and conducted local operations and joined the Caribbean Patrol (which had been initiated after the abortive Bay of Pigs invasion in early 1961).

'Cosby'

I went aboard the Fiske in February of 1962 while she was in the yards at Charleston S.C. After the yard period we went to Gitmo for refresher training. On July 17, 1962 we were at sea doing ASW maneuvers.

A young sailor by the name of Ronald Cosby from Birmingham Alabama was on fantail watch. His job was to sound the alarm if anyone should fall overboard and throw him a life ring. I and many other people had stood that watch before. I just happened to be there with him when the ship was making several turns and the waves [coming over the fantail] knocked the both of us down. We laughed and thought it was a big joke.

At that time I was supposed to be at my training station on the port hedgehog mount on the 01 level forward, so I left him and changed my wet clothes and went to my station. Not five minutes had passed when a sailor by the name of Hall came running up the port side and up the ladder screaming 'man overboard!' I could see the horror in Hall's face; I knew this was not a drill. The person on the bridge thinking this was a drill yelled what side port or starboard, Hall just wanting to get help said port, but in fact he (Cosby) went right over the stern. By the time we got back to where we thought he went over, all we found was many, many sharks.

I thought what horror must have been going through his mind seeing the ship going away and all that was around him. Nineteen years old and his life was over, how sad
William Loerning BMSN 1962-1965

There were other witnesses to this tragedy. A few of the ET's were on the 01 level near Mount 31. Another sailor was on the fantail with SN Cosby, EMFN Wadsworth. He was standing closer to Mount 53 than Cosby and was missed by the full brunt of the wave that broke over the fantail. Wadsworth ran towards Cosby as he was going over the stern and grabbed the cord of the sound-powered phone that Cosby was wearing. Wadsworth was left holding the broken end of the cable as Cosby was pulled down by the screws.

We have no firm information on whatever happened to EMFN Wadsworth. I do remember that he was not the same after we lost Cosby. He drank excessively and was frequently in trouble. There is no doubt he suffered from survivor's guilt. At that time we didn't understand nor treat PTSD. Everybody was expected to 'suck it up'

On October 21st 1962 *Fiske*, along with almost every seaworthy ship between Newport and Key West, got underway towards Cuba. It was reported that the USSR was bringing offensive missiles into Cuba and the US had pictorial evidence. Since this was the weekend many of the ships were short-handed. A general recall had been put out but a great many sailors missed their ships that day.

Transit barracks in Mayport were stripped of all available personnel and were divvied up amongst the ships that got underway.

Highlining crewmen back to *Fiske* from *Enterprise*

'Mayport to Fiske 10/62'

I was one of many that were not onboard their ships that weekend in October when Mayport basin was emptied of all the ships that were capable of getting underway. I was home in Hollywood, FL when the general recall of all military personnel was broadcast. I returned to Mayport as quickly as I could. All of us that missed our ships were bundled onto Navy R4D transports and flown down to Guantanamo Bay, Cuba for further transport to our respective commands.

A COD flight took us out to the USS Enterprise (your first night landing on a carrier at 'darken ship' is a never to be forgotten experience) where we spent the night. The Enterprise was so new that they opened a berthing compartment that hadn't had the mattresses unwrapped yet.

The next day all of the 'left ashore' personnel were then high-lined to our respective ships.
Gil Beyer ETR3 1960-1963

At the time of the Missile Crisis the *Enterprise* was a relatively new ship. She had only been commissioned in November of 1961 and only went into regular service in January 1962. When the COD flights came aboard with the many sailors that missed ship's movement she actually berthed those sailors in compartments that still had the protective paper wrappers on the bunks. For a young 'Tin Can' sailor coming onto the *Enterprise* it was an entirely new world.

Information recently released by the Navy Historical Center verified *Fiske*'s presence off Cuban shores but not as a member of the blockading force (for diplomatic reasons it became 'quarantine' because calling it a 'blockade' meant that a state of war existed). *Fiske* was part of TF135.2 centered on the USS *Enterprise* (CVAN 65). The *Enterprise*'s mission was to counter-strike in the event the balloon went up.

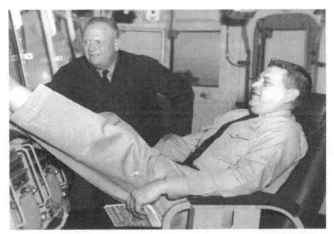

CDR Butt (R) and ComDesRon 8 on bridge during Cuban Crisis

Apparently the reason for all the years of secrecy surrounding TF135 – Comprised of TF 135.1 [the USS *Independence* (CVA 62) with screening destroyers] and TF135.2 [the USS *Enterprise* (CVAN 65) and screening destroyers] carried tactical nuclear weapons. There was, it appears, some potential political blow-back if the American people became aware of the fact that the United States would deploy nuclear weapons in the event of war. We found that a bit naive

It was during this period that *Fiske* earned the Navy Expeditionary and Armed Forces Expeditionary medal. She had also earned the National Defense medal previously (which is awarded to every unit and service member that had served after January 1960).

Fiske as part of TF135.2 in October 1962

Fiske returned to Mayport in early December after almost 6 weeks with TF135.2. Probably the two most memorable events of that time were: 1) spending about 48 hours straight at GQ with live rounds in the barrels early on during the crisis; and 2) when the forward refueling hose parted as *Fiske* was being fueled by *Enterprise.*

Port side 01 level after forward refueling hose parted

Several hundred gallons of NSFO (Navy Standard Fuel Oil) sprayed much of the Port side from the break aft and upwards to the bridge wing. Most of the bridge's refueling detail personnel were sprayed with oil as were many of the crew on the forward in-haul line. The *Enterprise* was kind enough to high-line a few bales of rags over after *Fiske* had used all of hers mopping up the spilt NSFO.

Fiske returned to Mayport in early December and spent much of the remainder of the year in a stand-down and/or in holiday leave period into 1963.

Most of the month of January 1963 was spent preparing for an upcoming deployment to the Mediterranean. February 5, 1963 found *Fiske* on her way to the Mediterranean.

Following the Cuban Missile Crisis, where the Fiske operated with Enterprise many times, the *Fiske* found herself operating with the "Big E" again. During the '63 Med Cruise she often served as Plane Guard whenever the Enterprise conducted flight ops. Acting as a guard for underway replenishments, flights ops or refueling was usually ordinary but on occasion the guard ship has to respond to an emergency. There are oft told tale of hours of boredom punctuated by moments of sheer panic.

'Quartermaster 'Steals' Snipes money!!'

During our Med Cruise of 1963, while at sea, it was time for watch change at 1545. Our quartermaster on watch, QMSN Gorman was on watch and Cooley, QM3 was scheduled to relieve him for the 1600/2000 watch.

Cooley could not be found and the search was on. By about 1700, I relieved Gorman as we continued to look for Cooley. As time went on, I became very upset with Cooley and his lack of his presence for his watch. Around 1800 I was pretty upset and low and behold, Cooley shows ups. Before I had a chance to lay into him for his actions, he said to me, "Tom, I just took $600.00 from the snipes".

As it had been payday that day and as we all know that also means the card games are going full blast. As it turned out Cooley ended up in one of the games with some snipes and he took them to the cleaners. Well, it was very difficult to say much knowing he hit the jack pot. I'm not sure how he settled this with Gorman, but hope he did something for him.

Charlie Thompson, QM2 1960-1963

'Highline Dunking'

Early 1963 off the coast of Florida (I believe). We were attempting to highline one of our officers to another destroyer. I don't remember which officer or which destroyer. The officer was half way across when suddenly both ships rolled towards one another, creating slack in the line dunking the officer into the water. I watched from the signal bridge as he went under and he was spinning in the bosun's chair, which for him must have seemed like a very long time.

Finally, after a short while in real time, the ships rolled away from each other. This pulled the slack out of the line and he popped out of the drink soaked to the gills. I'm sure it scared the hell out of him and I think that he was very relieved when he was pulled back aboard the Fiske.

Lee Dowling SM3 1962-63

There were port visits to Cannes, France; Piraeus and Rhodes, Greece; Palermo, Sicily; Naples and Taranto, Italy. During this cruise *Fiske* was detached from Sixth Fleet in April and transited the Suez

Canal on the 4th & 5th to participate in patrols off the Horn of Africa. The mission was to help in intercepting gunrunners between Africa and Asia Minor in the Red Sea.

Med Cruises always have routine evolutions: refueling, underway replenishing, chasing the stern of the carriers during flight ops et al. Most of these are done routinely but there are always exceptions to the rule. *Fiske* was on plane guard station astern of the Enterprise when a plane hit Enterprise's fantail. The following are two stories of the aftermath of that crash.

'Duty Swimmer'

I will start this by saying I can't tell you where we were at but we were on Plane Guard behind the Enterprise. It was 10:30 PM or so. Welliver and I were the Duty Swimmers when [a] jet hit the back of the flight deck of Enterprise. It was rougher than hell and we could not get the Captain's Gig in water so Welliver and I went to the fantail to get hooked up and swim.*

We swam a long way out to where pilot was at, we could see he was dead and tangled in the chute cords. Every time we got close to him the chute would pull him under. He would come up further away. This happened 3 or 4 times. At that point they [The Fiske] must have run out of rope. They started pulling us back. I guess we were so far out they started backing the ship to us.

When we got to the ship Welliver got pulled on. When I got close I looked and all I could see was the screws sucking me down. It's a blur from there on. I guess BM1 Rich jumped down on the screw guard and grabbed my harness and threw me over the railing and onto the deck. I got up and looked at Welliver. We were both shaking so bad from being cold and scared.

I think that BM1 Carr was on headset chewing on somebody in the Pilot House. Willhide [HMC] took us to his office [Sick Bay] and gave us a couple good drinks.

I have wrote this down in my Navy book for my kids and grandkids to have and to remember BM1 Rich who probably saved my life. I will be forever grateful. Larry Catlett SN 1961-64

SN Larry Catlett & SN B. Welliver

*There is confirmation that this incident occurred during the 1963 deployment with the Sixth Fleet.

'Plane Guarding'

One night, on the 2000 to Midnight watch, I was on the port lookout watch, while plane guarding the Enterprise. I forget the name of the Ensign that was OOD, but I remember the captain seemed to have a lot of confidence in him. Both the Enterprise and the Fiske on darken ship (not having any outside lights on). In addition, the planes did not have any lights on.

As I stood there, you could hear the grumbling of the aircraft, and just about see the shadow of the plane as it went over us. You could see nothing. Suddenly the sky lit up, one of the planes hit the stern of the carrier. The OOD started screaming into the 1MC, 'Captain to the bridge, captain to the bridge.' The captain, Cmdr Butt was a pretty stout fellow, but he flew up those stairs from the ward room. Thank God nobody was in his way. We turned on all our lights, and could see

one body in the water. I had a perfect view of all this and watched as we tried to retrieve the pilot, but he eventually sank beneath the sea. I thought to myself, 'May God have mercy on his soul.'
Bill Loening BMSN 1962-65

The *Fiske* was detached from Sixth Fleet and headed for the Red Sea. The HMS *Ashanti* (F117) and *Fiske* patrolled for ten days in the Red Sea and then made a port visit to Aden. It was the first time that most of the crew had had the opportunity to have a pint of beer with lunch as the Royal Navy never discontinued alcohol on their vessels.

Fiske was tied alongside the Ashanti to a 'camel' anchored out. Former Secretary of the Navy Josephus Daniels would not have approved, as the Brits still had beer with lunch and dinner and still offered their daily ration of grog. An Imperial pint of beer cost the equivalent of a nickel. They even keep it cold since the outside temperature was about 115 F. at noon. *Fiske* re-transited the Suez Canal on April 27th & 28th and re-joined the Sixth Fleet.

'Gibraltar 1963'

The Fiske departed Mayport on February 5th 1963 for another Med Cruise. A year or so earlier the ET Gang had gained 3 'strikers' - Reservists that were doing their 2 years active duty aboard. They were added to the ET Gang not because that they were ET 'A' Schools grads but because their combined GCT & ARI scores made them eligible to become ET 'strikers'.

This story concerns one of these strikers. His name was Jose Armin Longoria. He came from Mission, Texas. Now Mission, Texas is in the Rio Grande River Valley and his family has traced its roots in that area since King Charles the III of Spain handed out land grants in the 16th Century. In other words, they had been 'Texans' since even before there was a 'Texas'

Now Jose was very proud of his family heritage and in those long ago non-PC days he was constantly called 'Poncho' – by everyone. This caused him no end of upset and stress. And, to the best of my knowledge, continued throughout his 2 years of active duty.

Also onboard at this time was an ETN2 named Chas Slocum. Chas was from Casa Grande, Arizona. Chas was the intellectual of the ET Gang. He was older than most of us as he had 2 years of college prior to joining the Navy. Chas had the ability to tell the most convincing lies while maintaining a dead serious demeanor. That skill is the basis for this story.

Shortly after the Special Sea & Anchor detail was secured on February 5th most of the old hands were sitting around the ET shop telling stories about our last Med Cruise to the 'newbies' that had never been there before. A popular TV show of that time was "The Twentieth Century" sponsored by the Prudential Insurance Company. Prudential's logo was a picture of the Rock of Gibraltar with the word 'Prudential' in huge letters across its face. Somehow or another Chas got into telling all the newbies that one of the most unforgettable sights was seeing that sign as we entered the Mediterranean Sea. For the next nine days of our transit Chas continued to build the anticipation for that never-to-be-forgotten sight.

The afternoon before our entry to the Med Chas told everyone that we always transited the Straits very early in the morning to avoid going through all the fishing boat fleets that came out of all the ports on either shore of the straits – this was true. I had seen literally hundreds of radar contacts as we transited the straits during the '61 cruise.

Early that morning we were at breakfast when 'Poncho' stormed into the Mess Decks yelling at Chas. He called Chas every expletive he could think of in both English and Spanish. The context of his rant was that he never saw any sign after getting up at 0230 and watching on the 01 level until well after dawn.

Here, Chas demonstrated his evil genius. He looked somewhat confused and asked 'Poncho' what side of the ship he was standing on? Armin answered "the Starboard side". With an absolutely straight face Chas responded, "Well, there's the problem. You were looking south towards Africa. Gibraltar is on the north side of the Straits. You were looking in the wrong direction." A very chagrined Jose accepted this and went about his chores.

We had many interesting days over the next 6 months. Fiske visited Cannes, Athens, Palermo, transited the Suez Canal – twice, Aden, Naples, Taranto and Rhodes before heading west towards the Straits of Gibraltar. Again we planned on transiting the Straits early in the morning.

Later that morning Poncho came roaring up to Chas – again spewing expletives in both English and Spanish. After Jose exhausted his ire Chas put on his most serious, concerned face and asked the same question he had 6 months earlier, "What side of the ship were you on?" Poncho said, by way of explanation, "Well, since the Starboard side was the wrong side going into the Med, I spent the night on the Port side as we headed out."

I'm very glad I wasn't eating or drinking when this was said as I have learned that both liquids and solids really hurt when blown out your nose! Jose had spent the night facing the wrong way - again! To the best of my knowledge Armin was never told the truth that there was no huge neon 'Prudential' sign on the Rock of Gibraltar.

In the more than 50 years that have passed I sincerely hope that Armin has long since forgiven Chas for this incredible 'long con' at his expense. We were young and indestructible in the early 60's. We had survived the Cuban Missile Crisis and had a lot of fun along the way.
Gil Beyer ETR3 1960-63

ETN2 Chas Slocum 1960-63

From May 1st through the 20th *Fiske* was in port at Naples, Italy alongside a Destroyer Tender for repair availability. After leaving Naples *Fiske* visited Taranto, Italy and Rhodes, Greece before departing the Mediterranean and arriving back in Mayport on July 1st.

'Out of the Deep'

On one of our many visits to Naples during the '63 Med Cruise, Al Whitaker and I took the ferry to the island of Ischia along with some diving gear. We hired a local with a boat to take us to a small uninhabited island and drop us off with instructions to pick us up later in the day.

We spent the better part of the day snorkeling in the clear waters around the little island. Eventually we got hungry and noticed that another a few hundred yards away with what appeared to be hotel on it. We swam to the island and sure enough it was a hotel that was full of German tourists.

As we rose from the water in our wetsuits, masks and fins I think we scared the hell out of a group that was laying in the surf at the water's edge. The staff at the hotel was nice and fed us spaghetti for a small fee. We then swam back to the little island and later that day the local boatman came and picked us up. It was a really great time.
Lee Dowling SM3 1962-63

The *Fiske* participated in numerous operations with elements of DesRon 8 for the remainder of the year. In early 1964 she departed Mayport, Florida enroute to the Brooklyn Naval Shipyard in New York for decommissioning and commencing FRAM II conversion back to a DD.

A Chilly Lesson

A Midshipmen's cruise is where you'd take aboard these young Officer Aspirants to give them a feel of what the nautical world is about. Now the mark of a Midshipman is the blue band on the top of their ordinary sailor's white hat.

While some of them were civil and well mannered, some were snotty. They broke ahead of Enlisted Men in Chow Lines, and they tried to bark orders like the fledging Ensigns they aspired to be.

We were north of Halifax, Nova Scotia, on one of these cruises. The daytime temperatures were tolerable, but the nights were cold.

One particular "Young Gentleman" was almost intolerable in his arrogance. Worse, he was bunking with us in the Aft Berthing Compartment. Now, this compartment is built around the steel shaft that makes up the Handling Room for Mount 53, and there is a hatch that connects the berthing compartment with the Handling Room.

Now Mr. Obnoxious came down the ladder from the showers adorned only in flip-flops and a towel. Well, temptation could not be resisted. One of us lesser folk, grabbed his towel, and we shoved him into the unheated handling room. Then we dogged down the hatch and wouldn't let it open.

Well, the only way out, was to climb the ladder into the gun mount walk across the deck, and come below via the hatches on the weather deck. This, mind you, while buck-naked except for his flip-flops. It was, as far as we were concerned, a prank, nothing more.

Well, it was bitter cold out, and the Future Officer and pride of the Navy was warm, and slightly wet from the showers. He exited the gun mount just as the ship rolled, and he put his bare backside against the steel of the gun mount to balance himself. His epidermis froze to the gun mount and the ship's roll in the other direction caused him to part with a quantity of skin from his backside. Oh but it was a noisy parting. Even Chief Corpsman Wilhide thought it was funny. Of course, his antiseptic didn't help the situation.

Our young 'Ensign to Be' was more subdued after that. It was one of the few times I saw Lieutenant Guthrie, the Weapons Officer laugh. Apparently, the young man had earned no friends among the officers either.
Jerry Mosley YN3 1963-66

CDR Cyrus Butt was CO (Commanding Officer) from April 1962 until late spring 1964 when he was transferred to the *Charles R. Ware* (DD 865). He died on 19 July 1988 and is buried in Arlington National Cemetery.

Chapter V

(DD 842) Post FRAM

Call Letter – NBBU
Motto "Detect and Destroy"
December 1964 – June 1980

In February 1964 *Fiske*'s homeport was changed to New York, NY where she was decommissioned as a DDR. *Fiske* was going to undergo a FRAM (Fleet Rehabilitation & Modernization) conversion at the New York Naval Shipyard. The conversion consisted mainly of the removal of the after mast with its TACAN and ECM Radomes; the aft deckhouse containing the AN/SPS-8 Height-finding RADAR; Mount 52; much of the main deck superstructure; and, the remaining after 3"/50 gun mount. In their place was installed the ASW DASH helicopter hanger aft, an ASROC Launcher amidships and new ECM Radomes atop the DASH hanger. Other electronics equipments were upgraded and 01 level Port & Starboard triple tube torpedo launchers forward of the bridge.

Fiske was recommissioned as DD 842 in early December 1964 while in the Brooklyn Navy Yard. She underwent trials for much of

December and into 1965. *Fiske* was then sent to Guantanamo for Operational Readiness testing.

'Feel the Burn'

The Navy often accumulates a lot of outdated "Top Secret" papers. The military disposes of this with great care, usually. I remember, once, when we were in Norfolk, Lt (jg)'s Lipshur and Brown gathered together a working party of enlisted men, I was the only Petty Officer. Our Task was to burn six large bags of outdated Top Secret documents. They loaded us in the back of a pick-up with the two Officers riding up front, each with his web belt and .45 cal. pistol.

Our trip led us to a burn barrel set at the bottom of a sand hill. They showed us just how they wanted the job done, and then they retired to the Officer's Club. As the 'O' Club would not let them in with side-arms they left the pistols in my charge.

There we toiled, burning documents. After half an hour, a group consisting of a Lieutenant Commander and three men with Shore Patrol Regalia surprised us. It wasn't a great chore, we didn't know that we were doing anything wrong. Nobody was paying attention to whoever was sneaking up on us.

Well, they pulled a complete surprise attack on us. We were placed at Attention and asked what we were doing with these documents. So we explained that our officers were at the 'O' Club and that we were just following orders. They were very interested in this and, they got more interested when they found out that none of us had Top Secret clearances.

I was a sorry sight with two .45 Pistols draped over me like Poncho Villa. So, the Commander advised us that we were in violation of standing orders concerning disposal of Classified Material. Heck! I didn't know anything about their Standing Orders. All I knew was that an Officer had told me what he wanted done and I did it. Poof, period, plain and simple.

They positioned themselves over the crest of the hill and told us to continue burning the papers, but to remember that we were being watched. They relieved me of the .45s and the web belts at that time.

Well, in 45 minutes or so, the Navy Grey pick-up returned, and two somewhat inebriated Officers kinda staggered up. Lipshur put out his forefinger, tapped me on the chest, and demanded to know 'What the Hell I'd done with their guns' before I could reply, the Commander showed up and told them that he had them.

We enlisted men were driven back to our ship. Lipshur and Brown were detained at the Base Security Office. Thinking on my feet, I reported to Lieutenant Guthrie what had happened, and then to Commander Bradbury. After all, after our errant JG's I was next in command.

At that point, we enlisted types were out of the loop information-wise. The Scuttlebutt (Rumor-Mill) had it that both JG's had a close call and almost had serious problems. Were it not for the intervention of our Senior Officers (Ewing and Bradbury) it could have ended their Naval Careers.

For us enlisted people? We never heard another word about it. Candidly, I was hoping that the Navy would have both men shot. I had no use for either one. Ensigns and Lieutenants Junior Grade are pompous fools anyway.
Jerry Mosley YN3 1963-66

After Refresher Training in Guantanamo Bay, Cuba *Fiske* was assigned ASW duties. In 1965 *Fiske* patrolled Santo Domingo harbor during the crisis in the Dominican Republic. For this deployment *Fiske* received her second Navy Expeditionary award.

The DASH (Drone Anti- Submarine Helicopter) was an idea that never was totally successful. In concept it was a drone controlled by two operators – one for takeoffs and landings, another for the performance of its mission. The takeoffs and landing were controlled from the flight deck and the other by an operator within CIC.

DASH with torpedo

Since DASH was considered expendable it had no backups for its electronics. It is estimated that 80% of its failures were due to electronics, only 10% operator error and 10% mechanical.

Jr. Birdmen
Ltjg D H Olsen & Ltjg J R Rapson (l to r) DASH Operators

'Motor Whale Boat'

Oh, I remember "Little Creek" I was Coxswain of the 26' motor whaleboat carrying Ensign Singletary (Supply Officer) to Little Creek for parts to fix our Radar. To make it short, the MWB engine died in the middle of the tunnel section of the Bridge-Tunnel.

The USS Churchill County (LST) was bearing down on the MWB... The LST ran herself aground to avoid us. They tried signaling us with signal lamps but Singletary couldn't read it. They [the Churchill County] launched an LCM and towed us back to Fiske.

Commander Ewing met us when we came alongside. He and Singletary disappeared into his quarters. He and Singletary practiced for a week getting our Supply Officer back up to standards. I was issued a van key and told to drive to Little Creek and pick up the parts. The old whaleboat had a Model T- Ford Engine.

It, the MWB, was never trusted after that, and the Whaleboat was replaced with a plastic one later.
Jerry Moseley YN3 1963-1966

On January 19th 1966 *Fiske* left Newport for what was to become her second 'Around-the-World' cruise some 14 years after her first one. She transited westward through the Panama Canal and arrived in San Diego, CA on February 5th and arrived in Pearl Harbor, HI February 11th.

Fiske in Tonkin Gulf after FRAM conversion

Fiske crossed the International Dateline on at 0800 Friday, February 18th and it became Saturday, February 19th where *Fiske* entered the Domain of the Golden Dragon.

Fiske moored at Subic Bay Naval Station in the Philippines on February 28th and departed on her first war patrol during the Viet Nam Conflict on March 11th. When she entered the war zone on March 12th the crew of the *Fiske* became entitled to the Viet Nam Service medal and Federal Income Tax exemption.

"A Very Short Course in Fluid Dynamics"

Simple physics - a ship displaces its weight in water. The Fiske weighed (approximately) 2250 tons and therefore displaced 2250 tons of seawater as she steamed along. This displaced water is pushed outward from the bow and tends to 'pile up' much like a snowplow piles up snow. If it were possible to put directional arrows on the surface one would see that the water goes outward as the ship moves through it and back in again as the ship moves along.

This proves that the displaced water is moving back into the 'hole' that the ship leaves behind. When a ship is approaching another ship the forces tend to oppose each other and can create some problems. As you come alongside a moving ship you must do so very carefully. If you come too close to the stern ('abaft the beam' is an old sailors term for being past the middle but not behind) of the other ship your ship can be sucked into the 'hole' that ship leaves behind. A ship being sucked into that 'hole' can and has had bad results for the novice shiphandler.

Being sucked in can 'scratch the paint' on the ship you are approaching or your own ship. One must approach slowly and cautiously and ease into an equilibrium with these opposing forces. Remember that the bigger the ship you are approaching the bigger the forces and the greater caution that must be taken to avoid being 'sucked into the hole' and scratching the paint.
James R. Rapson Ltjg 1964-1967

On March 14th *Fiske* rendezvoused with the USS *Ranger* (CVA-61) and became the *Ranger*'s Plane Guard. *Fiske* subsequently was assigned as the Plane Guard for *Enterprise* (CVAN-65) and the *Hancock* (CVA-19).

Between Plane Guard duties for the carriers she served as a SAR (Search & Rescue) in the Tonkin Gulf. While performing SAR duties *Fiske* came under fire from North Vietnamese coastal batteries on April 4th. She suffered no hits in that encounter.

Guard station for refueling of *Enterprise* and *Dyess*

Fiske operated with the USS *Dyess* frequently during this deployment. On one occasion she assisted in the rescue of the crew of a small aircraft that had run out of fuel and had to ditch in the South China Sea. Both the pilot and navigator were retrieved from the water shortly after the plane crashed and sank.

April 14th found *Fiske* moored in Subic Bay, Philippines because of Typhoon '*Hester*'. Typhoon '*Judy*' found *Fiske* at sea with 20-foot waves and 40-knot winds.

A port call was made at Hong Kong June 10th through the 14th of 1966. *Fiske* began her fourth war patrol with her departure from Hong Kong. During this patrol *Fiske* provided shore gunfire support and is credited with destroying several targets and giving illumination support. *Fiske* departed the combat zone and made a port call at Kaohsiung, Taiwan June 25th through July 3rd.

'Extracts from Deck Logs – Jan 1966 to July 1966'

We entered the Combat zone 12 March, qualified for the VSM the next day...and combat pay. Worked with the Ranger and the Enterprise until 1 April then assigned to SAR in Tonkin Gulf. 4 April came under fire from NVA shore arty. Did not return fire. 10 April detached to Hancock, but rendezvous cancelled due to typhoon. Returned to Subic Bay 11 April. Underway to rendezvous with Hancock 24 April. 28 April SAR station. 29 April operations with Hancock. 1 May, Special SAR, then rejoin Hancock. 7 May detached Hancock, rejoined Ranger. 12 May Yokosuka, Japan. 21 May underway from Japan. 25 May, third war patrol...joined Ranger, 29 May rode out Typhoon Judy at sea. Assigned to AAW picket duty outside Combat zone. 31 May investigated wreckage off Tigre Island...recovered aircraft external fuel tank. 6 June assigned NGFS duties relieving squadron flagship USS Davis DD 937. Escorted Marine convoy 50 miles south to Danang. 10 June, visit to Hong Kong. 14 June, underway fourth war patrol, 15 June, on station NGFS off Quang Ngai province, I Corps, 119 rounds expended over four target areas, 18 structures destroyed, ten damaged. Trenches damaged. 16 June, NGFS Danang Area. 57 rounds expended, over 4 target areas, VC cave, assembly areas, and OP. All targets destroyed. Another target, 4 rounds, target destroyed. [If I recall correctly this was our main mission, an ammo dump right on top of a three hundred foot hill along the beach. The top of that hill lifted off after we fired two WP and two HE.] 17 June, on station NGFS Operation Dodge [2nd Battalion, 4th Marines, south of Hue]. Detached *to III Corps. 20 June. 21 June arrive at NGFS III Corps, off Mekong/Saigon River delta. Detached. 25 June, port visit to Kaohsiung, Formosa. 3 July, underway to Subic Bay. 6 July, underway, 7 July entered Combat zone for Market Time Ops. Departed same day.*

 8 July, Polliwog Day

 9 July, Shellback Day. Crossed Equator in Straits of Singapore, Long 106 deg. 27 min. east at 1733 local time.

 That was the last time we really operated in the Combat Zone. The last entry was crossing through the south end of the Combat zone to get the combat pay for July.

William G. Davis PNSN 1964-1966

Jam session on ASROC deck

According to official Navy records the *Fiske* operated in the Mekong River delta from June 16th through June 21st. Log entries imply that the *Fiske* was exposed to fallout from Agent Orange applications throughout these river drainages. Recent research demonstrated that components of Agent Orange were actually condensed when distilled by ship's evaporators (the freshwater making equipment). The end effect was that all ships that operated in the areas near Vietnam's river deltas were drinking, showering and eating components of Agent Orange - or other toxins.

Numerous naval personnel have been afflicted with a plethora of illnesses over the past decades since that conflict ended that have been connected with exposure to those compounds. Many of those exposed have died without recognition that these deaths may have been caused by that exposure. There, are as of this writing, numerous claims yet to be finalized for possible exposure to Agent Orange. There are also bills in Congress that would recognize the connection between Agent Orange exposure and those illnesses and provide compensation to those so afflicted.

Shipmates that are believed to have died as a result of Agent Orange are ETR3 George Hilt and Chris Billingsly. Only Hilt served during Fiske's Viet Nam tour. In late 2017 it was learned that SM2 Christopher Billingsley had passed from complications of that exposure.

Billingsley did not die as a result of being onboard the *Fiske* but rather as a result of his service in the Army as a Green Beret from 1963 to 1985. He served on the *Fiske* from 1959 to 1963. His wife, Virginia, informed the Fiske Association that when Chris was denied his request to go into UDT/SEAL training he decided to leave the Navy and join the Army. Chris rose to the rank of E-8 and made over 200 jumps "out of perfectly good airplanes" during his Army service. We cannot find information of any other *Fiske* personnel that may have been impacted by service in Viet Nam. Statistically it is entirely likely there are others.

MR2 John Frazier flying a kite

John Frazier, MR2, is one of the relatively few crewmen that served on the *Fiske* before, during and after FRAM conversion. He made the Med Cruise in 1963 and the Around the World cruise in 1966. EM1 John Frazer almost made the list but was transferred to shore duty just before the 1966 cruise. I believe that FTGC Brown was among them as he's in the '63 Med Cruise book and mentioned in one of YN3 Moseley's 'Fiske Tales' from 1966

Swift Boats coming alongside off Viet Nam

Short but Memorable

Sometime towards the end of our time in Viet Nam we were refueling from the USS Enterprise (CVAN 65)when a buddy came into CIC and told me that Ann Margaret was performing on one of the 'Big E's' elevators. Sure enough there she was dancing for us while some her band members played. It wasn't long before refueling was completed and she was gone. It isn't often that refueling was that interesting. Sure made the time pass quickly.
Dick Hersey RD2 1964-67

After a brief stop at Subic Bay *Fiske* headed westward and crossed the Equator on July 9th where all the ship's Pollywogs were inducted into King Neptune's Realm as Shellbacks. After a brief refueling stop at the ESSO fuel piers at Penang, Malaysia she spent two days in Cochin, India and then transited the Suez Canal. In route to Newport port calls were made at Piraeus, Greece; Barcelona, Spain; and, Gibraltar. The *Fiske* arrived in Newport, RI on 17 August.

'Last Night at Sea'

September 1966 – The day before pulling into our homeport from Viet Nam. 1600 - Knock off Ship's Work. Eat dinner and then retire to IC Room for nightly card game of Double-Deck Pinochle. Except this night's game didn't end until the Special Sea & Anchor Detail was set the next day.

We usually played until Taps at 2200 but this night went into the next morning. With the four of us standing around the Ship's Gyro all night playing cards.
George Hilt, ETR3 1964-66
Note: ETR3 Hilt died in 2010 believed to be a result of Agent Orange exposure

In late 1966 *Fiske* participated in LANTFLEX 66 – an extensive naval exercise held in the Caribbean. After the completion of that exercise *Fiske* departed for port calls at Massawa, Eritrea; Djibouti, French Somaliland and a six month long deployment to the Mediterranean and the Indian Ocean in May 1967.

During this deployment she again transited the Suez Canal. This time it was just days before the Arab-Israeli War closed the Suez Canal in 1967. She made; Bahrain, UAE; and, Mombasa, Kenya. The HMS *Nubian* (one of the UK's 'Tribal Class Frigates') was stationed in Mombasa. That became the unofficial 'homeport' of *Fiske* while in that area. The Oasis Bar in Mombasa served American beer and hamburgers.

'Fiske's Six Day War

The memories of Massawa, Ethiopia flowed like water to this old salt recalling Massawa in 1967. I was theDCA (Damage Control Assistant). That visit (or series of visits) was driven by the Arab-Israeli War of 1967 when Fiske was one of the last ships to transit southward through the Suez Canal before shooting broke-out in the Six Day War.

The Fiske was trapped with no way to return to the Med to complete our extended Med Cruise.

Fiske had loaded up with freight, CT's and other spooks in Alexandria prior to the transit and had been ordered to gather Intel on military installations down the length of the canal. That was easy: just count the number of sleeping soldiers next to their little guard huts along the way and watch the rust-bucket Egyptian Navy destroyers try to get underway at the mid-way transition point in Great Bitter Lake. Once clear of Suez we were ordered to Massawa to await further orders [subsequently to orbit at the south end of the Red Sea and report all traffic passing through the Straights of Mandeb (aka Bab-el-Mandeb)]. And thus started my memories of Massawa where the Fiske became "Station Ship Massawa". My first recollection was the awful stench that permeated everything long before we hit the sea buoy. That stench was Massawa, Ethiopia. Now a part of Eritrea, it was then a chunk of Ethiopia and the Eritrean Rebels made life miserable throughout the region. The only redeeming virtue I noted was a tiny US Army Corps of Engineer's base that had a cheapo bar with nickel beers and a slot machine. The Army worked to get us bootlegged supplies because fuel and food had been cut off once the shooting started. I can't recall how long we cycled through Massawa, but it made for some interesting tours up into the mountains to visit Asmara and the Navy Communications Station (which had come under attack by the Eritrean's at some point) and I suspect the Comm. Sta. guys figured Fiske would be their "Plan B" if things got crazy with the rebels.

The Red Sea was home for several weeks and included a quick sprint northward on June 8th 1967 when we intercepted a 'Flash' message from the USS Liberty that advised it was under attack and had provided an initial incorrect position that placed her in the north end of the Red Sea. It took a while (and multiple 'Flash' intercepts) to confirm that the Liberty was really in the Mediterranean, north of Suez. The rest was boredom (except for a civilian ship rescue near Jeddah, Saudi

Arabia) that eventually saw Fiske depart for other lovely garden spots throughout the Middle East. Ah, such memories.

I guess what comes around, goes around, because during the First Gulf War in the 90's, I found myself as the Harbor Defense Commander, responsible for port security for all coalition ports in the Middle East...old home week for this old salt.
W.C.S. "Skip" Mays III, Capt. USN (ret) ENS/LTJG 1966-1968

Fiske alongside Forrestal after the fire

Fiske rescued the crew from a grounded freighter and conducted two other at sea rescues during her stay in the Red Sea.

As she was about to return to the Mediterranean *Fiske* was called upon to rendezvous with the severely damaged USS *Forrestal* (CVA-59) off the coast of South Africa and escort her home from the war zone. Rather than transit the Suez Canal *Fiske* and *Forrestal* rounded the Cape of Good Hope and headed northwesterly toward the eastern seaboard of the USA.

Fiske outboard the *Tidesurge* (photo taken from *Forrestal*)

During the trip home *Fiske* and *Forrestal* refueled from the fleet oilers USS *Chemung* and the British ship HMS *Tidesurge*.

'Showing the Flag'

The whole purpose of this cruise was to "show the flag" as we steamed around the Mediterranean; playing war games, visiting friendly ports, etc. That was our intention. The CO announced that our port visit to the island of Malta would serve as an important event in promoting and strengthening maritime partnerships with European nations. Few of us really cared. The only question in our minds was "were the girls friendly?" Later, some said 'yes', others didn't comment. The whole episode is sort of hazy to me so I can't go into any detail. Probably just as well.

ST1 Ron White (center) with buddies STG3 Huber & ET3 Shields

Intentions aside Egypt and Israel had different ideas. Due to escalating conditions between them over who would control the Suez Canal, our Malta liberty was brought to a close and Fiske was ordered to transverse the canal, "Now!" But since some of the crew was still on the island, we waited until the following day to leave. Leaving Malta behind, we made for Port Said, the point where all ships wanting to transit the Suez had to wait. This included the USS Dyess (DD-880) which transited some days after us.

Port Said was a fueling station for ships that passed through the Suez. There was no liberty – just get in line and wait - a favorite past time it would seem. The Captain then took the opportunity to remind us that the next few days (days? little did he know!) would be used to "protect US shipping interests and also monitor all ship traffic in and out of the Persian Gulf." As we left Suez Port, we headed through the Gulf of Suez for the Red Sea, our patrolling area. And there we stayed. The big difference between the Panama and Suez Canals is that the latter has no locks because it's too flat. Therefore when it was Dyess' turn everyone was surprised at the greeting received from the citizens

along the banks. The tension between the UAR and Israel was known, but it was felt that the "flag-showing" missions were far removed from expressions of hostility. No incidents marred her transit, although protesters followed the ship in boats wherever they could and shouted jeers from the banks along the canal. Subsequently all military objectives along the canal were bombed by Israel, thereby cutting us off from the Sixth Fleet. The Red Sea turned out to be our Med Cruise."
Ron White ST1 1965-1967

Upon her return to Newport in September *Fiske* conducted local ops for the remainder of the year. In June and July 1968 she underwent refresher training in Guantanamo Bay, Cuba, and then in September departed for a five-month Mediterranean deployment. *Fiske* returned at the end of January 1969. The remainder of 1969 was spent conducting local operations.

January through mid-February of 1970 found *Fiske* in 'Modified Cadre' (reduced manning level) status. In late February she underwent a Navy Technical Proficiency Inspection and in March she was returned to full operational status and spent much of March and April participating in individual ship exercise operations and underway with 'Hunter/Killer' group off the Virginia Cape for ASW exercises.

In May 1970 *Fiske* was deployed with other units of DesRon 12, the USS *Wasp* (CVS-18), Marias (AO-57) and USS *Odax* (SS-484) on a five-month Northern European deployment. During that deployment she participated in two NATO exercises – "Night Patrol" & "Northern Wedding", conducted numerous ASW operations and returned to Newport, RI on October 6th.

Port visits made during that deployment included Lisbon, Portugal, Rota, Spain, Bremen, Germany, Brest, France, Plymouth, and London, England, Rotterdam, Holland, Aberdeen and Greenock, Scotland, Bergen, Norway, Cherbourg, France and Rosyth, Scotland (twice).

There was one tragedy during this deployment. On 16 June Lt Peter Zakis, USN – the Prospective Weapons Officer – committed suicide by stabbing himself several times and throwing himself overboard. He refused helicopter lifesaving attempts and drowned before ship recovery.

The Death of Lt Peter Zakis

North Atlantic 1971-Lt. Zakis and I had the Mid-Watch on the bridge. I was the Boatswain's Mate of the Watch and he was the OOD. During the watch the Lt and I would pass the time with small talk. Toward the end of the watch he began asking me questions about the ship, questions that a Lt should know.

The next morning the sea was rough, as the Atlantic usually was, and we were sitting around our compartment (1ˢᵗ Div) when we heard the door outside our compartment open. We wondered who was going out on deck in such weather. Plus, they didn't dog the hatch down. One of us went to shut when we heard the four blasts [on ship's whistle] for 'man overboard'.

A Wardroom Steward had gone to the Lt's Stateroom and found him sitting on his bunk bleeding. That was when he [Zakis] ran out and jumped overboard. He had stabbed himself four times in the chest.

We could see him bobbing in the rough sea. The Captain called for a chopper from another ship to rescue him. I saw a man being lowered on a cable but he went back up without the Lt. The Lt. still had scissors and tried to cut the rescuer. A volunteer was asked to go and retrieve him. BM1 Basteda tied a canvas belt around his waist and we handled the line as he swam out.

When we pulled them back to the ship BM2 Raymond Jewett and I pulled the body on board. The Lt had cut both wrists and slit his throat. I helped carry him down to the reefers until a chopper came for him. BM1 Basteda should have received a commendation for his brave swim.

Mike Walsh BM3 1970-71

Lt Marshall Lundberg was detached from DESCOL (Destroyer School) in Newport, RI to assume duty on *Fiske.* Lt Lundberg assumed the duties of Weapons Officer while Fiske was in Prestwick, Scotland.

LCDR Lundberg returned to the *Fiske* in 1977 and served as Executive Officer under CDR Turner until she was transferred to the Turks in 1980.

(l – r) GM3 Jim Bronice, BM2 Raymond Jewett, GM3 Stephen Wright, BM3 Michael Walsh

On 10 July, after departing Plymouth, England, SA David Larrow accidently fell overboard and was promptly recovered unharmed

During the London port visit in mid-July LCDR D.J. Curtiss relieved LCDR J.A. Stewart as *Fiske*'s Executive Officer.

After returning to Newport, RI on 6 October *Fiske* entered a 30 day period of leave and upkeep. On 30 November *Fiske* celebrated her 25th Anniversary with an official ceremony attended by Commander Cruiser-Destroyer Flotilla Ten, Rear Admiral Leslie H. Sell - *Fiske*'s first Weapons Officer and later Executive Officer. RADM Sell delivered the principal address and a silver anniversary plate was presented to the ship by the crew. The remainder of 1970 was spent operating with the Atlantic Fleet.

[Editor's Note: One cannot help but wonder where that silver plate is today.]

1971 found *Fiske* participating in exercises and made port visits from the Caribbean to Nova Scotia. Mid-January found *Fiske* acting as the 'School Ship' for officer students from the U.S. Naval Destroyer School in Newport, RI for 3 weeks. Operations were conducted in Narragansett Bay Ops Area with the USS *Yarnell* (DLG-17) and the USS *Voorhis* (DE 1028). A weekend port visit was made to Norfolk, VA on the 22nd & 23rd followed by ASW exercises with the USS *Clagmore* (SS 343) before returning to Newport on the 29th.

February 11th found *Fiske* underway for a ten day exercise in the Gulf of Maine. The primary reason for this exercise was the testing and evaluation of a new torpedo. The firing ship was the USS *Grayling* (SSN 646). Other supporting ships were the USS *Concord* (AFS 5) and the USS *Penobscot* (ATA 188). In addition to the torpedo testing ASW exercises were conducted.

'A Cold Shower'

We had been out to sea off Newport, RI for about a week and had just tied up and hooked up to shore services - electric, steam, telephone etc. Anyway 3-4 of us were sitting on the deck in After Diesel when the hatch flies open with this MM2 (Mitchell I believe) covered in nothing but soap suds. Dripping suds he reached over us and grabs the sound powered phone to find and ream out the fool who forgot to open the valve in Main Control to heat the hot water which ran out giving

the MM2 a blast of slightly above freezing water. After hearing cusswords that were new even I had not previously heard we were left speechless as he departed.
Frank Connell EN3 1971 -1972

Upon returning to Newport on February 21st *Fiske* began to make preparations for a tender availability with the USS *Puget Sound* (AD 38) on March 4th. *Fiske* entered the floating drydock (ARD 16) at Davisville, RI for hull repairs and continued her TAV with the USS *Puget Sound* until returning to the Destroyer Piers in Newport on March 25th.

After Easter weekend in Newport *Fiske* was underway for Cape Kennedy to act as a support ship for the test firing of a C-1 Poseidon missile from the USS *John C. Calhoun* (SSBN 630). On April 15th a team of specialists moved monitoring equipment onboard to analyze the launch and on the 19th 160 guests came onboard to witness the test. These guests were also treated to a fantail Bar-B-Q and tours of the ship. After the test launch *Fiske* disembarked her guests and headed north – arriving in Newport the afternoon of the 22nd.

On April 30th CDR William R. Pettyjohn relieved CDR Eugene K. Walling as Commanding Officer of *Fiske*.

Most of the month of May was spent in a TAV alongside the USS *Puget Sound* (AD 38). On the 24th *Fiske* got underway for ASROC test firings. *Fiske* also fired two torpedoes. The highlight of this excursion was that the ASROC and torpedoes had live warheads aimed at a submerged target. Following the tests *Fiske* ran the FORACS range off the coast of Cape Cod and returned to Newport on May 28th.

On June 7th *Fiske* got underway for an Antisubmarine Warfare Exercise off Bermuda. Acting in company with the USS *Garcia* (DE 1040) and USS *Barry* (DD 933) *Fiske* acted as a screen for the USS *Saratoga* (CVA 60). *Fiske* returned to Newport on June 12th.

From June 21st until June 29th *Fiske* was underway for NGFS at Culebra and a three day port visit to San Juan, PR. She returned to Newport on July 2nd and celebrated the July 4th holiday. She spent the next 14 days in an upkeep period. Much of the remainder of July was spent underway with Task Force 27.5 conducting ASW attacks against the USS *Sea Devil* (SSN 664). The Task Force also conducted ECM, Damage Control Drills, AA and Surface gunnery exercises.

From July 19th through the 28th *Fiske* participated in numerous ASW exercises as part of Task Group 27.5. The *Fiske* conducted simulated attacks on the USS *Sea Devil* (SSN 664). Also included in this at sea period were many engineering, damage control, electronic countermeasures, anti-air and surface gunnery, communications drills, underway replenishment and refueling exercises.

A ship's picnic was held at Sachuest Point, RI on August 1st and four days later found the *Fiske* steaming north to Winter Harbor, Maine to participate in their annual Lobster Festival. The USS *Bang* (SS 385) also attended. Both ships participated in the various activities and even as *Fiske* was anchored out over 1300 guests took advantage of the open general visiting during the short stay. August 15th found *Fiske* back in Newport for a five day upkeep period.

On August 15th thirteen Midshipmen from various universities reported aboard for a month of testing and indoctrination to shipboard life. The next day *Fiske* got underway for the Narragansett Bay Op Area to conduct ASW ops with the USS *Flying Fish* (SSN 673). After a short upkeep period in Newport *Fiske* was underway again on August 30th for a six hour cruise to provide at-sea orientation to 128 Navy League members and their families. The cruise featured ships tours, displays, a high speed run and a fantail cookout.

The following day *Fiske* was underway again for four days of operations off the southern coast of New England in with the USS *Van Voorhis* (DE 1028) and the USS *Atakapa* (ATF 149). Surface and air gunnery were emphasized.

Much of early September was spent in preparing the ship for her INSURV (Inspection & Survey). Preparations were interrupted on September 13th due to Hurricane Heidi when *Fiske* was required to move to hurricane mooring for one day. The INSURV Team came onboard September 20th and conducted a material inspection through the 22nd. Upon completion of the inspection *Fiske* began preparations for the next underway period scheduled for mid-October.

From the 27th through October 17th *Fiske* had a TAV alongside the USS *Puget Sound* (AD 38) that provided an excellent opportunity to correct the discrepancies found during the INSURV inspection prior to the next operations.

Following approximately six weeks in port *Fiske* was underway again on October 18th for local ASW ops with the USS *Hugh Purvis* (DD 709) and the USS *Sturgeon* (SSN 637). A torpedo and an ASROC were fired on October 21st before returning to Newport the next day. After a weekend break *Fiske* readied herself for the second Navy Destroyer School cruise of the year.

From October 25th through the 29th *Fiske* operated in the Narragansett Bay operations area with the USS *Adams* (DDG 2) and the USS *Davis* (DD 937) on the engineering phase of NAVDESCOL Cruise 35. After a weekend in Newport the three ships were again underway to exercise the students in the operations and weapons phases of destroyer capabilities. These two week exercises were broken by a weekend port visit to Halifax, Nova Scotia on November 5th to 8th.

After conducting ASW exercises with the USS *Clamagore* (SS 343) on the evening of the 10th *Fiske* and the sub collided when the *Clamagore* apparently tried to surface while under *Fiske*. There were no reported casualties to personnel but both vessels reported receiving minor exterior damage. Immediately after the accident the *Clamagore* was detached to return to New London, while *Fiske* continued to operate with the other two school ships.

'Fiske versus Sub'

The USS Clagamore (SS 343) [Now a museum ship at Patriot Pont, Charleston, SC] is intimately connected to Fiske. While acting as the 'quarry' during ASW exercises in late October 1971 it was reported that 'at approximately 2200 hours on 10 October Fiske and Clagamore collided'.

Apparently Clagamore tried to surface while under Fiske. Clagamore collided with Fiske's port side forward, rolled under, re-contacting Fiske's starboard side aft. The Clagamore immediately surfaced.

Both vessels reported 'minor exterior damage' but witnesses reported that many of the sail mounted antennas were missing from Clagamore. The Clagamore immediately detached from the exercise and headed for New London, while Fiske continued to participate in the exercise and returned to Newport in early November.
Russell T Sheridan Sr. BT2 1971- 1972

The *Clagamore* was decommissioned approximately 18 months after this incident and spent much of the late October 1971 through June 1973 either being worked on by shipyard workers or alongside the pier. No record of any deployments by Clagamore after the collision can be found and one can only conclude that she was more severely damaged than the reported 'minor exterior damage'.

The *Fiske* returned to Newport on November 12th where she began another period of general upkeep. In December LCDR B. J.Taylor Jr. relieved LCDR D. J. Curtiss as *Fiske*'s Executive Officer. The ship remained in port throughout the holiday season and the remainder of the year 1971.

YNI Michael Roach served on the *Fiske* from 1971 to 1973. He so enjoyed his time onboard that when he stationed in Seoul, Korea he had a portrait done of the *Fiske*. He found a shop near where he lived in off base housing that did portraits from photographs. The finished picture was hung in a prominent location in the home and when he retired after 30 years of service it was hung next to his shadow box.

He was Command Master Chief Petty Officer of VQ-4 after serving as an attaché at the embassy in Ankara, Turkey. He retired in November 1990 and passed in April 2014. The picture he had created is shown above. The frame is great addition to the portrait.

Very little official information is available for the 1972 calendar year. It appears that *Fiske* either failed to submit an annual Ops Report in early 1973 or that it was lost or misplaced during its travels up the chain of command. We do know that *Fiske* did make a few short term deployments before and after her time in Boston. That much is known. Between March and September 1972 *Fiske* was in Boston Naval Shipyard for a routine overhaul. Upon her departure from the yard she sailed for a brief Caribbean cruise and returned to Newport in October.

On January 4th 1973 *Fiske* deployed to the Mid-East and Indian Ocean where her operational commander was Commander, Middle East Force. In route port calls were made in the Atlantic at Guantanamo Bay, Cuba – for two weeks of intensive RefTra; Trinidad; Recife, Brazil; and Luanda, Angola.

While enroute to Recife, Brazil *Fiske* crossed the Equator entering into the Realm of Neptunis Rex, Ruler of the Raging Main on January 28th and the 'usual' induction of Pollywogs into Shellbacks took place. *Fiske* left Recife on February 9th and, after rounding the Cape of Good Hope, she entered the Indian Ocean on February 16th. After a short 'turnover ceremony on February 24th *Fiske* and the *Noa* (DD 841) became the "Indian Ocean Destroyer Group".

Between operations in the Indian Ocean calls were made at Lourenco Marques [renamed 'Maputo' after independence], Mozambique; Port Louise, Maritius; Nossi Be, Malagasy Republic;

and, Mombasa, Kenya. March 21st through the 24th were spent in the Red Sea with brief stop at Massawa, Ethiopia. During the port visit in Massawa [*now the major seaport of an independent Eritrea*], Ethiopia on March 21st and 22nd *Fiske* was honored by a formal visit from His Imperial Majesty Haile Selassie.

After leaving Massawa *Fiske* set a course for Bahrain where, on April 10th, she embarked several Royal Saudi Naval Officers and enlisted personnel for a training cruise. *Fiske* commenced local area training operations with the British Navy in the Persian Gulf. The Saudi's were disembarked in Bahrain in mid-April and *Fiske* headed for Karachi, Pakistan arriving on April 17th. After an enjoyable four day port visit *Fiske* departed for Mombasa, stopping enroute at Victoria, Seychelle Islands for a brief port visit. *Fiske* arrived in Mombasa on May 18th and relinquished the duties of "Indian Ocean Destroyer Group". During this period *Fiske* fulfilled her mission by 'creating a better understanding of the United States among the people of the countries of the Middle East and by her presence ensured the continued free movement of commerce in this area.' So says the official releases.

H.I.M. Haile Selassie, CDR Grady and Honor Guard

'FISKE VISITED BY TWO KINGS ON ONE CRUISE'

The Fiske departed its home port of Newport RI in early 1973. The plan was to head south for a port call in Recife, Brazil. From Brazil the plan was to continue south and turn under South Africa. Thence head north stopping at various ports along the East African Coast. The long range plan was to conduct an Around the World Cruise and return to Newport.

In late January Fiske entertained King Neptune as she crossed the Equator on and the awarded Shellback status to all deserving Pollywogs. His Highness, King Neptune, was pleased with Fiske and her Crew.

Continuing North, Fiske was to call upon each and every Shellback to perform in true Shellback fashion. The remnants of a cyclone blew in from the North East and while the Fiske navigation had a solid track on the impending storm, Fiske continued north at best speed to make its next scheduled port visit.

Fiske weathered the storm and was set to strike a heading to meet its next Diplomacy commitment when the Radio Gang messenger delivered a message to the Wardroom that would change the deal.

The message was:

"FISKE IS TO DIVERT FROM HER CURRENT PORT VISIT PLAN. FISKE IS TO SET COURSE FOR MASSAWA ETHIOPIA TO ARRIVE AT 0800 ON THE 23RD OF MARCH. FISKE WILL MAKE ALL PREPARATION TO HOST H.I.M FOR A STATE VISIT UPON ARRIVAL.

In the wardroom much head scratching took place. The question of the moment was:

WHAT'S A H.I.M? "

The answer became obvious. H.I.M is Diplomatic speak for HIS IMPERIAL MAJEST. That being Emperor Haile Selassie

The equivalent of General Quarters was sounded. The immediate issue was the condition of the ship. The storm had coated the entire ship with an ugly coat of brownish salt. The Boson Gang aided by the Second Division estimated that they could make either the Port side or the Starboard side presentable for a H.I.M. visit –BUT NOT BOTH.

Navigator team, front and center. Get in touch with the Port Authority and determine our birth location and to which side will we moor the answer came in less than 3 hours...Birth Number 4 and Starboard Side To. We had less than 9 hours to Clean Ship. Go First and Second divisions. In reality the job was an ALL HANDS requirement.

The next order of business was a message to the US Embassy Ethiopia. FISKE need to know (ASAP) what were the hot issues the US and Ethiopia were discussing that Fiske should be aware of. Secondly what are the current Economic and Cultural issues confronting H.I.M. that Fiske should know about? Talking Points that is. The US Embassy did a great job in a timely fission. **Fiske will be ready**

Well almost.

The pilot was aboard Fiske from his small boat at 0800. He was escorted to the bridge to brief the navigation team.

The briefing went well

Well almost

The navigation team was informed that because of the tide and weather conditions forecast on Fiske's departure date, it will be necessary to moor PORT SIDE TO.

A resounding **OH SH_____!** *was heard from the bridge to the fantail.*

A compromise was reached. Fiske would go Starboard to. Additionally Fiske would deploy her anchor 100 feet (about) into the channel apposite her birth. Three days later, at underway time, the anchor would be taken under a strain and keep the bow from being subjected to an adverse tide and wind.

It worked. Thirty minutes after securing the Sea Detail, H.I.M and his entourage parked at the brow. **Let the Visit Begin.**
Roger D. Grady CDR   August 1972 – March 1974

After a two day visit in Luanda, Angola *Fiske* set course for Recife, Brazil, arriving there on June 15th. From June 18th to the 20th conducted local operations with units of the Brazilian Navy and, after brief fuel stops in Trinidad and St. Thomas, Virgin Islands, arrived home in Newport, RI on July 2nd.

Fiske spent the remainder of July, August and most of September making preparations for her official transfer to the Fleet Reserve Force as a member of Destroyer Squadron 28, homeported in Bayonne, NJ.

Chapter VI

(DD 842) – Reserve Fleet

September 1973 to June 1980

On August 31st *Fiske* was officially transferred to DesRon 28 of the Fleet Reserve Force and her homeport was changed from Newport, RI to Bayonne, NJ. *Fiske* departed Newport on September 26th and after a brief stop at Earle, NJ to off-load 'special weapons' arrived in Bayonne. For the remainder of September and much of October *Fiske* was in port at Bayonne.

The last quarter of 1973 was spent either drilling with SAMAR 3-9 (Ship's Assistance, Maintenance and Repair Unit) or, for the last half of November until December 6th, in a tender availability in Norfolk, VA. The people that made up SAMAR 3-9 were experienced Reservists that used their past naval training and present civilian occupations in repairing existing equipment and manufacturing and installing new improvements to the ship.

Fiske spent an underway drill weekend in October, November and December with the members of SAMAR 3-9 in either the Narragansett Bay or Long Island Sound Ops areas. The assistance of this group proved to be invaluable and were a welcome addition to the *Fiske*. The *Fiske* returned to Bayonne on December 9th and spent the rest of the holiday period in port.

January 1974 found *Fiske* making preparations for a unit inspection by the Commander of DesRon 28. This inspection covered all facets of ship's operations, gunnery exercises, precision anchoring, engineering casualty drills and Damage Control drills. Also a PMS inspection was conducted by members of the staff of Cruiser Destroyer Force Atlantic. An overall grade of excellent was awarded to the ship upon completion of the IUC. This inspection may have been a contributing factor when the *Fiske* was re-activated from the Reserve Fleet to the active fleet in July and was deployed as a member of DesRon Four for a three month Mediterranean Deployment.

The remainder of the first quarter of '74 was spent either drilling with SAMAR 3-9 or her SELRES (Selected Reserve) crew. On February 16th *Fiske* disembarked SAMAR 3-9 and embarking her SELRES crew for a two week ACDUTRA (Active Duty for Training) period and on the 19th *Fiske* completed a Tender Availability alongside the USS *Shenandoah* (AD-19) and was underway to Bloodsworth Island and Naval Gunfire Support Qualifications. After receiving a satisfactory grade on the 20th *Fiske* returned to Norfolk. On the 24th *Fiske* departed Norfolk for the Norfolk/Jacksonville Ops Areas and spent the next 10 days conducting numerous exercises. After a very brief stop in Mayport *Fiske* headed for Bayonne and arrived on March 3rd. On March 8th CDR John F. Fitzgerald relieved CDR Roger D. Grady as CO of the *Fiske*.

In late March *Fiske* made a brief trip to the Naval Ammunition Depot in Earle, NJ to off-load ammunition in preparation of her upcoming conversion to NDF (Naval Distillate Fuel). The rest of March, April and much of May were spent in a restricted availability status while undergoing conversion of the ship's engineering plant to permit use of NDF. During this period *Fiske* conducted SAMAR drill weekends on April 6-7 and May 11-12. SELRES drills were conducted in port on April 20-21 and May 18-19. Conversion to NDF was completed by May 29th. On June 8th *Fiske* received word that she would be deploying to the Mediterranean in 47 days.

In addition to conducting SAMAR and SELRES drills in June *Fiske* also sailed to New London, CN and the FORACS (Naval Forces Sensor & Weapons Accuracy Check Sites) range. *Fiske* departed New London and arrived in Norfolk for a POM (Preparation for Movement) tender availability with the USS *Puget Sound* (AD-38). The POM was completed and *Fiske* returned to Bayonne on the 29th of June.

After conducting a combined SELRES/SAMAR weekend on July 13-14 *Fiske* departed Bayonne on July 16th for Norfolk. While enroute she conducted UNREP training with the USS *Noxubee* (AO-656).

On 19 July 1974, *Fiske* and *Harold J. Ellison* (DD 864) departed Norfolk for the Mediterranean Sea. They rendezvoused with the aircraft carrier USS *Independence* (CV 62) on July 20th. This three ship task force was joined by the USS *Garcia* (DE-1042) about mid-way to the Mediterranean.

Fiske's primary mission during this Mediterranean deployment was to train reservists in actual fleet operations. Every two weeks a new group of reservists – made up of approximately 60 enlisted and 5 officers – would arrive for training. *Fiske* demonstrated the viability of the total force concept which provides for the maximum effective integration and employment of both active and reserve assets.

During the transit with *Independence, Ellison, Noxubee* & *Garcia* the *Fiske* conducted three UNREPS and daily HIFR training arriving in Rota, Spain on July 28th. The transit was made with moderately heavy seas.

After departing Rota, Spain *Fiske* and *Ellison* transited to Malaga, Spain arriving on August 1st.

'"God"Overboard'

During the Med cruise of 1974 one port of call was Malaga, Spain. We had set the Sea and Anchor detail as we neared Malaga and we were about 15 miles from the dock. QMC Tom Nevitt was plotting our position and I was recording the bearings being shot by the Quartermaster group from the bridge wings.

Without warning one of the sound powered phone talkers, a small man maybe 5' tall, removed his headset, put it on the chart table, looked at Chief Nevitt and said "I'm God" then turned to me and said "I'm God". With that he left the bridge, walked down the port ladder to the main deck and jumped overboard.

I believe the young man realized fairly quickly that he was not God, he couldn't walk on water and in fact he couldn't even swim! I threw the man overboard buoy from the bridge wing to mark his point of departure and advised the OOD of what happened.

Watching from the bridge all I could see of the young man was the top of his head that appeared as a Brillo Pad floating in the ocean. Instantly and without regard for his own safety BM2 Jerry Pepo, a crazy NYC taxi driver, jumped over the side to assist the floundering young man.

With some quick reactions and nifty seaman ship we had both the hero and the victim out of the water in about 10 minutes. Upon arrival in Malaga the young man was removed from the Fiske never to be seen onboard again.
Dave Fitzgerald QM2 1973-76

After four days in Malaga the two ships conducted ten days of at sea operations in the western Mediterranean. *Fiske* conducted two UNREPs (Underway Replenishments) with the USS *Milwaukee* (AOR-2) and ASW exercises with the HMS *Opportune.*

Fiske and *Ellison* arrived in Naples, Italy on August 14th for a five day port visit. After departing Naples, Italy *Fiske* conducted a VERTREP with helicopters from the USS *Concord* (AFS-5). After completing the vertical replenishment *Fiske* and *Ellison* headed east to operate with the USS *Forrestal* (CV-59) off the coast of Cyprus for the next ten days. *Fiske* returned to Naples on August 30th for a ten day rest.

On September 17th *Fiske* and *Ellison* sailed for Barcelona, Spain. Enroute the *Fiske* conducted ASW exercises with the French submarine *Arianne. Fiske* and *Ellison* also conducted UNREPS with USS *Sylvania* (AFS-2) and USS *Milwaukee.* Both ships arrived in Barcelona on the 21st. After leaving Barcelona both ships sailed for Rota, arriving on September 27th. While in Rota *Fiske* was officially detached from the Sixth Fleet and on September 30th *Fiske* and *Ellison* began their transit across the Atlantic.

During this Mediterranean deployment *Fiske* conducted six reserve ACDUTRA periods of 14 days in length. Approximately 400 Reservists were trained onboard during this cruise. After a brief fuel stop in Ponta Delgada, Azores continued the transit and arrived in Bayonne, NJ on October 10th.

'Fires Out!'

I served on the USS Fiske during a Med. Cruise from mid-July through mid-October 1974. The Fiske was in the company of the USS John F. Kennedy (CV-67) and the USS Ellison (DD864) during our return voyage.

On or about October 7, 1974 the group encountered a severe storm about 3 days out of our home port at the Military Ocean Terminal, Bayonne, NJ. The Fiske was turned sideways into the trough of a wave, water washed up the side of the ship, extinguished the [fires in] boilers and we lost steam.

If you check the ships log you will find this event. I believe I was the log keeper during the event and the subsequent General Quarters period. As I recall we were without power for approximately 30 minutes. During our period of time without power we were badly battered by the rough seas taking rolls near 45 degrees and changes in elevation of at least several yards. I don't remember every day of my naval service but this is one event I will never forget.
David Fitzgerald QM2 1973-76

After returning to Bayonne, NJ from the Mediterranean *Fiske* began a 30 day stand down and post-deployment upkeep period. On 19-20 October *Fiske* conducted a combined in port SELRES/SAMAR weekend. On November 2-3 a SAMAR drill weekend was held. 9 November found *Fiske* underway again for the Narragansett Bay Op Area for her monthly SELRES drill weekend. Various drills including GQ, NGFS, Damage Control and ASW team training were conducted during this underway period. *Fiske* disembarked the SELRES component on the 10th and immediately sailed for Norfolk, VA for a TAV with the USS *Puget Sound*. She arrived 11 November and departed Norfolk on 3 December. *Fiske* arrived back in Bayonne, NJ after a brief stop at Earle, NJ Naval Weapons Depot to onload ammunition on 5 December. The weekend of December 7-8 found *Fiske* underway for another SELRES weekend. On the weekend of 14-15 *Fiske* conducted a SAMAR drill and remained inport throughout the holiday period and the remainder of 1974.

1975 found *Fiske* transferred from DesRon 28 to DesRon 30 on July 1st. CDR Fitzgerald remained in command for all of 1975. Much of January was spent preparing for *Fiske*'s annual Immediate Unit Commander (IUC) by ComDesRon 28. The SAMAR weekend of 18-19 January proved to be highly beneficial making final preparations for this event. The IUC was conducted from the 22nd through the 26th. During those five days all facets of destroyer operations were conducted: gunnery exercises; precision anchoring; full power run; and, damage control drills. The *Fiske* received and overall grade of Excellent in this IUC.

February found the *Fiske* preparing for yet another inspection – this time it was the Board of Inspection and Survey (INSURV). The INSURV was held in March and most of February was devoted to getting her in top materiál condition with the help of the SAMAR unit on the 8th and 9th. *Fiske* was underway on the 15th and 16th with other units of squadron for the monthly SELRES weekend. During that at sea period the *Fiske* completed the Annual Type Commanders' Communications Exercise with a grade of 94.

March 1st found *Fiske* underway for the monthly SELRES training weekend. This was devoted to Damage Control drills and Ship Maneuvering Exercises. After returning to Bayonne on the 2nd to disembark the SELRES personnel *Fiske* sailed for Norfolk, Virginia, arriving on the 3^{rd,} to undergo the INSURV which started on the 10th. For the first week in Norfolk *Fiske* completed final preparations for the Board. Upon completion of the inspection on March 14th *Fiske* was found to be in satisfactory materiál condition and was recommended she undergo her regularly scheduled overhaul.

On March 17th *Fiske* began her Quarterly Tender Availability alongside the USS *Shenandoah* (AD 26) and on the 26th SAMAR Unit 2202 embarked for their annual Active Duty Training (ACDUTRA). This group of experienced and skilled personnel contributed significantly in the repair of existing equipment as well as manufacturing and installing new improvements to the ship. In April the annual PMS (Preventative Maintenance Schedule) Inspection was held with *Fiske* receiving a grade of excellent.

On April 12th *Fiske* embarked the SELRES Crew for their annual two weeks ACDUTRA. The 13th found her underway for Bloodsworth Island and Naval Gunfire Support Qualification. Two days later *Fiske* had successfully qualified and was on her way to the Jacksonville Op areas. While enroute *Fiske* conducted daily General Quarter, Damage Control Drills and Gunnery exercises to improve her operational readiness.

Fiske visited Mayport, Florida from 18th through the 21st - departing early on the 21st for the JAXOPS (Jacksonville Operating Areas) areas where she conducted an ORE (Operational Readiness Exercise) with the Deputy Assistant Secretary of Defense for Manpower and Reserve Affairs and his Staff onboard as observers. A grade of Satisfactory was attained. On April 22nd-23rd *Fiske* participated in intense ASW (Anti-Submarine Warfare) Exercises with other units of DesRon 28 and units and aircraft from the Naval Air Station, Jacksonville.

Upon completion of those exercises *Fiske* began the transit back to Bayonne. While enroute north *Fiske* conducted numerous drills and exercises to improve operational readiness - arriving in Bayonne on April 27th and disembarking the SELRES crew.

Following the SELRES cruise *Fiske* remained in port from April 28th through June 21st for a restricted availability and upkeep. SAMAR weekends were conducted on 10-11 May and 14-15 June.

SELRES weekends were 17-18 May and 21-22 June. All were conducted in port. During the week of 19 May a 'Human Resources' availability was used to implement Phase II of the Navy's Equal Opportunity Program.

The week of June 23rd to the 27th was spent in Newport for Midshipman training. During this period *Fiske*, and other units of DesRon 28, went to sea daily and conducted engineering, gunnery and maneuvering drills for the benefit of the embarked midshipman. *Fiske* returned to Bayonne on the 28th of June. On July 1st *Fiske* was transferred from DesRon 28 to DesRon 30 commanded by Captain E. J. Mountford, USN.

Much of July was spent operating in the Narragansett Bay Operations Areas with a port visit to Halifax, Nova Scotia over the 11th through the 13th and a SAMAR weekend on the 19th and 20th. The next weekend was a SELRES weekend conducted at sea with units of DesRon 30 with emphasis being on surface gunnery exercises. On the 28th of July *Fiske* departed Bayonne on a "Go Navy Cruise" to Portland, Maine where she conducted an 'Open House' for the community. The 1st of August found *Fiske* in Winter Harbor, Maine for that town's annual Lobster Festival returning to Bayonne on August 5th.

Fiske remained in port in Bayonne from August 5th through the 22nd for upkeep and a SAMAR weekend on the 9th and 10th. *Fiske* was underway on the 13th for a SELRES weekend and disembarked them on the 14th and then sailed for Philadelphia for the change of command for ComDesRon 30, returning to Bayonne on August 30th where she remained until SELRES weekend of September 13th and 14th for Type Training. *Fiske* departed for Norfolk immediately after disembarking the SELRES crew and arrived there on the 15th for her quarterly tender availability with the USS *Shenandoah* (AD 26). While in Norfolk, *Fiske* made maximum use of all the Fleet Training Facilities, including the 14A2 Trainer and Damage Control School.

Upon completion of the TAV, *Fiske* returned to Bayonne on October 18th for upkeep. For the remainder of 1975 *Fiske*'s at sea time was limited to SELRES weekends on October 25th and 26th and December 13th and 14th for Type Training. The November weekend was spent inport due to insufficient fuel allowances. SAMAR weekends were conducted on October 18th and 19th; November 8th and 9th; and, December 6th and 7th.

1976 was much the same as 1975, homeported in Bayonne, New Jersey as part of DesRon 30. Her normal active duty ship's company consisted of 12 officers and anywhere from 150 to 180 enlisted personnel. *Fiske* was augmented by a two reserve units; a selected reserve unit (SELRES) composed of 5 officers and 100 enlisted that would be fill out the ships' wartime complement in the event of national emergency and Ship Activation Repair Unit 2202 with 6 officers and 90 enlisted whose job it was to provide material maintenance support for the *Fiske*. The new year of 1976 found *Fiske* still in Boston at the General Ship and Engine Work Shipyard while work continued on ship's systems. *Fiske* departed Boston on May 13th when she returned to Bayonne where she entered into a restricted availability for the completion of replacement of engineering space electrical wiring.

The *Fiske* had a TAV with the USS *Shenandoah* in mid-January in Norfolk, VA and her SELRES weekend of January 17th & 18th was spent preparing for the upcoming two week active duty period in February. SAMAR Unit 2202 arrived on the 26th of January for their 2 week active duty period. *Fiske* returned to Bayonne on February 13th after departing Norfolk on the 7th. The at sea period was spent in training underway details. On the 14th, with her SELRES crew embarked, *Fiske* departed Bayonne and steamed south to rendezvous with other units of DesRon 30 for type training. The first week was devoted to drills and exercises such as ASW, engineering and gunnery. On the 20th *Fiske* arrived in Mayport, FL for a 3 day port visit. Departing on the 23rd she participated in two days of intensive ASW exercises before heading north for Bayonne. The 3 days of this trip were spent drilling in tactical maneuvering and seamanship.

After arriving in Bayonne on the 28th of February *Fiske* remained in port until early April except for one SELRES weekend in March. During that SELRES weekend (March 20-21) she completed the type commander's annual communications exercise and received a grade of 93.

April 10-11 was a SELRES weekend and the at sea time was spent in gunnery exercises in preparations for the annual NGFS (Naval Gun Fire Support) qualifications scheduled for May. *Fiske* disembarked her SELRES unit on the 11th and set sail for her TAV alongside the USS *Piedmont* (AD-17) in Norfolk from April 12th – May 7th. On April 22nd CDR William R. Pressler relieved CDR John F. Fitzgerald as Commanding Officer, USS *Fiske*.

The first half of May was busy. Four days of NGFS off Bloodsworth Island with her SELRES unit embarked followed by four days of playing the role of a Kara Class cruiser in exercise "Solid Shield". The SELRES crew had been disembarked after successfully qualifying in the NGFS exercise. After disembarking the SELRES crew *Fiske* began her role as part of the aggressor force for "Solid Shield". *Fiske* returned to Bayonne on the 19th of May.

On May 24th ComDesRon 30 and his staff started three days of rigorous and thorough inspection of the *Fiske*'s material condition both inport and underway. She was found to be in satisfactory condition and spent the remainder of May and much of June in port. The SELRES weekend of June 19-20 found *Fiske* operating independently in the Narragansett Bay OpAreas (Operations Areas) the days devoted to practice battle problems for her upcoming annual "Operational Readiness Exercise" (ORE).

July and August proved to be interesting. *Fiske* remained in Bayonne from June 21st to July 16th for upkeep. From her berth at the Military Ocean Terminal *Fiske* served as a reviewing platform for the "International Naval Review" and "Operation Sail" held on July 3rd and 4th as part of our Nation's 200th Birthday Celebration. *Fiske* was host ship for the HMS *Britannia* for that period and on the 4th she held an open-house and picnic for crew and their families – with some 700 people attending. July 17th and 18th, a SELRES weekend, was the ORE. The exercise was observed by ComDesRon 30 and his staff. *Fiske* was given a grade of 'Satisfactory'. On the following weekend *Fiske* was again underway. This was for a dependents cruise around New York harbor coupled by a cook-out on the flight deck that was enjoyed by all.

Fiske remained inport until August 10th when she sailed for the Virginia Capes to participate in exercise COMTEX 7-76. Hurricane 'Belle', packing winds in excess of 70mph, made landfall in Jones Beach, Long Island, NY on that day. The exercise was delayed somewhat due to the high seas and strong winds. *Fiske* participated in four days of type training – ASW, gunnery, underway replenishment, communications and tactical drills. *Fiske* detached from COMTUEX 7-76 on the 14th and sailed for Norfolk to begin her pre-overhaul TAV alongside the USS *Piedmont* (AD-17).

After three weeks in the TAV identifying and prioritizing repairs and upgrades to be made during the upcoming overhaul *Fiske* returned to Bayonne on September 11th. The SELRES weekend of September 18-19 found *Fiske* underway off the Virginia Capes with other units of DesRon 30. On the 28th she went to NAD Earle, NJ to off-load ammunition and returned to Bayonne the same day.

October found *Fiske* in the Todd Shipyard, Brooklyn, NY for the drydock (Lot I) portion of her overhaul. During the Lot I period all below the waterline work is performed, including SONAR, hull cleaning, fuel and water tank repair. Lot I was completed on December 1st. *Fiske* sailed from Brooklyn for Boston on December 2nd and entered the General Ship and Engine Works Shipyard on the 3rd for the Lot II portion of the overhaul. This portion covered the overhaul and repair of ship's electronics and mechanical systems as well as installing new equipment and making much needed structural repairs.

The length of time spent in Boston and the immediate restricted availability in Bayonne leads one to believe that the Navy was in responding to some serious questions either of reliability or health concerns. It appears from the timelines that this was part of the Navy's Asbestos Abatement Program that was conducted during the mid to late '70s. *Fiske*, like every Navy ship built during WWII, was rife with asbestos in just about every compartment and space. Little consideration was given to its possible adverse health effects when we were trying to win a global war.

After successfully testing the entire electrical plant in early September *Fiske* was underway for Mayport, FL on the 12th. During this period *Fiske* conducted Damage Control, Engineering Casualty and gunnery exercises. The ship's Aviation Fire Fighting Team was established and trained at this time. *Fiske* remained in Mayport from the 12th to the 30th.

On October 3rd was enroute to Bloodsworth Island for her annual NGFS qualifications when the Commander, Carrier Group 4, aboard the USS *Nimitz* (CVAN 70) requested assistance in recovering an F-14 that had been lost after a ramp strike while attempting a landing. Recovery efforts were hampered by the knowledge that any Soviet submarines in the area would attempt to recovery any or all of the [at that time] state-of-the art aircraft. *Fiske* established a datum for the aircraft. On the morning of the 5th *Fiske* recovered the tail section and brought it onboard. Magnetic Anomaly Detection (MAD) gear from a *Nimitz* aircraft allowed the *Fiske* to positively locate the remainder of the aircraft on the 6th and that morning *Fiske* was relieved as on scene commander of the salvage operations by the USS *Fearless* (MSO 442). *Fiske* returned to Mayport to off-load the debris and departed Mayport for Bayonne, NJ, arriving there on October 7th.

Fiske participated in COMTUEX 1-78 from October 19th to the 26th and upon completion of that exercise steamed to Nassau in the Bahamas for a port visit and returned to Bayonne, NJ on the 31st. *Fiske* remained there until November the 19th when she sailed for Norfolk, VA for an IMAV on the 20th. She returned to Bayonne on December 15th where she stayed for the balance of 1977.

In December 1977 CDR John R. Dalrymple relieved CDR William R. Pressler as CO of the *Fiske* as an interim measure until a suitable replacement could be found. It has been hinted that CDR Pressler was relieved 'for cause' but we have only anecdotal information on this. CDR Dalrymple went on to attain the rank of Rear Admiral before retirement.

During much of the latter half of the 1970's *Fiske* was home to several female officers and enlisted personnel. Some became part of Ship's Company for qualification as Surface Warfare officers and other served with the Reserve SIMA Groups. The story below was submitted by one of those female Reservists that served onboard the *Fiske*.

And the winner is . . . .'

In true Navy fashion most of my stories involve liquor. Under the APG, as an E5 under 4, after my first duty station at NAS Willow Grove, I requested transfer as a Blackshoe and joined SIMA 102 in Bayonne, NJ. I recall that it was suggested that I not become one of the "boys". That never happened. How could one be expected to drink soda after chow when we could get a case of beer real cheap?

Early on at SIMA I wore my leather dress shoes because the Boondockers they gave me with my seabag were for men and much too big. That was the weekend I grabbed a Tektronix 555 oscilloscope from the ET Shop and headed down a ladder. My hand slipped off the railing and I went tumbling down with the 'scope. I hit the bulkhead and sprained my ankle.

Some months later we went from Floyd Bennett Field on a MATS flight down to Little Creek for a 'Wetaway Weekend'. There were 60 of us crammed into the smallest bus on the planet. We were one on top of the other, critically overloaded and in danger of toppling over but somehow we made it to our quarters.

That night, after a terrific meal at the Acey-Deucey Club, we went inside to listen to the band and have a few rounds – then a few more – then some more. I could see out of the corner of my eye that money was changing hands between our unit and the one next to us, but was oblivious to what was going on. The rounds kept coming – close to 2 or 3 AM - the place started to clear out.

It was then that I realized that the guys had been betting on who would outlast who, and I finally realized that I was the last "man" standing. Off to McDonald's we went, then back to our quarters to crash. The next morning, as I was walking up to the chow line, I see money changing hands again, and the guys started cheering. Turning around to see no one behind me, those buggers had been taking bets that I wouldn't show up! Finally, after chow, I was reworking a relay board – soldering – and feeling green at the gills with the neon lights above, and a blistering hangover. Suddenly, I see the Captain standing next to me as I worked. The conversation went this way:

Captain: - "Good Morning – I hear you were out drinking with the guys last night."

Me: - "Yes Sir"

Captain: - "I hear you drank quite a lot."

Me, Yes Sir, I had a few.

Captain: - "A few? – I thought I told you not to be like the guys".

Me: - Yes Sir, you did.

Captain: - "I hear you closed the place down"

Me: - "Yes Sir, we were having a good time".

Captain: -"I hear you out drank two units

Me: - silence

Captain: with a sly look and broad smile, "Well Done Sailor"

Walking the decks of the FISKE made me think of my father, who had passed away the year before. He served on a Destroyer in the Pacific during WWII, and was buried at sea in a ceremony off the USS Theodore Roosevelt. I tried to imagine the battles that had been fought, the incredible sacrifices that were made, and it made me humble. Although my part of a great tradition was very small, it was an honor to have served.

Do I drink today? Well, I wouldn't want to offend anyone who doesn't, but I do – just a little. But only one- I just won't say how big.

Sandra Ehlers Siciliano, ETN2 1977-79

Editor's note: ETN2 Ehlers was the daughter of a Destroyer man, a sister-in-law of a submariner and the Great Aunt of a crewmember on the flight deck of the USS Theodore Roosevelt (CVN 71) making her a true Navy family.

ETN2 Sandie Ehlers Siciliano

On January 19th, 1978 CDR Steven Lloyd Turner relieved CDR John R. Dalrymple as CO of the *Fiske*. CDR Turner headed a roster of thirteen officers and 179 enlisted personnel in the nucleus crew. Captain Turner and the XO, LCDR Lundberg, proved to a good team. There were 5 officers and 90 enlisted in the SELRES crew.

Fiske was also occasionally assigned repair availability to the Shore Intermediate Maintenance (SIMA) Unit 104. SIMA personnel were not considered part of the crew supplement but they were fully integrated into ship's operations while they were onboard.

CDR Steven L. Turner

CDR Turner was to be the last CO of the *Fiske*. He was a 1961 graduate of the U. S. Merchant Marine Academy, Kings Point. NY and in 1968 assumed command of the USS *Coconino County* (LST 603) followed by the USS *Outagamie County* (LST 1073). Both of these ships were homeported in Guam and served extensively in Vietnamese waters. After his Pacific tours he became a student at the Naval War

College in Newport. Following that duty he became Executive Officer of the USS *Brumby* (FF1044). Upon completion of that tour CDR Turner returned to academia as a student of Rensselaer Polytechnic Institute (RPI). After leaving RPI he was assigned to Headquarters, Naval Sea Systems Command in Washington, D. C. before becoming CO of the *Fiske*.

CDR Turner's Executive Officer was LCDR Marshall B. Lundberg. They served together until the *Fiske* was turned over to the Turks in June 1980.

Fiske commenced her regularly scheduled IMAV alongside the USS *Vulcan* (AR 5) at Norfolk, VA on January 23rd. During the next 30 day period *Fiske* completed a series of inspections, team training and following the completion of the IMAV she backloaded ammunition in Yorktown, VA prior to returning to Bayonne.

On February 24th *Fiske*'s SELRES unit began their annual Active Duty for Training. The combined crew participated in ASWEX 1-78 from the 26th to March 4th and made a port visit to Charlotte Amalie, St. Thomas, USVI from the 5th to the 8th. She returned to Bayonne on March 12th.

Fiske spent from March 20th to May 2nd in an IMAV with the USS *Sierra* (AD 18) in Charleston. During that period was certified to handle ASROC weapons as well as routine repairs and overhaul items.

Fiske arrived in Roosevelt Roads, Puerto Rico on May 9th and commenced FORACS/WSAT exercises that were successfully completed on May 16th. *Fiske* departed then and steamed for Guantanamo Bay for Fleet Refresher Training remaining in Gitmo until June 17th after successfully completing SELRESTRA. Underway again for Puerto Rico *Fiske* stayed in the Caribbean until the 21st of June to qualify in NGFS at Vieques Island, P. R. After a brief refueling stop at Norfolk, VA *Fiske* arrived back in Bayonne on the 25th.

Except for a brief SELRES on the 15 and 16th of July *Fiske* remained in port conducting upkeep and a Human Resources Availability (HRAV) throughout the month of July. On the 31st she got underway with the rest of DesRon 30 for operations in the western Atlantic.

Fiske arrived in Halifax, Nova Scotia on August 4th and participated in Navy Day activities in the Halifax/Dartmouth area along with other units of DesRon 30. *Fiske* steamed out of Halifax with ComDesRon 30 embarked on August 8th. *Fiske* was given an ORI (Operational Readiness Inspection) at this time and on the following day transferred ComDesRon 30 and sixteen observers to the USS *Johnston* (DD 821). *Fiske* remained with TU 40.0.3 until August 11th when she returned to Bayonne.

Much of September found *Fiske* in Bayonne for upkeep and INSURV preparation. She did make on Family Cruise to West Point, NY on the 23rd & 24th.

On October 10th the Sub-Board of Inspection and Survey (INSURV), Atlantic embarked at Bayonne for the underway Material Inspection. This was completed on the 14th in Norfolk, VA. The next day *Fiske* began an IMAV with the USS *Puget Sound* (AD 38) and a Restricted Availability (RAV) with NAVSURFLANT READSUPPGRU NORVA (Naval Surface Atlantic Readiness Support Group Norfolk, VA) for those fascinated by military acronyms. While in Norfolk *Fiske* conducted extensive off-ship training, including Aviation Fire Fighting Team training.

The IMAV/RAV was completed on November 22nd but *Fiske* remained in port for Thanksgiving before joining Task Force 21 for GULFEX-79. *Fiske* arrived in Key West, FL for refueling on the 27th and joined TU21.1.3 (in support of TU 21.1.5) until the 30th of November and on December 4th returned to Bayonne where she remained for the remainder of the year.

January 1979 found *Fiske* inport except for a SELRES on the 19th and on the 30th underway bound for Type Training in the Puerto Rico and Jacksonville Ops Areas. She and the USS *Hawkins* (DD 873) provided services for the USS *America* (CV 66) and returned to Mayport prior to steaming to Mobile, AL, arriving there on February

22nd and remaining there until the 27th. While there *Fiske* served as host ship for the Mobile, AL Mardi Gras festivities. After a brief stop in Mayport for fuel *Fiske* returned to Bayonne on March 5th.

Much of March was spent inport conducting upkeep except for a SELRES on the weekend of 17th and 18th and providing submarine services on 27th and 28th.

April found *Fiske* underway on the 6th, after embarking her SELRES personnel, headed for Norfolk, VA arriving on the 8th, and commencing an IMAV on the 9th. *Fiske* remained in Norfolk effecting repairs until the 9th of May when she headed back to Bayonne. She arrived in her homeport on the 11th, having conducted both surface and air gunnery exercises while enroute. The SELRES crew was embarked on the 18th and *Fiske* got underway for an ORI. *Fiske* returned to port to disembark the SELRES crew on the 20th and underway again on the 21st for NGFS Qualification at Bloodsworth Island in the Chesapeake Bay.

Due to adverse weather and sound propagation conditions NGFS qualification efforts were cancelled at Bloodsworth Island. *Fiske* refueled at Norfolk and returned to Bayonne on the 27th of May. On June 8th she embarked her SELRES crew for their annual ACDUTRA (two weeks) and was underway with other units of DesRon 30 for operations in the western Atlantic.

Fiske and other units of DesRon 30 arrived in Halifax, Nova Scotia on the 15th for a port visit and remained inport through the 18th. She arrived in Bayonne on the 23rd, having completed extensive ASW, surface and air gunnery exercise enroute.

On 30 June *Fiske* conducted a Family Cruise to Bridgeport, CN and remained there through the 4th of July. *Fiske* served as the Navy's representative for the P.T. Barnum Festival while there. Additionally, the ship conducted a 'Father and Son' cruise on the 5th and returned to Bayonne on the 6th.

A SELRES weekend was conducted on the 13th and 14th of July. Upon disembarking the SELRES crew on the 15th *Fiske* got underway for Vieques Island, Puerto Rico for NGFS qualifications. When these qualifications were successfully completely *Fiske* headed for Hamilton, Bermuda for a port visit from the 22nd to the 24th. She got underway on the 25th and arrived back in Bayonne on the 27th.

Fiske remained in Bayonne for much of August for upkeep with the exception of an ammunition on-load at NAD Earle, Colt's Neck, NJ on the 17th and a SELRES weekend on the 18th and 19th. *Fiske* got underway for Norfolk, VA on the 15th of September for repairs and ASW team training. The *Fiske* remained in Norfolk until the 21st and returning to Bayonne on the 22nd.

Fiske participated in COMPTUEX 1-80 from the 1st to the 11th of October; visiting Charlotte Amalie, St Thomas, USVI from the 12th to the 15th. After stopping in Norfolk for refueling on the 18th she embarked her SELRES crew on the 19th for underway training and arrived back in Bayonne on the 21st. *Fiske* remained in port for upkeep for the remainder of October and into November.

On November 14th *Fiske* got underway to participate in CNO Project 102, which involved a test and evaluation of the MK 48 torpedo. Exercises were conducted in the Gulf of Maine with the USS *Glenard P. Lipscomb* (SSN 685). After a brief port visit to Boston the *Fiske* returned to Bayonne on the 20th of November.

Fiske remained in port at Bayonne throughout the rest of November and the month of December observing Thanksgiving on the 22nd and going into a holiday stand down on December 15th closing out 1979.

January 1980 found *Fiske* in her homeport of Bayonne, NJ with a January 7th departure scheduled for a regular IMAV in Norfolk, VA. On the 8th *Fiske* was alongside the USS *Piedmont* where she stayed through February 8th.

On the 9th of February she embarked her SELRES crew for their annual two weeks of ACDUTRA and got underway for the Puerto Rico OPAREAS. Embarked onboard were two female officers, LT(jg)

Sheryl Krupski and Ens. Beulah Galvin, to garner at-sea experience for final qualifications as Surface Warfare Officers.

A 'Google' search revealed that Ensign Galvin went on to serve on several ships over a distinguished career that culminated in her being selected for Captain on the 1999-2000 Selection lists.

'Milk Crate Conning'

At the time those two young ladies reported aboard having females aboard ship was still quite new. I was a reserve Chief Quartermaster at the time and had been assigned to the Fiske on and off from the time she was transferred to the reserve fleet. If I remember correctly it was a 2 week ACDUTRA, and I spent a lot of time training the jg. and ensign in navigation, both open sea, inshore and celestial. We even had them steering the ship which they got a big kick out of.

Again it was quite a while ago, but I remember one of them being very short and we had to provide her with a milk crate to stand on when she was on watch so she could read the gyro for various evolutions. One time we did a practice unrep and she was conning from the milk crate. I believe it was Beulah and to see that she was CO of an AO makes me feel good I had a part in that career path. Anyway interesting story and it did strike some memory cords.
Jim Nordstrom QMCM (SW) ret.1974-1980

The *Fiske* conducted surface-to-air gunnery exercises, Electronics Warfare exercises, Air Tracking exercises and successfully qualified in Naval Gunfire Support (NGFS), at Vieques, during this two week period. ASROC and torpedo shots were conducted at mini-mobile targets.

Fiske arrived in Miami on the 19th of February for a 3 day port visit and returned to Bayonne on the 24th and remained there until March 15th when a SELRES weekend occurred. *Fiske* off-loaded ammunition at NAD Earle in Colt's Neck, NJ on the 26th. She also conducted an early morning ASROC and AWTT launch and returned to Bayonne on the 27th where she remained until early April.

On April 3rd Captain G. A. Archabault, USNR, ComDesRon 30, arrived onboard *Fiske* to conduct a personnel inspection of the crew and to present the *Fiske* with the Battle Efficiency "E" Award for 1979 along with other departmental and individual awards.

'Potty Principle'

I was FISKE's XO when Ltjg Krupski and Ens Galvin were onboard. We had been alongside USS Piedmont (in NORVA) for a Tender Availability that turned into an extended repair as cancellations by other ships made us their only customer. In those days, the "Potty Principle" was in full force as the Navy's tool to keep women off of combatant ships. Our forward officers' quarters, however, met all of the tests and especially the ensuite head.

Piedmont's XO asked if we were willing to take the women officers for hands-on training as their opportunities were limited on his ship. We were headed to the Caribbean for training exercises and NGFS qualifications among other things. Given the manning levels in those days, everyone was welcome! We had a group of sailors from the Navy's Ceremonial Guard in Washington aboard as well as sailors from ships finishing overhaul.

I was pleased to see that Beulah Galvin became a career officer. She was very bright, hard-working and a "natural" shiphandler ... unlike at least a couple of those in the ship's company wardroom. She overcame seasickness, which dogged her a few days but she never once complained.

Sheryl Krupski's husband was the Weapons Officer on one of the ships homeported in Brooklyn; I cannot recall which one. I want to say "DYESS" but am not at all certain.

We had a very successful cruise and did very well in our NGFS quals ... scoring high 90s. Had the high point of my career as a navigator when I shot a 7-star pinwheel ... didn't have to advance or retard one line ... as we left Vieques Sound and sped over the Puerto Rico Trench. A good fix and 20,000 feet of water! What greater

reward? Home entertainment, and barbecue and steaks on the flight deck. Liberty in Miami/Ft. Lauderdale and a stop to drop off our Virginia riders.
Footnote: Having decommissioned the ship in June, FISKE still won all that was to be had in terms of awards from DESRON 30 ... EVERYTHING.
Marshall B. Lundberg LCDR Executive Officer 1977-1980

Fiske was underway for Annapolis, MD on April 10th, arriving there on the 11th. She anchored off the US Naval Academy and was opened for general visitation for Midshipman and people from the surrounding communities. Fiske returned to Bayonne on the 14th of April.

On the 19th Fiske was underway with SELRES crew embarked for surface gunnery, air gunnery and tracking exercises. She also held a towing drill with the USS Corey (DD 817) returning to port on the 20th. Fiske spent the remainder of April and most of May in port for upkeep.

On May 16th she fired a '21 Gun Salute' off Battery Park, Brooklyn in observance of Armed Forces Day. She was then open for general visitation on the 17th while in port at Brooklyn. Brooklyn Borough President, Howard Golden, proclaimed the 17th of May "USS FISKE DAY". Fiske was underway on the 18th to undergo an (ORI) Operational Readiness Inspection administered by Fleet Training Group (FTG) San Diego. She returned to Bayonne that same day.

Fiske was underway for Philadelphia on May 22nd and returned to her homeport the same day.

On May 31st Fiske was informed that BTFN Gregory N. Lewis had died. He was a native of Huntington, WVA and was survived by his wife, Betty Lou and six children. A brief obituary notice from his hometown newspaper gave the location of his death as Philadelphia. Details were not readily available in the official records on how he died.

A newspaper clipping from the Philadelphia Evening Bulletin of June 1st 1980 stated that FN Lewis had died of multiple stab wounds to the back and that three Belknap sailors were being held by the police. It is somewhat ironic that on almost her last day of service *Fiske* lost a crewman to murder.

On June 2nd the Turkish crew reported onboard. On June 5th the *Fiske* was decommissioned and transferred to the Turkish Navy and re-commissioned the *Piyale Pasa* (D 350).

One can't help but think that the Turks got a good deal when they got the *Fiske*. Her record for her time in the Reserve Fleet was exemplary. For a Class of ships that was built to win just one war I can't help but believe they far exceeded that initial mission – and that the Fiske was one of the best of them all.

The transfer to the Turks became permanent when *Fiske* was stricken from the U.S. Naval Register on August 6th 1987.

Chapter VII

TCG Piyale Pasa (D350)
Ship's motto:
Denizler Var Oldukca
(We Own the Seas)*
June 1980 – December 1999

On June 5th 1980 the recently decommissioned USS *Fiske* (DD 842) became the TCG *Piyale Pasa* (D350) and began the continuation of a long and honorable career in service to the country whose flag she flew.

Ship's plaque for
Pilaye Pasa (D350)

- The 'Google' translation of the ship's motto on the previous page and the plaque is 'We have the seas'. It was decided that the more military interpretation of this would be 'We Own the Seas'. If this is in error it is entirely of the authors doing.

RETIREMENT
OF
USS FISKE (DD-842)

AND
COMMISSIONING
OF
TCG PIYALE PASA (D-350)

5 JUNE 1980

*Arrival of RADM C.A. BRETTSCHNEIDER—Ruffles & Flourishes
(Please remain standing for National Anthem)

*National Anthem of the United States of America
Invocation: Chaplain ANDREW JENSEN, CHC USN
Remarks by Commanding Officer, USS FISKE, CDR S. L. TURNER JR. USN

Remarks by Commander Destroyer Squadron THIRTY, Captain G. A. ARCHAMBAULT, USNR

Remarks by Commandant, Fourth Naval District, Rear Admiral C. A. BRETTSCHNEIDER, USNR

*Decommissioning of USS FISKE
Lowering of Colors
March Off (Guests be seated)

Introduction of Prospective Commanding Officer, D350, CDR KAZIM EVIRGEN

Commissioning of TCG PIYALE PASA
March On, Set the First Watch

*Hoisting of Turkish Colors—The National Anthem of Turkey

Remarks by Senior Turkish Officer Present,
Captain ILHAMI ERDIL, Naval Attaché of Turkey

Moslem Prayer
Petty Officer YAVUZ KAPLAN

Reception on Fantail

*Audience to Stand

Commander Kazim Evirgen

Graduated from the Turkish Naval Academy and was commissioned in 1961. He majored in Weapons Engineering, and began his career as Communications Officer and Operations Officer in TCG MORDOGAN. He then served as Fire Control Officer in TCG PIYALE PASA (the first ship to bear that name). He later became Weapons Officer of the cadet training ship TCG SAVARONA. This tour was followed by service as Executive Officer in TCG ICEL, a destroyer. He then served as Executive Officer in TCG C. G. HASANPASA, a frigate.

He became Commanding Officer of TCG ICEL in August 1978. He served there until being detached to assume command of TCG PIYALE PASA today. He has been selected for Commander. He is the father of a boy and a girl, and lives in Izmit, near Istanbul.

Commander Steven Lloyd Turner

Born and raised in Danville, Virginia, Commander Steven Lloyd Turner was commissioned in July 1961 upon graduation from the U. S. Merchant Marine Academy, Kings Point, New York.

Ensign Turner reported aboard USS CONWAY (DD 507) in December 1961. Following service in the CONWAY, he attended the Destroyer School at Newport, Rhode Island and upon graduation, served as Chief Engineer aboard USS HOLDER (DD 819), from May 1963 until June 1965.

Subsequently, Lieutenant Turner served as an NROTC instructor at the University of South Carolina. In 1968, he assumed command of USS COCONINO COUNTY (LST 603) followed by command of USS OUTAGAMIE COUNTY (LST 1073). Both of these amphibious ships were homeported in Guam, and served extensively in Vietnam.

Upon completion of service in the Pacific, Lieutenant Commander Turner became a student at the Naval War College at Newport, Rhode Island. He then served as Executive Officer of USS BRUMBY (FF 1044) before once again returning to academic life as a student at Rensselaer Polytechnic Institute. Following his studies at R.P.I., LCDR Turner was assigned to Headquarters, Naval Sea Systems Command, Washington, D.C.

Commander Turner took command of USS FISKE (DD 842) in January 1978. Commander Turner resides in Fairfax, Virginia with his wife, Louise, and three daughters Melanie, Natalie, and Suzanne.

The TCG *Piyale Pasa* (D350) with crew 'manning the rail'

Recent internet searches indicate that the first Commanding Officer of the *Piyale Pasa*, CDR Yazim Evirgen, completed his naval service and joined the Turkish Foreign ministry in the early 2000's.

Crew of the *Piyale Pasa* (circa 1990)

The TCG *Piyale Pasa* served in the Turkish Navy until she ran aground in late 1996 and was heavily damaged. She remained in limbo until she was officially scrapped on January 10th 1999.

It had been reported that when the *Fiske* was scrapped in Turkey parts were salvaged by the US Navy with permission from the Turkish Navy for use in other ships. The pictures below are of the *Orleck*'s Pilot House and it is believed that the helm and starboard side WTD (Water Tight Door) were taken from the *Fiske*

Photographs taken onboard the USS *Orleck* (DD 886) [a Navy Museum ship now berthed in Lake Charles, LA] by Leland East, EN2, supports the supposition that part of the *Fiske* lives on onboard the USS *Orleck.*

Pilot house of USS *Orleck (DD 886)*

"BURY ME WITH SAILORS"

I've played a lot of roles in life;
I've met a lot of men.
I've done some things I'd like to think
I wouldn't do again.
And though I'm young, I'm old enough
to know someday I'll die,
and to think about what lies beyond,
Beside whom I would lie.
Perhaps it doesn't matter much;
Still if I had my choice,
I'd want a grave, amongst Sailors when
At last death quells my voice.
I'm sick of the hypocrisy
of lectures of the wise.
I'll take the man, with all the flaws,
Who goes though scared, and dies.
The troops I knew were commonplace
They didn't want the war;
They fought because their Fathers and
Their Fathers had before.
They Cursed and killed and wept...
God knows, they're easy to deride...
But bury me with men like these;
They faced the guns and died.
It's funny when you think of it,
The way we got along.
We'd come from different worlds
To live in one where no one belongs.
I didn't even like them all;
I'm sure they'd all agree.
Yet I would give my life for them,

I know some did for me.
So bury me with Sailors, please,
Though much maligned they be.
Yes bury me with Sailors,
for I miss their company.
We'll not soon see their likes again;
We've had our fill of war.
"But bury me with men like them
Till someone else does more."

- Author Unknown

'FISKE TALES'
Take Three

In the course of putting this third edition together I have incorporated many additional stories and articles that, for one reason or another, I was unable to incorporate into the body of the history. Also while compiling this work I often thought about my years onboard.

To maintain my homage to the late Tom Clancy I've opted to add most of these submissions from shipmates and a few pieces that I've written added to the mix. Every submission is entered here as it was received and those that I contributed are as accurate and factual as my memory serves after the passage of almost 60 years and more miles than I care to think about.

While creating this work one thing became glaringly obvious. We were incredibly young. After three years onboard *Fiske* I was an 'Old Salt' just shy of 23 with two Med Cruises, enumerable shorter deployments and the Cuban Missile Crisis under my belt. The men that I went to sea with were smart, resilient, inventive, adaptable and tough. They personified the 'Can Do' spirit of destroyer men everywhere.

Today's military is much more professional than we were 'back in the day' but I can't help feeling that we had more fun dealing with the tedium of those long boring days at sea.

The stories that I wrote are presented as my words alone. There is no intent to hurt or demean anyone. If after fifty years we can't laugh at our youthful foibles and misdeeds we have lead a very empty and boring life. The *Fiske* was my first ship and the people I met on board helped shape the person - for better or worse – I am today. I sincerely hope that the readers enjoy the following stories.

Gil Beyer ETC USN retired

'ZERO'

His name was Zero. He was born in Naples, Italy in June (?) 1946. Zero's biological parents are unknown, but his next of kin in Fiske records was Raymond N. Fisher, TM2. Zero was a small white and brown pup when our father first acquired him during a Med Cruise on the USS Fiske DD842 in 1946.

Zero's given name was "Gennie" however since all sailors were given ID numbers and therefore Zero was given the number 000-Zero-Zero in his official records. Hence the nickname "Zero". It is unknown how Ray persuaded the Captain [Cmdr Charles H. Smith] to permit Zero to be aboard the Fiske, but he was certainly welcomed!

Zero – Master of all he surveys

Zero's rate was SM1c. Not Signalman - but rather Ship Mascot! By the proof of the many photos taken of Zero with numerous crew members, he was perhaps "King of the Ship"! During meal time, he was stationed atop a stool and had a bib placed around his neck to keep him clean when the officers arrived!

According to Zero's Official Health Record, he was a "Normal" dog and appeared to be healthy. In one account, it was listed that he had to stay in sick bay due to a simple fracture of his leg (left hind leg?). The leg was splinted and after one week he was discharged to resume active duty!

Zero served as Ship Mascot from June 1946(?) to October 1947. When the Fiske returned to port in Newport, RI, Ray had made an entry in his log book that "Zero had found a permanent home with John G. Bjelke, S1FC in Brooklyn, NY.

The story of Zero may not be dramatic or of high significance, but it exemplifies a humanistic approach of life aboard the USS Fiske DD842 and the effect that one small dog had on the lives of so many sailors. We wonder if there were ever any other mascots in the ship's history. If so, their stories should be shared!
Respectfully submitted,
Family of Raymond Fisher, TM2
Wife: Audrey; Children: Lynn, Barb and Ed

'That Voice from the Past'

This story has its beginning when I was in Boot Camp assigned to Company 311 at GLNTC [Great Lakes Naval Training Center]. Although it may seem to center mainly around Boot Camp it has its ending onboard the USS Fiske.

Our Company Commander, BMC Swain, was soon to retire long before our training could be completed. Being a short timer he was extremely lax in teaching us naval discipline. After his departure we were called out, front and center, before our Camp Lieutenant handing us a stinging rebuke. He stated that we were the most disorganized and undisciplined bunch of recruits to ever descend on GLNTC. Further adding we were a disgrace to the Navy. A. G. Muelman, MMC, was appointed our new Company Commander. Upon his arrival he wasted no time outlining his rules we would be expected to follow. Any disobedience (of) them would promptly result in immediate punishment. He then commenced explaining two types of punishments to be administered.

First - The Demerit System: The Chief felt this method would not be in our favor as an excessive accumulation of demerits could send one to 800D (Boot Camp Brig) where punishment was most severe.

Second – The Chief's Own System: A swift kick in the seat of the pants. This system, he said, only hurt one's pride, being humiliated in front of others and leaves no lasting harm to the recipient.

He gave us a choice – Demerits or his method. We all chose the latter, agreeing to the stipulation of not voicing any complaint later. None of us wanted to get the boot.

Enter W. G. McCarley, QM1, who was chosen to assist the Chief in reshaping Company 311. McCarley was every bit as strict, and even more so, than Chief Muelman, in enforcing discipline. He had a certain distinctive tone in his voice that demanded obedience as well as one's undivided attention to his commands. No ifs, ands or buts!

We quickly learned to listen and obey that voice of discipline. Had we not there would have been consequences to pay. Because like the Chief, he too would 'kick ass'. We became accustomed to hearing that voice of his. It would leave a lasting memory. A voice I had hoped to never hear again. Under the leadership of Chief Muelman and McCarley our Company was transformed into one of the sharpest and finest companies to ever graduate Boot Camp at GLNTC. Even our Lieutenant offered us his most sincere appreciation and congratulated us for the achievements we had accomplished.

Fast forward two years: After graduating from Radioman school in 1954 I was assigned to the Fiske unbeknownst the surprise awaiting me onboard.

One day while on watch in Radio Central I heard someone come into the room. As my back was towards the door I was unable to see who had entered. Then when I heard him address the supervisor of the watch, almost with disbelief, I recognized the voice. It was one I had had heard so many times so long ago.

It was the voice of my assistant Company Commander QM1 McCarley of Company 311 in 1952. McCarley, now a QMC voice had completely changed. Not as harsh, but completely opposite of that voice from the past. Sort of rather pleasant now.

What a coincidence! I had never expected to hear or see McCarley again let alone serving with him in the Fiske. Such a small world!
Merle G. Wagner, RM3 1954 – 1956

'The Arnheiter Affair'

My first encounter with Mr. Marcus Aurelius Arnheiter took place fully three years before I reported aboard USS FISKE. I was a Third-Class Midshipman on the Battleship USS Wisconsin (BB-64) on a summer training cruise. We had recently sailed from Lisbon, Portugal and were headed to across the Atlantic Ocean to Guantanamo Bay, Cuba.

As was my custom, I took every opportunity to record my adventures with my trusty camera. I took numerous pictures of classmates, events, ships, et cetera. On one of these forays, I was taking photos of various items of the ship's structure, armament and equipment, when I was stopped by Mr. Arnheiter. He was a First-Class Midshipman, and thus in a position to tell me what to do. He asked me what I was doing, and if I realized that much of the equipment on the ship was classified. I told him that at least some of the photos I took were likely to appear in his class's "Lucky Bag" (the class yearbook), which they eventually did. Actually, everything visible topside on this ship was of WWII vintage except for possibly some of the communications antennae. From then on I just tried my best to stay out of his way.

Fast forward about three and a half years. Fiske was in the shipyard in Boston, and I had been on TAD (Temporary Additional Duty) for several weeks attending the DesLant Gunnery School at Newport, RI, learning to operate the Mk 37 GFCS (Gun Fire Control System). I came back aboard and, lo and behold, there was my 'friend', now Ltjg Marc Arnheiter, who had reported aboard during my absence. Fortunately, he was in Operations and I was in Gunnery.

Marc seemed to take a liking to me and offered to take me down to New York (his hometown) when we both had a free weekend. This was shortly before Christmas 1954 and I took him up on the offer. He introduced me to a lot of people, including a number of attractive young ladies. He got me a date with one of them, a very statuesque blond, about as tall as I was with her high heels, very pretty and with, shall we say, a very well upholstered chest. Marc took us to the famous 'Stork Club', which was very crowded, noisy, smoky and not exactly to my liking. However, my date was absolutely enthralled! I guess that I didn't tip the Maître d' enough when we entered because he escorted us to a very small table, not more than two feet in diameter, right on an aisle. So small that one couldn't get his (or her) feet under it, and my right foot was out in the aisle. It got trod on a few times because the aisle was so narrow. I ordered a drink for both of us and we sat and talked for a while.

She suggested that we try the dance floor, which was very small and very crowded. It was so crowded, in fact, that we couldn't do much more than rock back and forth. There was no place to go! My date pointed out to me that the elderly gentleman dancing next to us was Charles Coburn, if I remember correctly. She obviously was thrilled to be in the company of the rich and famous, but I wasn't impressed. No big deal! About this time, we were both simultaneously rammed from behind and pushed together, hard. Normally, this would have been enjoyable for a young, single male like me but she must have been wearing an armor-plated bra because I felt like I had two big dents in my chest.

We danced a little while longer and then left the 'Stork Club'. I was glad to get back out in the fresh air. We took our dates home and then went to visit Marc's brother Theodore (named after their father I recently learned). We walked into his brother's house. I looked at his brother, and then over to Marc. "My God" I was thinking, "there's two of them!" If you stood them side by side you couldn't tell them apart! They were obviously identical twins. I don't remember much of the remainder of the visit, but when the weekend neared an end we drove back to Boston and returned to the ship.

I don't know where Marc had been before, during the two years since he was first commissioned in June of 1952, [Editor's note: Arnheiter may have served onboard the Battleship Iowa (BB 61) after graduation from Annapolis in 1946. Other duty stations between 1946 and 1954 cannot be verified.] but he quickly became known as a real pain to the enlisted personnel he stood watch with as a JOOW on the bridge. The Senior Watch Officer, Lt George W. Eidsness, who was also the Gunnery Officer, my boss) soon decided, with the concurrence of Captain Sweeney, that Ltjg Arnheiter was never going to be designated an Underway Officer of the Deck., the officer entrusted to run the ship when the Captain was not on the bridge. They both felt that he could not be trusted. At one point I was assigned a stateroom in After Officers Country directly across the passageway from the Executive Officer's stateroom. I overheard a conversation between Marc and the XO. Mr. Arnheiter was trying to convince LCdr Engelman to go to bat for him to convince the Captain that he should be designated an underway OOD. It never happened.

A Target Designation System (TDS) had been installed during our stay in the Boston Navy Yard. It gave the Combat Information Center (CIC) the ability to send the location of a target aircraft to the Main Battery Director automatically. The Director Operator could accept the designation by merely pushing a button, which resulted in the director slewing around rapidly in azimuth to point in the direction of the target, and setting it at 15 degrees of elevation. Mr. Arnheiter was assigned the job of operating the TDS, and this put him on the same sound-powered phone circuit with me and the Plotting Room Officer, Chief Petty Officer Jeremiah Patrick Murphy. Marc seemed to be unable (or unwilling) to use standard terminology in dealing with the others on the circuit, and caused a certain amount of confusion, particularly with the enlisted personnel, who couldn't understand what he was saying. This can be dangerous, particularly when you're dealing with gunfire. I tried to straighten him out, without a great deal of success, and one of our conversations on the sound-powered circuit was recorded by Lt Bob Enright, the Operations Officer, and played back to us later. Eventually, the Supply Officer was checked out on the system, and was far more successful, and the only problem, a minor one, was his southern drawl!

Mr. Arnheiter was sent to the Navy Justice School in Newport, and upon completing the course there, was made the prosecuting attorney on any future Court Martials. He was pretty good at it, and I can testify to that as I served on most of those Court Martials, usually as the junior-most member. Lt George Eidsness was the presiding officer on most of them. Most of them were pretty cut-and-dried AWOL cases, but one involved an assault by a petty officer from the Engineering Department, and it got pretty interesting. I don't remember any of the details as I write this fifty-seven years later.

After I left FISKE, in July of 1956, Marc was reassigned to the Main Battery Director, where I'm told that, he distinguished himself by narrowly missing a French submarine. I'm told that it nearly caused an international incident. I didn't hear anything more about him for quite a few years.

Apparently, he somehow got promoted to Lieutenant and then Lt Commander. He served as XO on a ship commanded by Captain Richard Alexander. Marc was very much the ingratiating type and he somehow convinced Captain Alexander that he was qualified for

command, resulting in a recommendation that he be given command of a ship. The fiasco that ensued nearly ruined Captain Alexander's career [Editor's note: In my opinion this did destroy Captain Alexander's career. He had been given command of the Iowa, slated for duty off the coast of Viet Nam. The Captain requested reassignment and spent the rest of his career in minor shore duty posts.] Marc was ultimately summarily relieved of his command over in Viet Nam. For further details read "The Arnheiter Affair" by Neil Sheehan. It seems that Captain Sweeney and Lieutenant Eidsness were right in their assignment of Ltjg Arnheiter's abilities.
George W. Post, Ens/Lt(jg) 1954-1956

Where's the Blimp?

At Sea: the Fiske was underway enroute to GITMO for refresher training exercises. One dark night south of Cape Hatteras area a message was received by radio that a US Navy Airship (Blimp) was long overdue at its Florida base. It had simply disappeared and it was feared that it might have crashed into the sea.

The Fiske was requested to join in the search for the supposedly downed blimp sparing no cost. A search of the area, where the last contact with it had been made, was given. We commenced a thorough search, combing the area inch by inch. All eyes were straining, peering into a sea of darkness and all that was on everybody's mind was, 'Where's the blimp?' After searching most of the night, exhausting all efforts to locate the blimp, we had nothing but negative results. The Fiske sent the message, 'No blimp found' and continued on to GITMO.

SIDEBAR:

1. *The Navy's Antisubmarine Airships (Blimps) was one of the most invaluable fighting machines of World War II.*
   Aside from outstanding escort and rescue services the Navy's Blimps greatest achievements were as submarine Hunter/Killers.

2. *They were armed with 50 caliber machine guns, depth charges, contact bombs, hedgehogs, Mk 24 mines, sonobuoys (listening devices to be used when a submarine was in the area) and RADAR.*
3. *The blimp could hunt down, detect, pinpoint location and hover over the enemy sub until surface ships arrived to assist in depth charging the area.*
4. *They were the U-Boats greatest danger. Once they homed in on a U-Boat the boat would be forced to submerge and had to stay underwater thus cutting off all its crucial attack positions.*
5. *As related by U-Boat Commanders the blimp was their most feared enemy.*

With the development of faster and newer submarines in the late 1950's and better SONAR systems the slower blimp was no longer deemed the best method of hunting submarines. The curtain came down on the antisubmarine blimp in 1961 when the airship program was terminated. They were no longer an asset for the Navy and ceased to exist. With the last flight in 1962 the Navy's flying service had come to an end. Surely the Navy's airships have earned their place in history.

As the Korean War is known as the forgotten war so it is with U S Navy's airships – the forgotten weapon.
Merle Wagoner RM3 1954 – 1956

A Navy blimp conducting joint exercises with *Fiske*-circa 1955

'Water Taxi Service'

I can't put a date on this story, but I believe it happened in late winter or early spring 1955. USS Fiske was assigned to escort the Battleship USS Wisconsin (BB-64) across the Caribbean to the coast of Mexico off the mouth of the Pánuco River. There we were to act as a water taxi to bring perhaps a hundred Mexican dignitaries from the city of Tampico, located a few miles up the river, out to a reception on board Wisconsin, anchored a couple of miles off the coast.

It seems there had been a hurricane in the area, and the U. S. Navy had provided relief and rescue services to the people of Tampico and the surrounding area in the wake of the storm. The Mexicans were very grateful, and wanted to thank the Navy for the help. Exactly how this came about I don't remember, but the reception was to be held on the battleship. Since the Wisconsin could not proceed up the rather shallow river to the city, and we could, we were chosen as the vehicle to get the guests out to the larger ship.

The first job was to figure out a safe way to get those civilians from the destroyer to the battleship. We maneuvered the Fiske starboard side to the port side of Wisconsin, and close enough that a large brow could be placed across the space between the two ships, for the Main Deck of the battleship to the 01 level of the destroyer. Life lines were taken down on both ships to accommodate the brow. One of the battleship's cranes did the lifting. I don't know if we anchored Fiske, but I don't think we did. As I remember, we maintained our position by use of our engines, which required some real seamanship by Captain Sweeney. The seas were rather rough, with a stiff wind blowing, and the two ships were headed straight into the wind and the seas, so we were not rolling or pitching. During this trial period, Fiske carried a banner on the starboard side of her bridge reading, "USS Fiske (DDR 842) Water Taxi Service, J. B. Sweeney, Coxswain". The banner was taken down before we headed up the river, and was not displayed when we had our Mexican guests aboard.

The test completed, Fiske steamed up the Pánuco River and moored starboard side to at a wharf on the city's waterfront. We stayed there until the day of the reception. Our guests came aboard; we cast off our lines and turned the ship around, so we could head downriver. The river wasn't much wider than the destroyer was long, and from my Special Sea Detail station on the fantail, I could see the mud our screws churned up. Once underway, I was able to take some pictures and now I wish I could find them to accompany this little tale.

We maneuvered alongside the battleship, the brow was hoisted into place, and our guests crossed over to the larger ship. The brow was hoisted clear, and Fiske then anchored about a half mile away. Some of the ship's officers, including the Captain, had been invited to attend the reception, so we lowered the ship's motor whaleboat, rigged our accommodation ladder and several officers, including yours truly, boarded the gig for the short ride over to Wisconsin. The battleship lowered her accommodation ladder as well, in order that we might come aboard. However, the boat was pitching and rolling so badly in the rough seas that the Captain decided it was too risky to attempt to jump from boat to ladder.

We returned to the Fiske, and by the time we got aboard and hoisted the whaleboat to the davits the reception was about over, and it was time to go pick up our passengers. Fiske again maneuvered alongside Wisconsin, the brow was placed as before, our Mexican guests crossed over, the brow was removed and Fiske again headed back up the river. We moored alongside the same wharf as before and stayed there for a few days.

My memory of the events that followed is somewhat hazy as I write this some fifty-plus years later. However, I do remember that some Mexican big-shot came aboard, and was given the red-carpet treatment, honor guard and all. Ltjg Marc Arnheiter was in charge of the honor guard, sword and all, and pulled it off almost flawlessly. After the VIP left the ship, things returned to normal, and we were able to a little time ashore in Tampico.

The ship was opened to visitors one day, and Ensign Post was put in charge of organizing the event. I chose the enlisted guides who would escort small groups of Mexican civilians around the ship, and make sure they stayed where they were supposed to. Unfortunately, we didn't have anyone sufficiently fluent in Spanish to tell them much about what they were seeing. Occasionally, one of the Mexican visitors understood enough English to translate what our guide was saying. All went smoothly all day long, and hundreds of Mexicans took advantage of our tour. I, of course, had the duty all day long, and had the 1200 to 1600 in-port OOD watch. As the end of visiting hours approached, however, there were a lot of visitors still waiting in line on the wharf. At this time, LCdr Engelman, the Executive Officer, saw them, and ordered me to open up the gangway and let them aboard. In nothing flat, it was pure chaos, and we had hundreds of Mexicans all over the ship. Concerned about security, I protested, and was promptly ordered to my stateroom. When it was all over, and after a lecture by LCdr Engelman, I apologized, and all was forgiven.

Another event of note while in Tampico. I was the in-port OOD again, and we had stationed a couple of armed guards on the main deck to keep uninvited visitors from simply jumping aboard, on the fantail and another about half-way between the Quarterdeck and the fantail.

My Petty Officer of the Watch, an SOG1 named Johnson, saw a woman jump aboard, and informed me. I told him to go aft and investigate. She was a prostitute, of course, and by the time he got back to the fantail, she had already set up shop in the after gun mount, and a number of the crew were lined up, ready to take advantage of her services. Johnson dragged her out of the gun mount and dumped her over the life lines on to the wharf. Obviously, someone had planned this little caper, and put out the word where she would be, and arranged for the fantail watch to look the other way! We never did figure out who the culprit was.

This happened in broad daylight, and if it had been after dark, she might have done a booming business.
George W. Post, Ens/Lt (jg) 1954-1956

In Disarray

During our 1955 Med Cruise the Fiske was visiting Leghorn (Livorno), Italy located on the west coast of Tuscany. Also, Livorno is the home of the Italian Naval Academy.

While in this port a somewhat bizarre experience happened that put the crew in a very stressful situation. Captain's Inspection was scheduled for Saturday at 0800. On Wednesday a representative from a local laundry/dry cleaning came onboard offering free pickup and delivery prior to the Saturday inspection.

Several of the Fiske crewmen readily accepted the offer and sent their uniforms over to the beach laundry for a professional cleaning. We felt there would be no problem having it back in time for inspection as we would have a two-day leeway from pickup to Saturday's inspection.

Our hope was to have our uniforms brought back to their true white color as we were tired of the ship's laundry returning them in an off-white color from its overuse of harsh detergents.

Early Saturday morning came without the promised uniforms. LCDR Engleman, the Executive officer, was instrumental in getting Captain Sweeney to delay the inspection from 0800 to 1000. This would give more time for the delivery of our uniforms.

At 1000 hours the inspection was delayed again to 1100 hours as no uniforms had materialized. At 1030 Captain Sweeney announced that the inspection would commence promptly at 1100 hours. There would be no more delay.

Now this nearly caused pandemonium among those of us that had sent our uniforms to be cleaned. That left us without suitable uniforms for inspection. We had only one option left - that was to beg, borrow or steal whatever we could to stand inspection in. Even the XO had sent his uniform to the cleaners.

When we fell out for inspection several crewmembers were wearing mismatched uniforms, some slightly wrinkled, some even soiled. Some of the rated men were wearing lesser rates on their jumpers.

As the Captain started through the ranks he no longer saw the neatly dressed, sharp looking Fiske sailors that we normally were. What he saw now was some misfits looking unpresentable who had put this inspection in disarray.

Captain Sweeney was well aware of our dilemma thanks to CDR Engleman. However, he was not pleased with what he had seen. He humbled us with comments about how improperly we were dressed. Then the Captain reminded us that when in the Navy, while onboard the Fiske, there was no excuse for not always being ready for inspection.

The XO was caught up in the uniform crisis as we were. He was wearing a uniform he borrowed from the Supply Officer. It was in need of a hot iron and the sleeves were about 2 inches too short. We got a big laugh seeing him trailing behind the Captain wearing a slightly wrinkled borrowed uniform that was way too short in the sleeves on him.

Merle Wagner RM3 1954-1956

'Ski'

I first met Louis B. Schmeiske in October 1960 when I reported onboard the Fiske. He was the first ET I met. It was a Friday afternoon. He welcomed me onboard and then told me to disappear until Monday morning when I would officially check-in. I was an ETRSN just shy of 20 years old. He was an 'Old Salt' ET3 of 22 or 23 so I did as I was told. I dumped my seabag, grabbed my AWOL bag and headed back towards my home in Hollywood, FL.

Shortly before 0800 on Monday I officially reported onboard the Fiske. I met up with the rest of the ET Gang and the other 'newbie' ET onboard, Charles W. Slocum. Chas will be the subject of other stories.

Schmeiske quickly became known as 'Ski'. As a senior Communications ET he was responsible for the AN/SRT-14 transmitters. They were our primary long-range and medium range transmitters. They were almost the size of a phone booth and just full of hi-voltage danger points. Ski was probably one of the best technicians I ever served with. He could make those damned SRT's work in spite of themselves. It was routine for Ski to practically live in the Transmitter Room anytime we were underway.

The second most impressive thing about Ski was his understanding and ability to use all of the parts of speech. He could use the 'F' word in every conceivable grammatical way imaginable. Subject, noun, verb, adverb, predicate, adjective and I believe he, on more than one occasion, used it as a split infinitive!

To say his language was 'colorful' did not give him his full due. The breadth and depth of his mastery of profanity made him a man to be respected and, in my case, emulated.

Ski's mastery of profanity was on full display one day when he was working on the modulator drawer of an SRT. Now the SRT was state of the art back in the 1950's. It had many features that would make today's technicians gasp in horror.

One such feature was a 'spark gap' that was designed to protect a portion of the modulator circuitry from excessive voltage. This spark gap had two small aluminum balls spaced a certain distance apart so that if the voltage exceeded 'x' level a spark would jump the gap and protect the modulator. Before I get too 'techie' let's just say SRT's were not user friendly.

We were underway out of Mayport and the ship was experiencing 'moderate' seas. In other words rolling and pitching unpredictably. Ski was trying to adjust one of the mechanical relays in

the modulator drawer when we took a pretty significant roll and his hand fell onto both balls of the spark gap. There was a big flash of light, a cloud of smoke and a shout of pain following by a virtuoso performance of profanity. When we looked at his hand it looked like someone had taken a melon baller to the base of his thumb. There was no blood flowing as the wound had been instantly cauterized. To the best of my knowledge Ski carried that scar with him for the rest of his days.
Gil Beyer ETR3 1960-63

Louis B 'Ski' Schmeiske ETN3

Bored

We were bored – very bored. Fiske was near the southern end of the Red Sea. The Big Picture of this operation was that the US Navy was tasked with conducting Interdiction Patrols. The purpose of these patrols was to try to intercept any gunrunners that were attempting to smuggle arms from Asia minor to sub-Saharan Africa.

It was the 60's and there was much unrest in Africa. So, it seemed like a good business model to sell guns to whatever factions wanted them. Our job was to stop these shipments from getting to Africa.

The smallest portion of this Big Picture view was an aging WWII destroyer sitting in the middle of the Red Sea. There were approximately 230 very bored sailors onboard. The temperature at mid-morning was near 115 F (46 C) in the shade. The temps in the Engineering spaces was 15 to 20 degrees hotter. Those below deck couldn't stay there for longer than 2 hours. No ship's work was done between 1000 and 1400 in any space.

We were steaming in a square 50 miles on a side at approximately 5 knots. Not even fast enough to create a breeze. It was enervating – and boring. We would have loved to see an arms smuggler but that did not happen.

Earlier in the cruise somebody had found an entire case of lacing twine in a long unopened storage space. And, several cases of teletypewriter paper – long past usability. Lacing twine is what they used to use before zip-ties came into being. It is a woven nylon ribbon about ¼" wide that was used to bundle wires together in electronic equipment. That one case had 40 spools of lacing twine and each spool was about 100 yards. Lacing twine is incredibly strong.

Somebody came up with the bright idea that we could make hammocks out of the twine. This could be done using what is called a 'fisherman's net knot' and a shuttle made of wood or-in our case-a wire coat hanger. Several of us enthusiastically started weaving away.

We soon realized that it was going to take a very long time to weave a net long enough and wide enough to be used for a hammock. The weavers found themselves with several 3-foot square nets without a purpose.

Bored sailors are nothing if not inventive. Another sharp-eyed shipmate had noticed that we were sailing through tens of thousands of small jellyfish. We quickly started trying to net them. It quickly became apparent that this was easier said than done.

The biggest problem was that our quarry were jellyfish. Our nets worked much like a cheese slicer. Netting a jellyfish results in slicing them into several pieces. But again, sailors are nothing if not inventive.

By using the laws of physics that deal with relative motion we soon were able to net jellyfish with varying degrees of success. Picture a line of dungaree and t-shirt clad young men running full tilt down the deck while dipping a net into the water and in smooth, fluid motion depositing a jellyfish into 5-gallon bucket.

The endeavor soon became a contest as to who could net the most intact jellyfish. In this heat we soon ran out of energy and enthusiasm. You can only run full tilt in that heat for a short time. I don't recall who won but whoever did I'm positive that they only netted a small number of jellyfishes. However, it did break up the day.

For a brief period, we weren't bored. That was a high point of our being the smallest part of the Big Picture.
Gil Beyer ETR3 1960-63

'440 Volts'

I think that about everyone knew MM1 Jess Davis. Jess was working, I think, in the Reefer Room. I was working on a vent controller in the compartment above the Reefer Room, ergo the Mess Line. As was usually the case on Fiske we were at sea, going from someplace to someplace else - standard operation. I had my hands in the controller when Jess came over.

Out came the hands and we engaged in conversation about some inane thing. The ship was going soft and smooth at the time, a really nice ride. During the course of the conversation I put my hand on the door of the controller. Jess put his hand on my shoulder and the conversation continued. Suddenly the ship lurched, my pinky touched a hot contact, my other reflexed and Jess went flying to other end of the compartment.

Jess came back, somewhat puzzled and angry, demanding to know why I hit him!!!! After I told him what had happened we both had a roll on the floor laughing fit and got to conversing again. Pretty soon up came the hand to my shoulder again, up came my hand to the controller door and ----LUCK being a fickle lady the ship lurched, finger on hot contact again and Jess went flying again!!!!! We both laughed at the sheer stupidity of our actions that tears rolled down our collective faces. Both his and my job of the time was finished and we left the area. I think that Jess would agree that 440 volts can pack a pretty hefty punch. I hope he still smiles at the remembrance.
John Frazer EM1 1960-1965

'Slush Funds'

We all know that slush funds were illegal in the navy. But, on the bridge we had a department slush fund. Being that most of us were younger sailors, we had a couple of older Signalmen that could lead us to their advantage. One of these Signalmen was a guy by the name of Turner. He helped organize this fund with the idea that we would each put in $5.00 per pay day and we would lend this money out to only guys in our division. The old 5 for 7, a great deal for us investors!!!

So it started and the first person that borrowed money from the fund was, you got it, Turner. Well the next payday came and we each put in another $5.00 per person and guess who borrowed from it immediately, Turner. Well, when the next payday came and we asked

Turner to pay up he refused. He was a Second Class and the second most senior person on the bridge. Our Chief Signalman was the most senior, but he wasn't on the bridge much. Anyway, when Turner refused to pay up, what could we do? Who could we turn to? No One!! So this individual got us for about $60.00 and there wasn't a thing we could do about it. Welcome to the real world young sailors!!!!
Charles Thompson QM2 1959 -1963

'Smitty'

William Arthur Smith Jr. was 6' 2", 210 pounds and twenty-one years old. He was the oldest son of a career Army Senior Noncommissioned Officer. He had spent the majority of his life moving with his father, mother and brother from one Army Post to another since his birth in 1942. His father was not present at his birth. World War II intervened. I don't believe Dad was there for the birth of his brother either, Army first, family second. Somehow in the late 50's the Smith family landed in South Florida. Maybe his Dad got a tour of recruiting duty, I don't know and it's not critical to the story.

With Dad gone a great deal of the time, Mom was the central authority figure. She was responsible for day-to-day operations and family discipline. William used to say that she had the fastest large wooden spoon in Florida. Whenever sibling disputes arose there she was to mete out order and structure. Smitty always knew when he was in major trouble if she ever shouted, "William Arthur Smith Junior, get your butt over here!" It wasn't the mild reference to a portion of his anatomy. It was the use of his full, baptismal name that was the dead giveaway.

With a family history of service it wasn't too unusual that Smitty joined the military right after High School. What was unusual was that he joined the Navy. His avowed reason for this break with family tradition was that he didn't want to walk everywhere he went. His mother always claimed that he was too lazy to walk to the corner store much less across a country like his Dad did in Korea. Anyway, Smitty joined the Navy Reserve unit in Miami, Florida and, because of various test scores, was assigned a job classification in the electronics field.

Then, as now, most Reservists meet monthly over a weekend to learn their military and professional skills. They also have to some active duty time, usually two weeks, in the summer. Smitty opted to 'go active' for two years after the troubles that the United States had with the new regime in Cuba. Actually he went into the Regular Navy shortly after the Bay of Pigs debacle. After his Boot Camp and Basic Electronics schooling he was given orders to the USS FISKE (DDR 842), home ported in Mayport, Florida, down river from Jacksonville.

That is where I met William Arthur Smith Jr., ever more to be known as 'Smitty' by the crew of the FISKE. I was another junior enlisted man that had been onboard the FISKE for about a year. I started this with a brief description of Smitty, now I'm going to fill it out some. Smitty was indeed about 6' 2" and 210 pounds. He also had dark brown hair, hazel eyes and the type of beard that went immediately from freshly shaved to five o'clock shadow in approximately three hours. He, when freshly shaved, had the most innocent, cherubic face you can imagine. At age twenty-one he could have been used as the poster child for Gerber's Baby Foods. He was always good humored and easy going. The more he was put upon the happier he seemed. No task was too onerous or tedious but he was lazy.

His mother later told me that both Smitty and his brother were so lazy that they had hair on the soles of their feet like Hobbits. But that's another tale. This story is about our trip in early 1963 to the Mediterranean. This was Smitty's first, and probably last, Med Cruise because his two years Active Duty would be up in September and he had already decided not to re-enlist.

We left Mayport in early February and entered Cannes, France on the 25th. Cannes represented everything sophisticated and very European to us naïve young Americans of the early 60's. Hell, they had topless beaches before we ever even heard the word 'topless' in the

States. It was too cold to go to the beaches, but the thought was there. What the Cote d' Azur did offer were some very friendly and pretty ladies at each and every bar you entered. It would have been rude not to be friendly back. This was done in the best interests of international relations, of course.

A group of us were having a couple of beers at a local waterfront bar downstairs from a 'hotel' that rented rooms by the hour. Smitty looked especially young and naïve having just left the ship. Smitty had already committed to saving every penny he could so that he could buy something nice for his Mom. Anyway, there we were enjoying the cold beer, the warm and friendly young ladies when Smitty realized that he might be tempted to spend more money than he should during our stay in France. Being a good friend I accepted his request that I hold his money for him. Not to give it back to him, under any circumstances, until we got back to the ship.

That was when the dark side in me took over. There were eight of us in a booth and around the table, four sailors and four enticing young ladies all speaking fractured French and English, drinking the local beer and feeling good to be alive. I was talking to the young lady that occupying a good part of my lap when I looked over at Smitty.

There he was, radiantly innocent and un-worldliness. Did I mention the cowlick that no amount of Brylcream would subdue? Anyway, I looked at him and whispered into the shell-like ear closest to me, "He's a virgin", indicating Smitty. The chorus rippled around the table in rapid French. Many a "no", "incredible" and other expressions of disbelief were heard. Smitty responded just as I expected him to. He turned beet red from the collar of his jumper to his hairline.

The word spread throughout the bar. I keep assuring my French friends that what I said was true. Smitty stayed bright red as all the girls immediately focused their attentions on him. The other two sailors at the table thought that this was great fun and supported my story.

Smitty's three companions, were settling up the bar tab as the intensity of the bargaining was escalating. You don't often see ladies of this profession arguing their fees downward against each other. It seems that I had struck a chord within them. These ladies wanted to the 'first' to initiate Smitty into manhood.

The fact that this event had occurred several years before, and thousands of miles away, didn't have any bearing. The ladies believed their eyes when Smitty was labeled with this unhappy state. His response was classic. He asked for his money that I was holding. He demanded his money. He begged for his money. I was steadfast and unyielding. What kind of friend would I be if I let him waste his money this way? The eager French girls joined in pleading his case. The ladies were almost as distraught as Smitty was as we went out the door of the bar.

The memory that I still carry with me after these many years was the expression on his face. The same expression you see when a child is told, "No dessert, you didn't finish your carrots." That look, coupled with the inventiveness, depth, breadth, scope and imagery of his profanity. It took about a week for him to even speak to me, aside from work related conversation. The following month I helped him to pick out a nice set of cameos in Naples, Italy for his Mom. Wherever he is I hope he remembers that MED cruise with all that fondness I do.
Gil Beyer ETR3 1960-1963

'Blueberry Pie in Norfolk'

Now, I have written several times about a Chief Fire Controlman named Brown. He was an Institution aboard the Fiske. He had been a seaman aboard the Battleship Pennsylvania at Pearl Harbor. There were those, aboard ship, who predicted that he'd been in the Navy so long that his blood was Haze Grey - just like the ship. Now I remember having the Mid-Watch (Midnight to -0400) watch in Norfolk, Virginia. It was a warm summer night and the Watch was wearing White Uniforms. he duty cook was supposed to fix the Mid-Watch a special meal called 'Mid-Rats'. That night, though, the cook was bent out of shape because he hadn't passed the promotion test. He decided that he wouldn't fix us Mid-Rats. Did we need them? Of course not! We were not that hungry, but we had our rights! And Mid-Rats were part of our inalienable rights!

Chief Brown was the 'Officer of the Watch'. I was Petty Officer of the Watch, and a kid named Bowser was Messenger.

Well, I sent Bowser forward to the Galley for Mid-Rats, and he reported back that there were none. The cooks replied that there wouldn't be any. Well, that just wouldn't do! Now, Chief Brown was standing his watch in the Chief's Quarters and I didn't want to wake him up for that. he was a fierce man when angered.

So, I waited until 0200 and sent Bowser forward again. His instructions were simple. If the cooks had gone to bed, consider his mission a foraging raid. If nothing else we could get a loaf of bread.

To our surprise he came back with a whole Blueberry Pie, and it was still hot! No doubt about it, there would be the devil to pay if we were caught eating that 'Pilfered-Pie'.

There was nothing to do but destroy the evidence, and we did! Every morsel and crumb of that pie was gone by 0345, and the pie tin went overboard. Well, you just can't eat Blueberry Pie without getting stains on white uniforms. We were standing there damned by our own uniforms.

The next day, we slept late. It is one of the advantages of the Mid-Watch. Chief Brown dropped by the Weapons Office and asked, "Mose, do you know anything about a Blueberry Pie that went missing from the cooling racks last night?" Of course, I told him I didn't. He looked at me with that glance that said that he knew I was lying, and said, "Yea, and my mother is a virgin!" But he left and I never heard from the incident again.

My jumper was another matter. I had to smuggle it off ship to a commercial cleaners to get the stains out. The Chief could have hanged both Bowser and me. Yet, he had been a Seaman once, and he'd probably stolen a pie or two in his day. On the positive side, Mid-Rats were always available after that. Jerry Mosley, YN3 1963-1966

'Striking a Blow for Freedom'

Guantanamo Bay was an interesting place. One of our jobs in 1964 was to escort Soviet merchant ships past our naval base to their port of GITMO city.

Now the Bay itself was international waters. We could not refuse them access to the middle of the bay...We did, however, object when they moved the line to as close to our piers as they could come. Russian sailors lined the rails of their ship with cameras and photographed everything in passing.

To thwart this we sailed about 20 yards off their starboard side at the same speed they made. Then we had the engine room make as much black smoke as they could.....Because we sat lower in the water than they did, this plunged their decks into utter blackness.

They were handsome ships. I remember a single smokestack, oval in cross-section with a broad red band on it bearing the Soviet Hammer and Sickle in gold.

The first time we carried out this tactic, the Russians called us every bad name in English they knew. They even called us names in Russian. I do not speak Russian and it didn't bother me....Joel does speak Russian, and he translated. His translations simply added fuel to the fire.

By the time of the second ship, I was ready. I had taken two 1/2" bolts from the gun shack. They were about 1 inch long. I had the remnants of my expensive bicycle inner tube and I fashioned a large slingshot and used two stanchions as part of the weapon. Along came Comrade Ruskie and I was ready. As the name calling started, I stretched my slingshot and fired.

There was a fairly gratifying twang from the Ruskie, I had at least hit the hull, but I needed elevation.....By lying on the deck and drawing back to fire the second bolt, I got the elevation....I heard what sounded like glass breaking.

As an Officer had been dispatched to investigate, I ditched the weapon overboard and went back to the Weapons Office.

To this day, I don't know what I hit, but I struck a blow for America!
Jerry Moseley, YN3 1963-1966

'God Chuckled'

Our ship was underway for routine training exercises after completing our stay in Charleston Naval Shipyard and RefTra in Gitmo. We were operating independently conducting various drills and exercises in the Navy's Operating Areas east and South of Norfolk, Virginia.

Underway periods become routine very quickly. For most of the crew not directly involved with exercises and drills it's fairly boring so we do a lot of regular maintenance and upkeep work. When not doing our chores and/or during off duty time sailors of all ratings tended to gather in small groups on topside. Destroyers are still small enough that everyone knows everyone else onboard in a short period of time. Every one onboard has to do their job in order for the community to be successful.

That doesn't mean that it was a totally integrated society. Deck Department people didn't normally 'hang' with Engineering Department. But usually you at least knew each other to say "Hi" to. What mostly happened was that the Deck, Operations, Gunnery, Supply, Engineers all had their usual gathering places. But overall it was a fairly close-knit group that worked well together.

One of the normal periods that groups formed was after the mid-day meal. On this particular day a small group of us were gathered on the 01 level between the stacks smoking our after lunch cigarettes and talking of various things most of which involved girls, woman, females and /or alcohol. The group consisted of myself, a friend nicknamed Bunny (Paul Bunzick) who was a Boatswain's Mate seaman, a couple Gunner's Mates, and one or two others. We were taking shelter near the Paint Locker and just chewing the fat while lunch settled. Now all of us were in different Divisions and had different responsibilities so when the 1MC System passed "Turn To" at 1300 we all had places to go. The group was breaking up when along comes BM3 Eugene Abercrombie. Abercrombie was an anachronism even in 1962. He had been in the Navy over twelve years and had never risen above pay grade E-4.

He chose this particular moment to climb all over Bunny for not being at his place of duty and was threatening extra duty hours for being tardy in reporting to his duty station. Well, Bunny's duty station was the Paint Locker, about five feet away from him and he had the keys in his hands to open the doors. It was his responsibility to issue the paint, rollers and brushes that were needed throughout the ship and that they were returned clean and ready for the next day's use. The formerly dispersing group slowed its movement just to see what was going to happen.

Bunny was a slender, blond haired kid of average height from central Florida. His eyes were the palest blue I had ever seen. In certain lighting conditions they looked white. Bunny looked at Abercrombie with a look of utmost seriousness and told him that he was at his duty station, he was ready to do his job and if he, Abercrombie, didn't lay off he, Bunny, would have him struck by lightning! I've already mentioned that we had been running into squalls all day and one was just passing at this moment. Abercrombie said something really cogent like, "Oh yeah" and proceeded to chew Bunny some more.

Bunny stepped back and said, "If you don't believe me watch this." and he pointed towards the top of the forward mast. Then, as if on cue, a lightning bolt shot out of the sky and struck the RDF antenna with a loud crack and it started raining little chunks of fiberglass. Now, never let it be said that even if he was the sharpest knife in the drawer, Abercrombie couldn't recognize real power when he saw it.

I would have loved to gotten his expression on film. It was a unique combination of primal fear, awe and, even reverence. The group

witnessing this manifestation was gazing upward, in stunned silence, with their mouths agape. It was a moment of pure magic. All eyes were focused on the top of the mast. Because of my position, slightly behind and aft of the group, out of the corner of my eye I saw that one of the group was not looking upward. With just as much intensity, awe and wonder as everyone else there, Bunny was staring at his finger. At that moment, quietly, God chuckled.
Gil Beyer ETR3 1960-1963

SN Paul 'Bunny' Bunzick

'Lightning Strike! - The Aftermath'

Chas Slocum and I stood facing each other about two feet apart. We were separated by the 8" diameter of aluminum pipe. It's a good thing that Chas was probably 5 inches taller than me so that we could stand on different foot pegs. Just below our chin level were the eight ½" mounting bolts on the flanged circular base of the antenna that extended another 42" above our heads atop the forward mast.

The Fiske was underway East of Mayport, Florida. Chas and I had tied ourselves off as best we could. Not much room for error up there. The lines from our safety belts were carefully wrapped around the mast. By doing this we wouldn't have to worry too much about using both hands to work on the antenna. We weren't saying more to each other than what was necessary and there was no one else around to talk to since we were about 100 feet above the surface of the Atlantic Ocean. Just looking into each other's eyes was enough conversation. Neither one of us was ever going to admit to being scared almost to the point incontinence. That is part of the indestructibility myth. At age 'twenty-something' you are immortal.

Our task was simple. Undo the eight bolts, lift the antenna sufficiently to unscrew the cable connection in the antenna's hollow housing and lower the antenna to the AN/SPS-10 platform fifteen feet below. The antenna then could be lowered to the 03 level and carried down to the shop for inspection and, possible, repair.

The task was considerably complicated by circumstances. We were 100 feet above the ocean. The ship was underway in what the Navy calls 'moderate seas'. Standing on the main deck no one would have a problem moving with the ship. The movement, however, becomes much more amplified the further up one goes. This is much like being on the end of a 'crack the whip' line while skating.

Couple the motion with an occasional whiff of stack gas and it was not a pleasant experience. The seas had actually calmed somewhat after the squall lines had passed. It was the lightning from these squalls that was reason that Chas and I were up here in the first place.

With lengths of light line tied to our wrenches and the other end tied to our belts we started in on those 8 bolts. The reason for the wrenches being tied off should be fairly obvious. We are over a hundred feet up and we didn't want to drop a wrench - not to mention the danger anyone walking below us. A simple, "Damn!" just doesn't cover the inconvenience of having to go down the mast to get the wrench. In accordance with the prime Navy directive of "If it moves, salute it. If it doesn't move, paint it." it was obvious that these bolts hadn't moved in a great while. The removal of these bolts took about a half hour.

With the bolts removed and tucked safely into various pockets, the antenna was balanced on its 8 inch circular base. This is fine on the kitchen table at home but when it's over 100 feet in the air, with 10-15 degree roll, along with the pitching, as we climbed one wave and slid down the other side, and the ship traveling at about 12 knots the antenna didn't want to stay balanced. Again, it's a good thing Chas was five inches taller than me. He went up two pegs and with his safety line looped around the mast just under the flange he wrapped his arms around the antenna and lifted it up so I could undo the cable connector. Since the connector was protected inside the base it came undone fairly easily.

At this point, the antenna was completely free and only prevented from falling to the deck, or into the ocean, by Chas' grip. Slowly, we maneuvered the antenna down between Chas and the mast until the butt end was just above his knees and the top extended above his head by a foot or more. I carefully tied this antenna to Chas's body by looping a number of turns of light line around him. Chas slowly started down the mast to the AN/SPS-10 platform. I taped up the cable connector and went down too. The rest of the journey down the mast was slow but uneventful.

During one of the squalls lightning had struck that antenna on top of the forward mast. When hundreds of thousands of volts of electrical energy strikes sensitive electronic equipment it tends to smoke and stop working. When the lightning hit the antenna the watch officer in CIC (Combat Information Center) noticed that his AN/URD-4, UHF Radio Direction Finder had stopped working. He called the EMO (Electronics Material Officer) to report the problem. The EMO in turn called the Leading Electronics Petty Offer, who in turn sought out Chas and me. Chas and I verified that the RDF was indeed not working and reported back to our LPO. It was during our discussion with the LPO that the plan to remove the antenna from the mast was first formulated.

The antenna, having been removed from the mast, was lying on the workbench in the Electronics Shop (Starboard side just off the Aft Thwart ships passage) with about six people gathered around doing the electrical equivalent of a post mortem. What we found was the entirety of the metal portions of the antenna had been melted and fused together just like it had been welded into one piece. The fiberglass covering had been shattered as though a small bomb had been placed inside it. The consensus of opinion, EMO, LPO, Chas, a couple of other Techs, and me was that this antenna would never work again!
Gil Beyer ETR3 1960-1963

'Yokosuka, Vietnam & Hong Kong'

After Sonar School I reported onboard the Fiske at Newport, RI we headed south for Gunnery and Anti-Submarine operations off the coast of Georgia. We had liberty in Savannah – it's a pretty city. Afterwards we went into drydock in Boston where it was very cold, 5 degrees F.

From Boston we went down to Guantanamo Bay, Cuba where I was put into the hospital after spilling boiling hot coffee on my left ankle. I stayed in the hospital while Fiske visited Jamaica and San Juan, Puerto Rico then returned to Guantanamo to pick me up.

We left Cuba and headed for the Panama Canal. Before going through the Canal we were told that there was a submarine (one of ours) off the coast of the Yucatan Peninsula and if one of us could find it we'd a weekend in Hawaii. Not true it turned out. Well, guess who found the sub? I did, and reported it to the Chief Sonarman. We tracked that sub he finally answered up on the underwater telephone. I won some respect from my superiors – just a little – not much.

Upon going through the Panama Canal we headed for Subic Bay, Philippines where we stayed for a day or two. From there we went to Yokosuka, Japan to have the ship's generator replaced or fixed. Me and a buddy, Jimmy Stewart – not the actor – went to Yokohama for 2 days, had some fun and came back to the ship by train.

Jimmy was ahead of me and went up the gangplank. I was too late; they pulled the gangplank away from the ship and it was pulling away from the pier. There was one mooring line left; I threw my bag on the bow and grabbed the mooring line as the ship was backing out. I climbed the mooring line to the bow of the ship. The captain didn't look happy!

Once we were underway we headed to Viet Nam for patrol. After the patrol we went back to Subic Bay for a day and then left for Hong Kong. While enroute we ran through a massive hurricane where I lost a trashcan full of scrap food – I was on Mess Cook duty. Just about the entire crew was sick.

I developed a toothache while we were in Hong Kong. A British dentist aboard another ship there pulled the tooth.

The Fiske was used for Search & Rescue of downed airplanes and pilots; Gunfire support for the Army and Marines near the coast. I believe that we were fired upon twice; once from land-based artillery and another time by some kind of gunboat from inland waters. We detected a Soviet submarine but no action was taken.
John Naldrett STGSN/STG3 1964-1967

'Plane Guarding & Sharks'

I was only onboard Fiske a short time when we completed our yard period at Charleston Naval Shipyard and returned to Mayport. The only thing we did was routine ops for most of the summer of 1962. All that changed in October when we spent a lot of time following the Enterprise around off the Cuban coast.

Early in 1963 (I forget the month) the Fiske left Mayport and headed to the Med. As a civilian I have been to Europe a number of times and it only took 6 or 7 hours, depending on where I was going. On that trip over to Europe on the Fiske it took (I think) around 25 days. I had a tooth filled on the Enterprise while we in a port (maybe Palermo). Years later my wife and I visited Palermo and other cities in Italy. Believe me, seeing all those places as a civilian, sure beat the waiting for liberty.

One night, on the 2000 to Midnight watch, I was on the port lookout watch, while plane guarding the Enterprise. I forget the name of the Ensign that was OOD, but I remember the captain seemed to have a lot of confidence in him. Both the Enterprise and the Fiske on darken ship (not having any outside lights on). In addition, the planes did not have any lights on.

As I stood there, you could hear the grumbling of the aircraft, and just about see the shadow of the plane as it went over us. You could see nothing. Suddenly the sky lit up, one of the planes hit the stern of the carrier. The OOD started screaming into the 1MC, 'Captain to the bridge, captain to the bridge.' The captain, Cmdr Butt was a pretty stout fellow, but he flew up those stairs from the ward room. Thank God nobody was in his way. We turned on all our lights, and could see one body in the water. I had a perfect view of all this and watched as we tried to retrieve the pilot, but he eventually sank beneath the sea. I thought to myself, 'May God have mercy on his soul.'

After the Med Cruise we started making preparations to go into the yards for FRAM conversion in Boston. FRAM was a major change to the Fiske. She was completely reconfigured from the main deck up. This changed Fiske from a DDR to DD to better hunt submarines. At the end of this yard period we were sent to GITMO for refresher training since we had mostly a new crew that had to start working together. On September 5th 1964 I married my girl friend and found that it was a lot harder to leave my wife than a girl friend.

During of refresher training whenever we were cruising around GITMO someone would always put a piece of meat on a hook and drag it behind the ship in the hopes of snagging a shark which we never did. One night we anchored out in the harbor instead of tying up to the pier. Just as 'Taps' was being piped someone that had put the hook in the water earlier noticed that the slip knot he had tied to the handrail was gone. He started to pull on the rope and you would not believe the size of the head of a shark that came out of the water. Someone attached the rope to a nearby deck winch and pulled the biggest shark I've ever seen completely out of the water.

When you see a shark in the water he looks streamlined. When this one was hanging vertically out of the water it looked more like a light bulb with fins. Somebody somehow sliced the belly of the shark open, which was not easy, and blood poured out all into the water and on the whaleboat, and at the time I was the coxswain, and had to clean all the blood off the boat. Later that night I had to make a run into the dock, and I could not get that shark out of my mind I don't remember the officer, but he took a picture of the shark.
Bill Loerning BMSN 1962-64

'Splish, Splash'

Early in our '61 Med Cruise I was standing MOW (Messenger of the Watch) on the mid-watch on the Quarterdeck. The OOD (Officer of the Deck) asked me to get him a cup of coffee from the Wardroom. The Wardroom was just forward of the Galley. As I was walking by I heard water running. Since the Galley was supposed to be closed at this hour I got curious.

As I peeked in the little circular window set in the door I was amazed at what I saw. There was CS2 (Commissaryman Second Class) Joe Bourgoin relaxing neck deep taking a bath in one of the Galley coppers! His clothing was hung neatly nearby. Being a mere seaman I didn't let him know I was there. I went on to the Wardroom Pantry, got the coffee for the OOD and tried to forget what I had seen.

It was quite a while before I could bring myself to eat soup.
Anonymous 1960-63

The Commodore's Ham

This is a story of just one of the many capers that took place during my tour of duty. I cannot recall the port of call the Fiske was visiting at the time.

The Fiske was serving as flagship for DesDiv 42 with the Commodore and Staff onboard. The Flag call letters were DTQI.

It all happened on a night the Commodore was on liberty. Radio Central's night patrol was on the move and decided to check out his [the Commodore's] icebox. In that icebox was a nice, juicy ham. Temptation was too great to resist, the ham was lifted and delivered to the Radio Shack.

All the Radiomen were summoned to Radio for a feast upon the Commodore's ham. Leftovers went to the deep six.

When the Commodore returned and found his ham missing he was outraged. He ordered all the officers and chiefs to be on a closer look out in the future for these kinds of activities onboard the Fiske.

Again all the Radiomen were summoned to Radio, this time by our Chief Radioman. Not pointing a finger at anyone Chief Leroy issued a stern warning pertaining to the Commodore's orders. We all knew that there was no doubt in his mind who had pulled off this heist of the Commodore's ham.

The ham was delicious!

Merle Wagoner RM3 1954 -1956

'Evaporators'

USS Fiske DDR-842 was in drydock at the Boston Naval Shipyard after suffering damage from a storm when I boarded her for the first time. It was January, 1959 and I was an MMFN assigned to aft engine room. Arriving late in the evening, the OOD had me throw my seabag down the hatch to the sleeping quarters for the engineering department. Climbing down the ladder into a semi-dark space, I didn't know where to go so I lay on my seabag (and as I found out later) on a pile of laundry bags for my first night's sleep on a Tin can.

A year later I advanced to MM3 and was put in charge of the ship's fresh water systems. This duty required the operation and maintenance of the fwd and aft evaporators as well as hooking up to the fresh water line whenever we docked after our time at sea.

Get a bigger hammer

In March of '61 the forward engine room evaporator ceased providing water pure enough for our boilers and personal hygiene. Unfortunately, this was in the middle of some naval exercises. The salt content was too high and could not be corrected, so a major overhaul had to be done. Working around the clock for three days (the picture is from the cruise book, and that's me in the evaporator), several of our crew chipped and clawed our way back into production. This was to the great relief of our ever-present Engineering officers, LTJG William Merritt and LTJG Peter McKenna-who were on our butts most of the time-because they had to report to our Captain, CDR Clifford Hunter, on the progress.

Although we were exhausted, we were proud to have finished in such a short time. It was a "Job Well Done" - and I'm also sure the rest of the crew was glad to get real showers again.

Wayne Peterson MM3 1958-61

'Surface to Surface Gunnery Exercise'

They probably don't shoot surface to surface exercises anymore, with the modern emphasis on missiles, but in the mid-1950's, the missile age was just beginning, and there was still the possibility that one ship might have to fight another ship using guns. To prepare us for this eventuality, the Navy still had a suitable exercise in its training manuals. To fire such an exercise a "sled" target was used, towed by a fleet tug. The sled was a big wooden float that vaguely resembled its winter namesake, but with a pipe frame that stood perhaps fifteen to twenty feet above its waterline. Stretched across this frame was a big fabric sail to make the device visible from a distance, and a radar reflector was carried to produce a better image on the ship's fire control radar. The sled was attached to the tug by a steel cable a couple of thousand feet long. When firing on the sled at relatively close range, the firing ship set in an offset of a couple of degrees in its fire control computer to avoid excessive damage to the target, which was considered pretty expensive. When firing from a range of several miles, however, we aimed to hit, but since the sled was only about fifty feet long, this didn't happen very often!

The target was "acquired" by the radar and then, under normal conditions, tracked automatically, with the gun director pointer and trainer just watching through their sight telescopes, ready to take over in case of a radar failure. The director was providing inputs of target bearing and range to the computer to enable it to determine the necessary lead angle and angle of elevation for the guns to put the big projectiles on target. When the range closed to the "maximum effective range" of our 5"/38 caliber main battery weapons, the Captain ordered a course change so that all gun mounts could be brought to bear, and when the director officer had received the word from the safety observer in each gun mount that he had the target in his sights, the Captain gave the permission to "Commence firing when ready."

At this point, the order went to out to all mounts to load one or both guns, and when the Mount Captains reported that they were loaded, a "salvo" was fired, meaning that all guns fired simultaneously, and all the projectiles landed at the same time. The director officer, watching the fall of shot through his binoculars, then corrected as necessary by sending "spots" to the computer crew, left or right in 'mils', and add or drop in yards. By the time the 'spots' had been cranked into the computer, the guns had been loaded again for another salvo. If the solution was perfect, of course, no spotting would be necessary, but this was rarely the case, most often because our wind data was not completely accurate, and the wind could push those projectiles quite a distance on the long flight to the target. Salvo fire would continue until the director officer decided that he was "on target", at which time he would shift to "Rapid Continuous Fire", and all firing would be closed, so that the guns would fire just as soon as a round was rammed home. At this time each of our six guns was putting out twenty or more rounds per minute, and the hail of projectiles raining down around the sled became pretty intense, sometimes hiding the target from view if your solution was really good.

As the projectiles landed, observers on our ship and on the tug were also watching, and measuring the distance left or right and long or short of the fall of shot relative to the sled, and grading the exercise accordingly. Included in the grading criteria were the number of spotting salvos necessary to bring the rounds on target, and the time required expend the allotted number of rounds. The surface target the sled was supposed to represent was a ship more than four hundred feet long, several times the length of the sled, and much wider and higher, so that you did not have to score any actual 'hits' on the sled to get a passing grade. However, your numerical score would be higher if all rounds fell close to the sled.

On this occasion, the sled was being towed by the USS Luiseno (ATF-156), and we were in an operating area south of Newport, Rhode Island. It was a cold, wintery day, but the sun was shining, and the North Atlantic was relatively calm, with waves perhaps four to six feet high. We had made one "dry run" to make sure everything was working properly, and it seemed that all was in order. We steamed away from the target again, and upon confirmation from the bridge, I passed the word to the gun mounts that the next run would be a firing run. No matter how many times you practiced the procedures, this was the time that something was most likely to go wrong, because everyone tensed up, knowing that this time the big guns were actually going to make noise, and lots of it! We turned and started our run in, and soon had a computer solution. When the range had closed to about twelve thousand yards, the ship changed course to the right, and the word went out to the gun mounts "Match up and shift to automatic." The guns were now on target, and I soon had the safety observer's reports that they all had the target in sight. LUISENO was out there too, about a third of a mile to the right of the sled, and we had to be sure that the guns were not pointed in her direction!

We received permission to fire, and all firing keys but one were closed. The upper handling rooms loaded their powder and projectile hoists, sending ammunition up to the gun crews. I gave the command, "All mounts, load one gun." Seconds later, the reply came back, Mount 51, 52, 53 loaded." Upon my command to fire, my computer operator closed his key, and there was a tremendous roar. Each of the three guns belched fire and smoke, as I kept my eyes glued to my binoculars, waiting for the rounds to land. Three columns of water appeared close to the sled. My spots went to the plotting room: "Left ten, drop 100." Another command to the mounts was "to each load one gun". The plotting room advised that the spots had been entered, and once again I gave the order to fire. The guns belched fire, smoke and noise again, and I watched for the rounds to land. Right on! "All mounts, rapid continuous fire!" Now we were putting out an average of two fifty-five pound projectiles per second, and it sounded like all hell had broken loose! The ship was engulfed in a cloud of brownish colored smoke, and I had to strain to see the target! The first rounds landed a little to the right of the sled, but right on in range. I sent down a spot; "Left five". The fall of shot seemed to move a little further to the right. I asked Plot if they had entered that spot in the right direction, and they assured me that they had. Another; "Left ten". Again the fall of shot seemed to move to the right, and in fact, the sled had moved out of the field of my binoculars! Something was wrong! The projectiles weren't falling anywhere near the tug, yet, but I sounded the "Cease Fire" buzzer and screamed "Cease fire, cease fire!" into the 17MC microphone, simultaneously nudging the man with my right foot to make sure he had released his firing key. There was sudden silence, and one more blast from Mount 52, just to my right, just forward of the bridge. The projectiles stopped falling, as far as I could see, well to the left of the tug. No harm done, I guessed, but what had gone wrong?

When the cease fire order had gone out the director was moving rapidly to the right. I had heard stories of radars tracking the steel cable between the sled and the tug, but I had never believed them!

A discussion followed over the sound-powered phone circuits between the bridge, Plot and the director, and we decided to make another dry run, to check out the system, and anther firing run if everything checked out OK. The dry run went like clockwork, and the second firing run went equally well. We literally smothered the sled in splashes, and we got a pretty good grade on the exercise as a result. I knew it had gone pretty well the second time, and as I scrambled down from the director I was feeling pretty good! As I passed CIC on my way down to the wardroom, one of the radarmen called out to me; "What were you trying to do Mr. Post, to sink the tug?" Puzzled, I asked him what he was talking about. He informed me that the last round from the first firing run had landed about 200 yards beyond LUISENO, and that they had received a voice radio call from the tug telling us to cease fire. In fact, he said, it sounded like the person calling us needed to go change his skivvy drawers, he was that scared!

It was a wonder that LUISENO (ATF 156) allowed us to make that second firing run, in the light of what had transpired. Later in the day, we conducted an informal investigation to find out why that last round had been fired. I had given the cease fire order in plenty of time to keep from hitting the tug, and once the firing circuit had been broken, theoretically, at least, the guns should have stopped firing. There was only one hitch, however. The 5"/38 can be fired by percussion as well as electrically. Also, once loaded, it can only be unloaded "though the muzzle". In other words, the projectile, once seated in the rifling of the gun barrel, cannot be backed out. The powder case can be removed, and in such a case, it is normally replaced with a "short round", containing a smaller charge of powder, sufficient to get the projectile well clear of the ship. Of course, the gun has to be pointed in a safe direction first, to make sure no one gets hurt. The investigation revealed that the Mount Captain of Mount 52, an old First Class Gunner's Mate who should have known better, had found himself with a loaded gun when the firing circuits were broken. He decided he did not want to go through the rigmarole of reporting the loaded gun, and the unloading procedure that would follow, so he ordered his pointer to "Fire By Percussion" by pressing the firing treadle provided for the purpose. In a way, I can understand his decision, because those guns barrels were getting hot by that time, it could "cook off", and the resulting explosion in the chamber could kill the whole gun crew, and anyone else in the vicinity as well. This fact, plus the fact that we did not actually hit LUISENO, probably was instrumental in getting him a verbal reprimand instead of a court martial. If we had hit the tug, that Gunner's Mate, the Skipper, and I would have been hung side by side.

Leaving CIC, having been informed of my near miss, I was just a little bit shaken, and needless to say, I was no longer "on top of the world!" The Captain was already there when I entered the wardroom, and he turned to me and said quietly, "Well, George, by the grace of God and a little luck, we don't have to paint a tug on your director!" George W. Post Ens/Lt(jg) 1954-1956

'Fiske versus Sub – Take 2'

I'm not certain about the date of this incident but I'm sure that there were reports in the newspapers.

We were on a sub training mission out to sea from Massachusetts. The sub would hide and we would find them. I was on the Evaporator Watch when the sub tried to surface under the Fiske. I was thrown five feet when the sub's conning tower hit our hull. I believe that General Quarters was called and the Damage Control teams closed off several compartments. We took on quite a bit of water. It was dark and the sub (badly) damaged.

The Fiske towed it back to port – about 100 miles. The Fiske went in for hull repairs. The sub was in much worse condition. This must have been late '71 or early '72 – wish I would have kept a diary. Larry Hovland EN3 1971-1972

'Swim Call'

After departing the Red Sea, Fiske headed for the Persian Gulf. The folks in the Middle East were still uncertain which way the wind was blowing and a port visit to Chittagong (Bangladesh) had been scrubbed weeks earlier, and schedules were tweaked to include several visits in the Persian Gulf. A key stop was Manama, Bahrain where the Brits maintained a shore base known as HMS Jufair. Since the start of the Six Day War, there were no US logistic support ships south of Suez, so fuel and food replenishment had been sketchy at best. Most Arab countries in the region had an oil embargo that generally prevented US Navy ships from refueling in port and causing a stir among Arab natives who were convinced the US was up to no good. The Brits had been at HMS Jufair since 1935 and had a reasonably good relationship with the Sheik who ran Bahrain and thus had access to fuel and food.

The British Navy Oiler, HMS Plumleaf, was homeported in Bahrain and was an obvious "gas station" for the Fiske. The downside was that the Brits were not eager to upset their Arab hosts by allowing an obvious refueling of a US Navy Destroyer in plain sight on the commercial pier where the Plumleaf was moored. As a result Plumleaf would get underway and steam just over the horizon, drop the hook and Fiske would get underway and moor alongside her and refuel. HMS Plumleaf was somewhat unique as most oilers go - she boasted a swimming pool for her crew on one of the higher decks back aft.

As many old salts are aware, the British Navy also has slightly different rules when it comes to the consumption of alcoholic beverages. Once Fiske had come alongside and refueling had commenced, the Plumleaf Commanding Officer invited off-watch Fiske officers and crew to go for a swim in her pool.

CDR Bill McKinley, Fiske's CO, thought that was a wonderful gesture and authorized swim call on Plumleaf. What Captain McKinley did not realize was that the route to the Plumleaf's swimming pool was right past the crew's mess and the Officer's wardroom. Both the mess and wardroom were nicely stocked with all sorts of liquid refreshments of the alcoholic variety and only a few Fiske sailors or officers made it to the pool. I personally recall some absolutely wonderful gin and tonics being consumed before the Plumleaf's 1MC chattered that the Fiske guests should return to their ship to get underway.

I headed back across the lifelines with my shipmates and paused to grab some breath mints before heading to my Sea Detail post on the bridge. Captain McKinley was a teetotaler and frowned on drinking of any sort so most of the Bridge Watch steered clear of him to avoid triggering awkward questions regarding their swim call. Sea Details were typically a high energy, somewhat noisy evolution as commands were barked and checklists were confirmed. Not this time. Getting underway from alongside Plumleaf had to be the most quiet and civilized evolution I had ever recalled and even amazed the Captain who monitored things from his chair on high. Clearly, a significant number of the crew were somewhat mellow and delighted with British hospitality. Unfortunately the Captain eventually figured out what had gone on and future refuelings were without a swim call. Can't win 'em all, but I realized that Fiske Sea Details did not have to be the Chinese fire drill I had come to know.
W. C. S. 'Skip' Mays III Ens/Ltjg 1966-1968

'Duty Swap'

My second most favored story involves a First Class Radarman - whose name I cannot remember. When standing in port watch my duty section was required to have any "Chits" requesting a duty swap turned in before 1630 for approval. The only exception would be if the

Sailor requesting a swap could tell me a story I had never heard before.

I do not remember the date of the occurrence, but it was a beautiful evening, about 1800 when I was approached by the First Class with chit in hand. I immediately reminded him of the 1630 rule. To which he smartly replied: "Sir, my wife is going to get pregnant and I want to be there." I think I almost died laughing, but told him "Get out of here." for 45 years I have wondered just how that shore liberty turned out. If that Radarman reads this I hope he'll answer up.
David Taylor, LT USNR 1965-67

'My First 48 Hours'

Directly out of Boot Camp in San Diego I reported aboard the USS Fiske at Newport, RI in December of 1965. Within 48 hours we departed on a short cruise to New Jersey for ammunition. Fresh out of Boot Camp as a Seaman Apprentice, I was still saluting Chiefs and just didn't have a clue. For my first night at sea I stayed up quite late trying to see all I could see and finally retired to my bunk late and still couldn't figure out why I was being called "the new Deck APE". Within a few hours some sailor was with a red flashlight was waking me up to tell me I had the watch. Quite sleepily I told him that he had the wrong guy. He said that if my name was LaVille to get my butt up to the bridge because I DID have the watch.

After getting directions, I arrived at the bridge for my watch. WOW, was all this real? The night lights, the Combat Board, the crew and the silence. That's what struck me, the silence. The Boatswain's Mate of the Watch got me acquainted and I started to learn my way around as we rotated from station to station. When it started to get light outside the Boats told me that I needed to take the helm. He explained to me to approach the OOD and salute, while keeping the salute, say 'Request permission to take the helm sir' then state the compass and course reading, state the RPM's, state the knots, state the ... blah, blah, blah, blah. Well, I thought that just because I was the new kid and he was playing a joke on me and I wasn't going to fall for this nonsense. O.D. Williams – the BMOW – escorted me into the hallway off the bridge and had a short chat with me as to just what was what and I became an immediate believer. After my third attempt at requesting to take the helm (of which I must say the OOD got quite a kick out of) I was granted permission to take the helm.

Now this helm thing was just crazy – if you wanted the compass to go in one direction you had to turn the helm wheel the opposite. I thought that I was quite mechanically gifted but I was really having trouble keeping the Fiske on course. Then the Captain entered the bridge and had Williams relieve me from the helm. The Skipper took me out onto the port bridge wing and stood there with his hand on my shoulder as we looked aft. He pointed aft, but he didn't need to. I could see it. There it was: the biggest zig-zag wake ever created by a U. S. Destroyer without being under combat conditions. He had a short but encouraging word as to my helmsman abilities, patted me on the back and returned to the bridge. As I stood there looking at the wake, I then realized that I was receiving applause and whistles with hoots and hollers of praise, as the entire breakfast chow line was directly under the wing, down on the main deck and they had caught the whole thing. Warren D. LaVille, HM3 1965-1967

'Sonar Games'

Any vessel whose job is ASW (Anti-Submarine Warfare) is a noisy place.

Learning to sleep while the Sonar is "Echo-Ranging" is one of the things
you learn to do. There is a loud PINGGGGGGGGGGGGGGGGG! that gradually fades into the distance to be followed by yet another PINGGGGGGGGGG! And that is repeated over and over again......You get used to it! Though Lord knows how you manage.

I remember being in the Caribbean just East of Culebra
Island and bound for the Florida Straits in mid 1965......Briggs,
Sonarman 1st was our leading "Ping Jockey"

I was sitting in the Weapons Office trying to look busier than I
was. I noticed something different! We still had the loud PING but now
we had a returning echo.   The call was PING------Pong, PING-------
Pong......We had ourselves a submarine down there. Ears perked
up,   Hearts beat louder,   what was next? We weren't at war with the
Soviets! We couldn't just sink their submarines. Maybe Briggs was
bouncing signals off a wreck, a water logged reminder of our "Father's
War."

If so, we would hear the signal get stronger and stronger, then
fade as we moved on beyond it.....There was a way that Sonarmen used
to identify a wreck I didn't know what it was, I presumed Briggs did

We waited; looking at one another....One thing was certain, we
weren't

getting any closer.....The target was just out there. It wasn't
trying to evade us, there were no course changes. The Superheaters on
our boilers weren't lit off, that meant we were making less than 21
knots In fact Joel had just come up from below and let me know we
were making about 14 knots.

Nobody seemed alarmed.......Hey! There was a submarine
down there! Were they crazy?   It was filled up with genuine Russian
speaking Communists who might be planning to launch a missile on
Washington! My young and belligerent heart wanted to squash them
like a bug for their impudence.

We had them cold!   We should launch an ASROC (Anti-
Submarine Rocket)

We weren't even at General Quarters!!!!!   Was I the only sane
man on the ship.

Then the Sonar shifted to empty Echo Ranging again.....We had
possessed a submarine for an hour or so, now it was gone.

I looked at Joel, his face was filled with complete indifference. He had his blue working cap on the back of his head, and he was concentrating on emptying a coffee cup he had in his hands.

He just smiled and remarked "Calm Down, Moose, you'll live longer!"

He then commented on the gun shack coffee, "Don't you guys ever clean that coffee pot??"

Found out later that Briggs was tired of playing games and had played Sonar School training tapes....It almost cost him a chevron......Me? I learned to be just a little more "laid back" Such is the life of a seaman.
Jerry MoseleyYN3 1963-66

'Bits & Pieces – Dates uncertain'

1. *As we proceeded down the channel at Pensacola for plane guard duties for carrier qualifications we got out of the channel and in the process we scuffed off the SONAR dome, buffed up a portion of one screw along with messing up one shaft. We still proceeded on one shaft.*
2. *While escorting the Enterprise during the Cuban Missile Crisis a F8U (Crusader) had a flame-out and went into the sea. The pilot ejected and was Okay.*
3. *While steaming off Florida in a rain storm the UHF Radio Direction Finder was hit by lightning. The Navy said that was not possible.*
4. *Anchoring in the harbor of Monaco while the Gran Prix was going on. [May 1961]*
James Hanner RD3 – RD2 3/1961 – 12/1963

Pilot ejecting from F8U Crusader

'CO's – Ying & Yang'

When CDR C. H. Butt relieved CDR C. E. Hunter in April 1962 the entire crew wondered what difference it would make. Our morale and spirits were at low ebb. We'd been in the yards in Charleston, SC for 3 months under less than ideal conditions and wondered what new burdens were going to be placed on us. CDR Hunter appeared to some to be losing it.

We had had Dress Inspections on the Crew's Mess Decks in the evening where one of the commands given was, "Lift pant legs, Hut". This command was so the Captain could ascertain if we had any cigarettes in our socks. Those that had them were gigged. During the remainder of my twenty-one year Navy career I never again heard that command given.

There were rumors that one of the crew had contacted his Congressman over this, and other, events. Other rumors told of the consequences of contacting ones Congressman. Reports of having a big 'PI' stamped on your service record ['PI' meaning 'Political Influence']. This is the atmosphere into which CDR Butt entered.

CDR Butt had been onboard the Fiske before. He had been Weapons Officer and XO back in the 1950's. It didn't take long for the differences to be felt. If CDR Butt wanted to know the answer to a question he went to the person he thought best knew the answer. If it was the Leading BT, that's who he talked to. It was the 'new normal' to see a pair of white bucks and white uniform trousers descending the ladder into the Sonar Shack area. Under CDR Hunter you could count on your Leading PO, your Division Officer, Department Head and XO to visit but you seldom saw the CO.

In very short order it became known that CDR Butt expected you to work hard but play just as hard – if not harder. Case in point-we had just completed our RefTra in Gitmo after the yard period and returned to Mayport. I was sitting in the ET Shack after evening chow when in walked the Captain. He asked me if I had the duty and I replied 'No Sir'. He then asked why I wasn't on the beach and I told him that I was broke. He reached into his pocket and handed me a $10 bill and told me to get off the ship.

I heard similar things from enough people to know that if the Captain had asked just about any of the crew to move a bulkhead we would have tried to do so. CDR Butt was a chain-smoker of non-filtered Kool cigarettes. They say imitation is the sincerest form of flattery. I'm willing to bet that the sales of non-filtered Kool's sky-rocketed in the Ship's Store. I know I helped.

By the by – the Ward Room became much more interested in the opinions of the CPO's and senior LPO's because they were afraid that they wouldn't know what was going on in their Departments or Divisions. We became a much better ship because the crew knew we had a CO that cared.

Out of the dozen or so CO's I served under I rate CDR Cyrus H. Butt number 1. I hesitate to give a number to CDR Hunter.
Gil Beyer ETR3 1960-1963

'Memories – Fond & Otherwise'

Most of my fond and otherwise memories of my time on Fiske are already published in the Fiske Association records. I have honest and forthright in praise and less than praise.

My time there (was) from mid-1960 to shortly after the (re)commissioning in the Brooklyn Navy Yard in 1965. My transfer orders were not welcomed by me as I really wanted the world trip. Alas, that was not to be as the Navy decided that my services were REQUIRED on the Reserve trainer. I was being sent to New Haven, Connecticut. It turned out to be true, unfortunately.

I remember Captain Hunter. I did not think much of him then nor do I now. I remember inspections to be more important than ship's work. "Paint it and make it pretty" the way it was. Operational equipment to Capt. Hunter was optional. Inspections (were) mandatory. The one that really got to me was in Whites on a COLD, WET SNOW on the ground, UNDER THE CRANE (dripping) where we got gigged for spots, spots and more spots.

Inspections under Capt. Butt gave way to operational readiness and paint gave way to grease and elbow grease. Things got done, equipment started working and in short order morale improved.

From Charleston the ship went to Gitmo. On the way the Engine Order Telegraph quit working. Entry into had to done by tug if the 'EOT' didn't work. We found drawings and traced (the wiring) box by box to a connection box in the After Fire Room behind a boiler that was filled with water. Guess what the PROBLEM was!? We had to remake the box, cut new Bakelite, install new connectors, dry out the many wires, reconnect, test and with 2 hours to spare were operational. The Electricians and IC men were very tired and proud. Fiske entered Gitmo unassisted.

I remember the Cuban Missile Crisis when no one knew where or why we were rousted out of our beds at midnight and told to get underway with 50% of the crew on board. We did that and several crew members had thrilling tales of their trip to catch up with us. Some came by helo, some by highline. I remember GQ because an unidentified aircraft was approaching Enterprise. I remember being told that two Phantom jets identified that aircraft as the Enterprise's mail plane. We had terrific gunners and that plane was in our crosshairs. How close can you get?

I remember NOT going aground in the bay by Pensacola. I also remember the mud 'darkening' our wake.

Med trips, Liberties, places we went, things we saw – all are memories that we all have. I have mine, you have yours. So does every (crew) member of every ship that ever left a homeport.

There are a couple of things of note though that I think speak to the professionalism of (the) Fiske crew under Captain Butt. I doubt the same could be said for Captain Hunter.

On the way to the 1963 Med Cruise while transiting Cape Hatteras – I think – there was a terrible storm. I think (the) Enterprise lost (an) aircraft off an elevator during the storm by waves. A young striker in Fiske's After Engine Room decided to use the outboard hatch to run an errand. Green water came in through the hatch and shorted out the After Switchboard and the Degaussing Panel. Asked if we could continue to the Med or go back home for repairs our answer was to continue on. The estimate to repair was 48 hours. There wasn't much sleep by any of the electricians but the job was successfully completed and on the line during that time. The Degaussing Panel took longer but it also was successfully made to work (while) underway.

Another shipyard job done by the Engineers was replacing the tube nest on one of the evaporators. Parts were delivered to the ship during a quick stop in Sicily and the repaired during the underway period.

I understand (that) there were antenna problems corrected underway that normally be an in-port job. I'm sure that there were many other jobs that this crew was able to correct with the ship at sea. It seems our motto could have been 'Work at sea, Play in port'. That's pretty much what we did.

During that cruise several of us were advanced in rate after a RARE personnel inspection in the port of Monaco. Following the inspection and announcement of advancement several crew members were thrown over the side in celebration. At least I was able to get my shoes off and wallet out first. The water was wonderful. Remember?

I probably haven't given anything new here. Maybe I'll think of else at another time. This is it for now. I hope you can read it and make some sense of out of it.
John Frazer EM3/ EM2 1960-1965

Suez Transit 1963

In February 1963 the Fiske departed Mayport, Florida for duty with the Sixth Fleet in the Mediterranean Sea. After visiting Cannes, France; Athens, Greece; and Palermo, Sicily in February and March Fiske was detached from the Sixth Fleet to transit the Suez Canal and enter the Red Sea for duty with units of the Middle East Forces.

This was a period of some unrest in that region. Syria had seceded from the UAR (now only consisting of Egypt) and there was a great deal of tension between Syria, Egypt & Jordan. In concept the UAR was designed to be a union of Arab states for better trade and to present a consolidated front to Israel. A coup d'état in Syria in 1961 sounded the death knell for the UAR but the name remained until after Nasser's death in 1971.

The UAR was very much a client state of the Soviet Union. Most, if not all, the weapons the UAR's armed forces had were of Soviet manufacture. The Suez Canal may be an international waterway but it runs right through Egypt. Fiske took onboard an Egyptian pilot at Port Said on April 4th and began the southward transit.

As an ETR3 I spent a great many of my working hours in CIC. The Combat Information Center is nerve center of any warship, collecting and collating data from a great many sources. Our ECM suite was primitive by today's standards but it was working well enough for us to detect and define many of the signals that we received.

From the time we entered Egyptian waters at the north end of the canal until we exited at Port Suez on the south end of the canal there was one constant. From beginning to end we were tracked by various Soviet Fire Control Radars. The radars were of just about every conceivable type from artillery to missile. The signals were not intermittent or random. They were 'locked on' to Fiske for the entire trip. They only ended after we were outside Egyptian waters on April 5th.

The rest of the stay in the Red Sea was fairly routine and boring. The most exciting things we did were to visit Aden, Yemen for a few days and trying to net jellyfish while we steamed along at about 5 knots. The return trip through the canal was a repeat of the inbound transition.
G. Beyer, ETR3 1960-1963

No collection would be complete without an example of the January 1st Mid-Watch log entry. Here is one that was submitted by its author.

DECK LOG – REMARKS SHEET

*USS FISKE (DD 842)___ zone description + 5 R_ date SATURDAY 1 JAN 19 66_*
AT PIER 1, U.S. NAVAL BASIN NEWPORT, RHODE ISLAND
REMARKS

00 – 04 ON THE FIRST DAY IN SIXTY-SIX
HERE IN NEWPORT, BERTH THREE-SIX
PIER ONE, WEST FACE,
WHERE THIS CHRONICLE TAKES PLACE.
THIS SHIP, AND OTHERS IN THIS NEST,
TIED WITH BOW, STERN, SPRINGLINES AND A BREAST.
THE FIRST LIEUTENANT, SO SHE WON'T GET 'WAY
HAS LED A WIRE TO THE QUAY.
THE SHIP OUTBOARD "ROAN"
SHIFTS AGAINST FENDERS WITH A GROAN.

IN BOARD, HAPPY NOT TO BE ALONE,
IS DESTROYER "BASILONE"
"DYESS" TOO, IS IN THE NEST,
ENJOYING A DESERVED REST.
"AD-28", WITH UNTOLD PLEASURE
ISSUING OUT HER ENDLESS TREASURE
OF CANVAS, ELECTRONIC PARTS AND WOOD
MAKING ALL OUR HURTINGS GOOD.
OUR ENGINEERING PLANT, BECAUSE OF LEAKS,
HAS BEEN WRAPPED UP STONE COLD FOR WEEKS.
A SKINNY STEAMLINE FROM THE PIER
WINDS ITS WAY FROM HERE TO THERE
TRYING WITH ITS LEVEL BEST
TO REACH EACH SHIP IN THE NEST
FAILS TO PROVIDE, WITHOUT INTENTION,
A MODICUM OF HEAT, (THAT'S NO INVENTION).
SET CONDITION IV IN EACH DIVISION
IS MON CAPITIAN'S DECISION
TO STRIKE A HURTING, TELLING BLOW
TO AN ENEMY, SHOULD HE SHOW.
BELOW THE MAIN-DECK, EVERY SPACE
CONDITION YOKE PREVAILS THE PLACE.
AND SOPA's PENNANT, WHITE AND GREEN
DAYTIMES ON "AD-19" MAY BE SEEN.
SHIPS FROM THE MIGHTIEST OF FLEETS
FOUND HERE TONITE INCLUDE THE "WEEKS"
THE "DAVIS" TOO, ACROSS THE PIER
IS CELEBRATIMG NEW YEAR'S HERE.
FORGIVE ME NOW, IF I DO CLOSE,
THIS HUMBLE VERSE AND HUMBLER PROSE,
MY TENURE HERE IS GETTING BRIEF
AND NEAR AT HAND IS MY RELIEF.
//s// D. J. OLSEN LTJG   USNR

'Boston-GITMO-Vietnam'

After Sonar School, I reported onboard the Fiske at Newport, RI we headed south for Gunnery and Anti-Submarine operations off the coast of Georgia. Enroute we had liberty in Savannah – it is a pretty city. Afterwards we went into drydock in Boston where it was very cold, 5 ° F.

From Boston, we went down to Guantanamo Bay, Cuba where I was put into the hospital after spilling boiling hot coffee on my left ankle. I stayed in the hospital while Fiske visited Jamaica and San Juan, Puerto Rico then returned to Guantanamo to pick me up.

We left Cuba and headed for the Panama Canal. Before going through the Canal, we were told that there was a submarine (one of ours) off the coast of the Yucatan Peninsula and if one of us could find it we'd a weekend in Hawaii. Not true it turned out. Well, guess who found the sub? I did, and reported it to the Chief Sonarman. We tracked that sub he finally answered up on the underwater telephone. I won some respect from my superiors – just a little – not much.

Upon going through the Panama Canal we headed for Subic Bay, Philippines where we stayed for a day or two. From there we went to Yokosuka, Japan to have the ship's generator replaced or fixed. Me and a buddy, Jimmy Stewart – not the actor – went to Yokohama for 2 days, had some fun and came back to the ship by train.

Jimmy was ahead of me and went up the gangplank. I was too late; they pulled the gangplank away from the ship and it was pulling away from the pier. There was one mooring line left; I threw my bag on the bow and grabbed the mooring line as the ship was backing out. I climbed the mooring line to the bow of the ship. The captain didn't look happy!

Once we were underway we headed to Viet Nam for patrol. After the patrol we went back to Subic Bay for a day and then left for Hong Kong. While enroute we ran through a massive hurricane where I lost a trashcan full of scrap food – I was on Mess Cook duty. Just about the entire crew was sick.

I developed a toothache while we were in Hong Kong. A British dentist aboard another ship there pulled the tooth.

The Fiske was used for Search & Rescue of downed airplanes and pilots; Gunfire support for the Army and Marines near the coast. I believe that we were fired upon twice; once from land-based artillery and another time by some kind of gunboat from inland waters. We detected a Soviet submarine but no action was taken.
John Naldrett STGSN/STG3 1964-1967

A Cool Ship

In January of 1968, Fiske entered the Boston naval Shipyard for an extensive four month overhaul. On May 6, 1968 Fiske completed her modernization and returned to Newport to prepare for refresher training at Guantanamo Bay, Cuba. That's where the story begins. The signal gang's leading petty officer SM/1 Bob Mitchell was going to make sure that the signal bridge space was something to be proud of and that Guantanamo's training score's would be exceptional. I can recall that Bob was always looking for a better way to do things, and was therefore always open to suggestion.

The signal bridge shack was the best you had ever seen. From inside, you had a 360 degree view. Always a fresh pot of coffee and sometimes we boiled hotdogs in a second coffee pot. Somehow bread and mustard was always available. This signal shack was well insulated and well heated for the cold weather. Therein lay the problem as we steamed toward the hot Cuban environment. With this well built insulated shack, how could we keep cool? As per Bob's instruction, the signal gang painted the roof of the signal shack white, which really helped in keeping the shack somewhat less hot. I can recall a conversation when someone jokingly suggested that the shack needed an air conditioner. The response was, yea, right how is that going to work?

We arrived at Guantanamo and spent the week training. That first Sunday there, I went to Navy Exchange and Commissary to look around. Son of a gun, they had A/C units for sale. It was something to think about as I recalled a previous joking conversation. I mentioned my discovery to Bob. Like I said, Bob was always open to suggestions and seemed quite interested in pursuing the idea of an air conditioned signal shack.

After some discussion, the signal gang agreed that cooling off the signal shack was a great idea and figured out the engineering of such an endeavor. All that was left to do was to purchase the A/C unit and somehow get it on board for the install. Next, where was the purchase money coming from? I thought that perhaps with the money I was making from the use of the signal bridge sewing machine we could purchase a couple of picnic coolers.

We would then all chip in and buy caned soda from the commissary and get ice from a supply division shipmate who wanted to be paid off in soda. We pooled our money and purchased forty cases of soda.

The Commissary delivered them to the ship and for some reason I never been able to figure out, the officer of the deck called for a working party to report to the gangway to receive supplies. The soda was delivered to the signal bridge and was stowed in a flag bag and a deck locker. The two picnic coolers were filled with soda and covered with ice. We put out the word that ice cold soda was for sale and business took off.

A few days later while we were performing an underway maneuver the captain called Bob to the starboard bridge wing and requested a can of coke. I remember Bob telling me that the captain wanted to pay for the soda but Bob refused to take the money.

We did sell all of the soda and doubled our money. We purchased the a/c unit and just carried it on up to the signal bridge; no questions asked and installed it in the signal shack. An unseen problem cropped up. Everyone wants to stay inside. Somehow we worked out the problem.

A few weeks later the XO came up to the signal bridge to check out the rumor of an a/c unit installed in the signal shack. He came in and savored the cool comfort and told me that it was against navy regulations to install such an appliance and, not only that, the weight of the a/c unit would unbalance the ship.

Are you kidding me? Jokingly, I told the XO that we had not better have too many of ship's company stand on either side of the ship at the same time. That comment didn't go over too well. However, as the conversation continued I mentioned that the captain really enjoyed the soda that he requested. That was the end of the conversation. We never heard another thing about the soda or the installed a/c unit until one day, while being underway and taking on fuel when the oiler signalman via semaphore asked us if it was true that our signal shack was air conditioned. He wanted to confirm the rumor. Bob told him to use the big eyes and check it out and confirm the rumor himself because through those 360 degree windows, you could see people inside drinking hot coffee on a terribly hot day with the doors closed.

I've often wondered that on Friday June 5, 1980, as the Fiske was decommissioned in Philadelphia and turned over to the Turkish Navy and renamed the Fiske TCG Piyale Pasa, did the signalmen give out a big woweeeee.
Daniel Gilroy SM3 1966-1970

"Cool Ship – A Footnote"

On the occasion of that bit of skullduggery I was the OC division officer. I was well aware of the soda sales operation - hardly a totally legal operation by Navy standards. This was facilitated by the Mess Deck Master at Arms - a 1st class Signalman - and the possessor of the only key to the ice machine. Funny how those things work. Sailors came from all over the ship, including snipes from the engine room, and that is a long climb. At the time I decided it could be dealt with only if necessary.

I did have one very nervous moment however. As fate would have it, I would ride back to the ship, which was at anchor, in the Captain's Gig with the illegal A/C unit and some wary Signalmen. Of course the OOD had to be the Ops officer, my boss and the Department Head for the Signalmen. I doubt if that gig had ever before or since been unloaded faster of both passengers and cargo. A lot of snappy salutes and this Division officer headed left to the bridge. The Signalmen headed right and up with the A/C. With unbelievable speed that A/C unit was installed in the wall of the signal shack, wired and even painted gray. It was operational in less than one hour!!

Absolutely nothing was said to me about the subject for about a week. Then one sunny afternoon, while we were underway, the Ops Officer approached me while I was standing at the chart table in the pilot house. He simply asked if I knew about an A/C unit in the Signal Shack. I answered "What A/C?" That was, to the best of my knowledge, the last word....case closed. This is one of my favorite sea stories from the Fiske.
Dave Taylor (Lt USNR) 1965-67

'Cumshaw'

Cumshaw? This is a good old navy term for the unofficial transfer of goods or services within the navy without the benefit of proper government authorization. In short, trading or barter. The best deal I ever took part in occurred in the old Brooklyn Navy Yard while we were undergoing FRAM-I conversion sometime in 1964.

It all centered on a couple of facts: 1- The Navy Yard's M-1 rifles of World War II vintage were in the hands of the Shipyard's

Marine Garrison. They had just been replaced by M-14 Rifles, a more modern version with full auto capability, chambered for the new 7.62 NATO round. 2- Now, our small arms locker was filled with bolt action Springfield 1903 rifles of World War I vintage. It was plain to anybody that Uncle Sam wasn't spending money upgrading our ship because he thought we looked pretty. Sooner or later, we were going to Vietnam

Lieutenant R. E. Guthrie worked out the trade with the Captain in Charge of the "Jarhead" (Marine) Garrison. Twenty-five of our bolt action rifles for their sniper teams in exchange for the 25 M-1's they were turning in.

The only problem was that the Greenies wanted "Cumshaw" in the form of 4 cases of Sea Stores Cigarettes. Well, we had two cases. No more! The deal was on the verge of going sour.

So, I pointed out to the Lieutenant that we had 4 bottles of Scotch in the Weapons Office Safe, and a couple of bottles of rum, besides. In short order, I had arranged to trade 4 Bottles of Scotch for 2 cases of Sea Stores Cigarettes that the USS Dyess (DD-880) had.

Phase 1 was complete. We arranged for the transfer to take place at the loading dock of the Marine's Supply Building. Lieutenant Guthrie went into the Captain's office. The signal was simple. If he came out of that office with his hat on his head, the deal was off, and we were to drive off in the truck. If he came out with his hat in his hands, the deal was good, we would wait for the Marine guard to go inside, offload the cases of cigarettes and load two cases of rifles, plus two 8 round clips/weapon.

Well, we spent a nervous 10 minutes in the truck. There were four of us, two in the cab and two in the bed of the truck. Out came Lieutenant Guthrie with his hat in his hand. The Marine guard got a phone call, and had an urgent mission inside the building.

We jumped out, and in less than three minutes had given the Marines 4 cases of smokes while we got their rifles and clips. .When everything cleared, we were a block away going back to the yard building allowed our ship with our treasure.

That, dear readers, is the pinnacle of my career in "Cumshaw". I could never top that one. As far as I know, the Navy is still looking for those rifles.

Jerry Mosley YN31963-66

Dominican Republic Crisis–One White Hat's Perspective

Newport, Rhode Island. Liberty had gone down at 1600 Hours. (4 PM). It was a Thursday Afternoon. It was now 1630 and I sort-of casually went below, got out my "Dress-Blue-Bravo" Uniform and got ready to go ashore. There was no rush. I was looking forward to a good dinner at my favorite Italian Cafe followed by a movie. The movie didn't start until 7:20, so there was no rush.

I had just squared away my Dixie Cup (white-Hat) and started for the ladder to the Weather Deck. The "word" over the 1MC system was terse, and to the point. "All Liberty Is Cancelled! Make preparations for getting under way!" Ha, Ha! This was funny, who turned that idiot loose on the "Squawk-Box" anyway?

Well, it was not an idiot. Close to it though, it was the XO. Now, the job was to get our men back on board who had gone on Liberty at 1600. I found Lieutenant Guthrie and asked him what was happening. I was even hoping that I could get a little Liberty. The good Lieutenant was silent. His only comment was that we would be at sea in two hours. He was upset, his wife was expecting him home, and he couldn't even phone her and let her know that he wouldn't be home.

It still seemed like a joke! A cruel joke, to be sure, but a joke nonetheless. As we spoke, The Shore Patrol was gathering up Ship's Company from every dive and bar in town. At 1800 Hours we went to Quarters. If I expected information about our trip I was mistaken. They were just counting noses to see who wasn't there. There were still men missing. We went to Stations for Leaving Port at 1830 Hours. We were still short some of our crew. Then, we cast off and went to mid-channel.

Dyess was going with us, and she was having trouble getting steam on her boilers. They brought the rest of our crew aboard by launch while we were in the channel. One man was still missing-a kid named Davis.

By 2000 hours, Dyess joined us, and we started down Narraganset Bay. She had enough steam to move, but little more. There were still problems. It was a long sea detail. Rumors abounded - Vietnam? A Russian Attack on America?

We found out when well at sea that there was a crisis in someplace called the Dominican Republic. Basilone, Forrest Royal, A.H. Fox, the whole squadron had pulled an Emergency Sortie and for what? Who had ever heard of the place anyway? If the Russians wanted it, let them have blasted country. There was no reason to spoil a good evening of Liberty.

Alas, the U.S. Navy didn't feel that way. 25 year old Destroyers were going in Harm's Way. Bat Blind Dyess, unsteady Fox, and Fiske with her doubtful fire brick. Our side would need lots of luck.

As for Davis - our missing sailor? Uncle Sam flew him down to Charleston to be brought aboard by a launch. Where was he? Well? That is a subject we can't get into.
Jerry Moseley YN3 1963-1966

Six Day War Prequel

I was on watch as we were waiting to transit and some US embassy official or whatever he was came aboard and needed to get a message sent out to POTUS and everyone else in command at the Pentagon that something was about to HAPPEN SOON!

I was unable to get up a phone link so tried finding "CW" link. Wished I had called for help from Mallory (he was much better with the key). But I finally got up with a Navy Com Center in Turkey and got message sent. In other words......The 6 day war was starting!

We then started transit of the Suez and a LOVELY 2-3 months in the Red Sea. Beard growing contests, fishing contests and any other contest we could think of.

OH BTW.....WATER RATIONS. PHEW!

All this time we under Radar from both sides. KINDA SHAKEY!
Terry Oldham, RM2 1966-1968

'First Contact'

I was back by the scuttlebutt by the Ship's Store one afternoon shortly after being transferred to the ET Gang, when a young Ensign came though the aft hatch. He looked like a deer in the headlights.

He asked me, "Where's the wardroom?" In a moment of unthinking brazenness, I pointed forward and said, "It's on the pointy end of the boat, Sir. Go that way 'til you run into a door. You can't miss it."

Later I thought maybe I was out of line and decided to stay clear of the young Ensign. The next morning at quarters in CIC, I found out just how difficult that would be when he introduced himself as our new OI Division boss. I tried to hide behind radar repeaters and stay out of sight. Thankfully, he didn't remember me. I am still occasionally in contact with that Ensign, now Captain Dale Paquette, USN Retired.

During the '68 Med Cruise, Reserve Sailors were offered an early out; after an informal meeting on the mess deck, most of the guys turned it down until we returned to Newport in February of '69. I never regretted that decision and hope my shipmates didn't either.
Jim "Ace" Melvin ETN2 Sept. 1967-Feb 1969

'The Sacrifice of Sailors Thanks to BMC Cornell'

Rough seas-20 to 30 foot swells in the North Atlantic. The Motor Whale Boat was breaking loose from the davits so our good chief orders the Boatswain's Mate petty officers to secure it. BM2 Raymond Jewett and BM3 David Enwright tied canvas belts around their waists while I fed the line out. I had 3-4 Seamen holding on the line behind me including SN Donald Spaith. As soon as Jewett and Enwright stepped out on the deck a wave washed them down the passageway pulling me out also. Thankfully the operation was aborted and everyone was safe.
Mike Walsh BM3 1970-71

'Suddenly'

We were at the crossover section of the Suez Canal. A HOT place even on a cool day. The command was going to have a 'fantail bar-b-que'. It was generally a pretty lazy – did I mention HOT – day. Bar-b-que drums were set up, someone with a line out trying to catch FISH for the Grill!!!! Crew members offering thoughts - some not printable - other encouraging. Some more or less supporting the fisherperson to catch a BIG ONE!!!

SUDDENLY

A Hit!!!! Cheers went up from the observers and the HOPEFFUL!!!!! Then we waited, wondering what gastronomic delicacy would come forth from the sea!! The fisherperson with a few stalwart helpers fought the beast on the other end with great effort and tenacity!!! Several minutes passed, the fisherperson heaving mightily as feet, nay, yards of line piled up on the deck around him. Finally, after a long hard fought battle, out of the sea flew the big PRIZE of the DAY!!!

A pair of dungaree trousers someone on some ship had lost when they tried to drag them clean behind the ship. The fish bar-b-que was a bust but the steaks we had were really DELICIOUS!!!!
Anonymous

'Shore Patrol Duty (?)'

Malaga was a great liberty port on the Spanish Costa del Sol. The Fiske operated with 3 section duty. Not one to enjoy remaining onboard every third day I always volunteered for Shore Patrol duty.

Terremolinas is a resort town about 8 miles down the coast from Malaga. I was fortunate enough to draw shore patrol duty one evening and served my watch with QM2 Strum from the USS Ellison. The town of Terremolinas was a great host to the sailors from the Fiske, Ellison and Independence.

Faithfully executing our shore patrol duties Petty Office Strum and I visited every bar and disco in town. Being a welcoming people the local residents offered us a drink at each establishment we visited. Needless to say by the time our watch was over we were feeling no pain.

Our last stop on patrol was an establishment called the Boga Boga Club, a disco and the most happening place in town. Most of our crew ended their evening there. Petty Officer Strum and I parted way when I poured him into a taxi and sent him back to his ship. I removed my shore patrol arm band, duty belt and nightstick and joined the Fiske crew for the rest of the evening just to be sure that all remained safe. I returned to the ship about 6:00am.

Legend has it that upon his arrival at the Ellison Petty Officer Strum was unable to exit the taxi and required assistance from the Quarterdeck watch. Petty Officer Strum was placed on report and the legal officer from the Ellison requested an affidavit from me questioning our actions that evening.

My response was the Petty Officer Strum conducted himself in accordance with the finest traditions of the US Navy. I explained that we had only one beer and that was with dinner. I went on to suggest that it must have been something that he ate that caused his symptoms.

The charges against Petty Offer Strum were either dropped or he was found not guilty at Captain's Mast. At our next liberty port Petty Officer Strum contacted me and we celebrated his exoneration, once again upholding the finest traditions of the Navy.
David Fitzgerald QM2 1973-76

'Old Age & Treachery Win – Again!'

Fiske never missed an operational commitment and was frequently scheduled to fill holes created by the no-loads in Philadelphia as well as the "ACDU" [Active Duty] Navy. During my tour of some two-and-a-half years, we were out of homeport well over

50% of the time - not bad for a ship that was viewed by the "real fleet" as a non-steamer.

The Fiske, as a part of ResDesRon 30, was often tasked with providing the 'Opposing Force' for exercises held by the 'Regular Navy'. One such exercise was conducted with the USS Virginia (CGN 38) acting as 'Blue Force' commander on a cruise toward Vieques Island. As part of the 'Red Force' Fiske was to disrupt, harass and – if possible – attack the 'Blue Force'

Captain Stephen L. Turner and I used a variety of tactics such as using total EMCON save for surface search radar, voice communications (CH 16) as necessary, carefully prepared our MOVEREPS, perfected our times of filing reports and staying pretty close to the beach. Along the way we did a lot of damage as we fired upon the unsuspecting 'Blue Force' with HARPOON and other weaponry allotted for gaming purposes.

We popped into the Caribbean through Mona Passage, caught up with the Virginia Group and took station during the mid-watch. The next morning we announced our presence with, "Good morning, Commodore! This is the good ship FISKE steaming in Station A-2. We just did what we weren't supposed to be able to do. Have a nice day! Out!"

No plaudits that I remember as the "greyhound of the sea"... er ... "junkyard dog" escaped detection and mysteriously appeared as a part of the formation. I would have liked to have attended the debrief onboard the Virginia. I wish that we had had the balls to put that one out over PRITAC when we actually joined up during the midwatch.
Marshall Lundberg LCDR, XO 1977-1980

Marshall Lundberg, LCDR Executive Officer 1977-1980

'Music & Vietnam – Part I'

Around the beginning of 1965, the Fiske and crew were off to Vietnam to engage in the war. When we arrived in the South China Seas we were assigned to patrol and escort the convoys up the coast of Vietnam.

Also, was assigned emergency sea rescue for aircraft carrier pilots. Also included was Gun Fire Support for a number of weeks. The Fiske was making its presence known with her 5" guns. The shelling was pretty intense on some occasions. So much so that we had to go back to Subic Bay to have our 5 inch guns recalibrated.

While we were in port getting of guns refurbished, some of my shipmates - Amato SN (singer); Burdge, SMSN, (drums); Bradbury BMSN, (singer); Rick, FTG3 and myself (guitar) formed the band, "The

Frisky Fiske's". On liberty, we often headed into town (Olongapo, Philippines).

We would play for our own amusement - and also free drinks - in some of the local bars. THE SPORTSMAN CLUB, THE GHESHIA HOUSE, THE WHITE HAT, GEMINI 2, PAULINES were a few of our favorites.

One night while we were jamming, my guitar string snapped. One of the employees at the bar offered me a lift to find a new guitar string. I packed up my guitar and followed him out to his vehicle. To my surprise it wasn't a car or jeepney cab. It was a motor bike. I had never rode as a passenger on a motor bike before. Especially while carrying an electric guitar. I was a wreck, carrying my guitar and case in one hand while hanging on with the other. That was the only time and the last time I would ever be a passenger on any type of motor bike or motor cycle. I survived my wild ride and bought a new set of strings.

The "Frisky Fiske's" played at a number of places whenever and wherever we could but, one of my favorite places was the President Hotel in Kowloon, China. We ferried from Hong Kong to Kowloon and would play at the hotel. We had a great time there.
Larry Altero ETN3 1964-66

'Music & Vietnam – Part II'

Another time, while spending my R & R in Tokyo, Japan, I bought an acoustic guitar and some Japanese sheet music. I was playing solo for free drinks at this time in a bar for a great group of Japanese patrons.

I have found that no matter where in the world you are, music is a universal language. It was always fun and appreciated whenever we played on the Fiske for our shipmates.

The crew loved good old American Rhythm and Blues, especially the way Ray Bradbury would belt them out those oldies. Whenever I hear Ray Charles singing, "Crying Time" I would reflect *back to those memorable days aboard the USS Fiske DD-842. She was a great ship with a great crew of sailors.*

At our 2015 Fiske Reunion, I had the opportunity to introduce my wife to some of the men that I served with on the Fiske. I also had the honor and privilege of meeting other men and women who served aboard the Fiske during other years.

Thanks Gil for challenging me to write about some of my experiences during my tour aboard the Fiske. As you say," If you don't write about it, it never happened".
Larry Altero ETN3 1964-66

Death Grip

We were high-lining 5" VT shells from an ammo ship when we did the break away. I was still carrying a shell as we sped up. I knew that the Captain was going to put the wheel hard over causing a 'greenie' to wash down the (main) deck. I being an old hand ducked into a manhole to wait for us to complete the turn and then to continue to the Aft 5" Magazine. As I turned around one of the new kids is coming down the deck – 110 lbs. soaking wet but he was still dry. The expected wave swept him off his feet landing him flat on his back. He had a death grip on that shell. As I helped him to his feet I didn't know eyes could get that big!
Frank Connell EN3 1971-1972

'Dedication'

After the Fiske had returned home to Newport, 'Stew' (Jim Stewart) was transferred to the separation barracks for his final physical. Jim wrote... "While there, the Weapons Officer, LT. A. L. Cahill., visited me; 'Stewart he said, we've been hit with an NWAI (Nuclear Weapons Acceptance Inspection) - please come back on board and help us. I don't have anyone to operate the ASROC Station

computer the way you can'. So, I did. And oh yeah ... the Fiske passed the NWAI!"
John Naldratt STG3 1966-68

Editor's note: This is a prime example of the commitment and cohesiveness of Fiske sailors and Destroyermen in general. GMM3 Stewart had been transferred off the ship prior to his release from active duty and volunteered to aid his shipmates to pass a readiness inspection.

Doing it the Right Way

One day in '64 or '65 while I was on the bridge as Bosun's Mate of the Watch, my only duties were to assign sailors to various jobs and pipe messages over the 1MC.

After a while a sailor came up to the bridge and said he wanted to speak to the OOD. I looked at the OOD, who saw what was going on, and nodded his head, that he would talk to this sailor.

The sailor saluted the OOD and said he wanted to speak to the Captain. Aboard a navy vessel, one does not talk to the captain; at least I never saw this done.

The officer looked at the Captain, who was sitting in his seat, looking out over the ocean, and the Captain nodded his head that he would talk to this sailor.

The sailor saluted the Captain, and showed him his freshly painted red left arm. The sailor said that his division officer made him do it because he did not know the difference between port and starboard.

The sailor said that this was against the UCMJ and was not allowed. You could almost see smoke coming from the Captain's collar as he said to me "get [name redacted] here now!"

Whatever happened to that division officer I do not know.
Anonymous

'Char Shine'

Char Shine to the uninitiated is Moonshine that has been filtered through charcoal. The resultant libation is much smoother than the run of the mill stuff. We became acquainted with the subtle differences when John Clifford Towe ETR3 (formerly a BTFR but that is another story) returned from leave after our '63 Med Cruise.

He came into the ET Shack with his AWOL bag and set it on the bench. The bag softly clanked. He opened the bag and, after ensuring the shop door was closed, lifted 2 quart and 2 pint mason jars out of the bag.

Now JC's hometown was Old Hickory, TN and he was well versed on the cottage industry practiced in that area. This Moonshine was his present to the ET Gang. We each had a drink of the regular stuff and it was definitely raw and powerful. Then JC offered us a small glass of the better product. Let me tell you I have since drank single malt scotch that wasn't as smooth as that char shine.

We husbanded those 2 pint bottles for quite a while, quietly sitting in the ET Shack in the evenings listening to Country music.
Gil Beyer ETR3 1960-63

'Numbers'

One thing about being underway, it is boring. We were going somewhere after leaving someplace else and aside from normal shipboard routine we weren't doing much. At this time ET's (Electronics Technicians) were not standing regular watches – we were 'On Call' 24/7.

Between the evening meal and Taps we usually sat around the ET Shop and tried to find something interesting to listen to on the radio with English voices. When you are in the Med the choices were limited. We had BBC International, the Voice of America and Radio Moscow. These three could be counted on to provide hours of entertainment for the very bored.

One night we heard a story on the BBC about a tribe in sub-Saharan Africa whose number system consisted of only 1 and 2. Anything more than two was 'many'. Chas Slocum and I considered that to be totally unacceptable. One had to be able to better define the number of enemies one was facing. If for no other reason than how many re-enforcements one requested.

It might have been that we were very tired but we decided to expand this number system. We would use the 1, 2 and 'many' but added 'lots' and 'bunches'. 'Lots' was defined as 'many²' and 'bunches' was 'lots²'. This seemed to work for any number above two.

Over the years this numbering system has served me quite adequately under multiple situations.
Gil Beyer ETR3 1960-63

Afterword
Author's/Editor's Comments

Thus ends the story of the USS *Fiske,* a ship that served honorably and well from 1945 through 1998, a total of almost 54 years. She was one of many of her Class but unique in the minds of all those that served onboard her.

I won't say that all my time onboard *Fiske* was all 'Beer & Skittles' but she was my first ship and many of the shipmates that were onboard with me in the early 1960's continue to be some of my best friends all of these many years later.

My greatest single regret is that I have so very little to add to my stock of "Fiske Tales" for the first decade of her life. It seems we started this project too late. Falling back on the oft quoted Tom Clancy, "If it isn't written down it never happened."

Any errors found, mistakes made in time and/or place are mine alone. As I was finalizing this revision/update I realized that this isn't really a history. This is in essence a scrapbook. A scrapbook put together by many people over many years.

It is hoped that this 'scrapbook' will bring everyone that ever served on a 'Tin Can' in the Cold War Era memories – both good and bad – and encourage them to tell their own stories to those they love.

To those that never had the honor of serving it is our hope they get some small idea of all the sacrifices that are made daily in your behalf and just what the ordinary and routine heroism of 'just doing our jobs' entails.

To all that served, their families and friends it is my fondest wish that some of these 'tales' bring back thoughts of an era long gone. I wish the very best always to all with fair winds and following seas.
G. E. Beyer USN retired

Contributors to 'Tin Can' and 'Fiske Tales' include the following:

Armin Longoria ETNSN/Bill Loerning BMSN/Bill Davis PNSN
Charlie Thompson QM2/Daniel Gilroy SM3
David F. Stone SN1c/David Taylor LT USNR
Dennis Stead EM3/Dick Pettingill DK3/Douglas Bracken
Edward Barncord/Eugene Peloquin Ens/Lt(jg)/ Frank Connell EN2
Frank Nicastro SOG3/George Hilt ETR3/George Hodulik BT2
George W. Post Ens/Lt(jg)/Gil Beyer ETR3/Iain Hines
Jerry MoseleyYN3/Jim Hanner RD2/Jim Melvin ETN2
Jim Stewart GMM3/Jim Taylor FTG/John Naldrett STG3
Herb Foy FCT3/Jeff Kovite SOG2/Jerry Hanson IC3
Jerry Moseley YN3/ John Degnan Jr/SOG3/John Frazer EMCS
Lee Dowling SM3/Leyland East EN3/Lou Palermo FT2
Marshall Lundberg CDR/Mike Petro SK3/Mike Walsh BM3
Millard Wagnon FTSN/Milt Kramer/Paul ShipeTM3
Robert Johnson/Sandie Siciliano ETN2/Terry Oldham RM2
Warren D. LaVille HM3/William Chandler RDM1
William Loening BMSN/W. C. S. 'Skip' Mays Ens/Ltjg

Reference Sources & Acknowledgements

Navy History & Heritage Command
Washington Navy Yard
Washington, DC

U. S. Navy Destroyers of World War II
John C. Reilly Jr.
Blandford Press 1983

The U. S. Navy, an Illustrated History
Nathan Miller
American Heritage Publishing Co., 1977

Jane's Fighting Ships 1969-1970 & 1997-1998
Jane's Yearbooks

Jane's American Fighting Ships of the 20th Century
Edited & Foreword by Captain John Moore, R.N.
Mallard Press 1991

Navy Department
Naval History Division
Washington Navy Yard

Combat Fleets of the World 1986/87
Naval Institute Press
Annapolis, MD

Navy Historical Center
Operational Archives (War Reports)
Washington Navy Yard

Wikipedia – World-Wide-Web accessible Encyclopedia

The USS Fiske (DE 143) in World War II:
Documents and Photographs
E. Andrew Wilde Jr., Editor

War in Manila Bay by Rear Admiral B. A. Fiske

Blood on the Sea
American Destroyers Lost in World War II
Robert Sinclair Parkin

Naval History & Heritage Command
Washington Naval Yard, DC

Charlotte Sun Port Charlotte, FL

Society of Ship Sponsors of US Navy

USS *Fiske* Cruise Books
1950, 1953, 1961, 1963, 1966, 1967 and 1973

Boston Globe, November 2008, Obituary of Oliver F. Ames

Dictionary of U.S. Navy Ships
Vol. II 1963

Naval Officer's Guide – 1943
Arthur A. Ageton

Plus a host of unnamed individuals at the Navy History & Heritage Command, The National Archives, The Tin Can Sailor Association, newspaper archivists from across the country, family members of former *Fiske* officers and crew.

I must give credit to my proofreaders, my wife Sherry and daughter Jana Beyer-Kelley, for their eagle-eyed efforts to keep me grammatically correct and structurally cohesive.

Without the entire team's efforts this work simply could not have been accomplished. It is our hope that we have given life to the *Fiske* and to an era that has passed.

Commanding Officers
Special Thanks to Wolfgang Hechler & Ron Reeves

(Commissioned as DD Nov 1945)
CDR Charles Hubert Smith - Nov 1945 - 1947 (Later RADM)
CDR Robert Irving Olsen - Jun 1947 – Feb 1948(?)
CDR David F. Stone - Feb 1948(?) – Feb 1949
CDR Newell Edward Thomas - Feb 1949 - Mar 1950
CDR John Enoch Pond Jr. - Mar 1950 - Sep 1951
CDR Carl R. Dwyer - Sep 1951- Apr 1952

(Decommissioned as DD Apr 1 1952 –Recommisioned as
DDR Nov 25 1952)
CDR Powell Prestridge Vail Jr. - Nov 1952 - Oct 1954
CDR James Blaine Sweeny - Jun 1954 – Oct 1956
CDR Cyril G. Griffin - Oct 1956 - Sep 1958
CDR John B. Hough - Sep 1958 - Jul 1960
CDR Clifford E. Hunter - Jul 1960 - Apr 1962
CDR Cyrus H. Butt III - Apr 1962 – Oct 1964

(Decommissioned as DDR Feb 1964 & Recommisioned
as DD Dec 1964
CDR John Robert Ewing - Oct 1964 – Apr 1966
CDR William McKinley – Apr 1966 – Nov 1967
CDR James Sylvester Brunson - Nov 1967 - Jul 11 1969
CDR Eugene Kirtley Walling - Jul 11 1969 – April 30 1971
CDR William R. Pettyjohn - April 1971 – August 1972
CDR Roger D. Grady - Aug 1972 - Mar 1974

Transferred to Naval Reserve Fleet (DesRon 28 & 30)
1973
CDR John F. Fitzgerald - Mar 1974 - Apr 1976

CDR William Raymond Pressler Jr. - Apr 1976 - Dec 1977
CDR John R. Dalrymple Jr. - Dec 1977 - Jan 1978 (later
RADM)
CDR Steven Lloyd Turner - Jan 1978 - Jun 1980

Transferred to the Turkish Navy in June 1980

- To the best of my knowledge CDR Cyrus H Butt III was the only officer to serve onboard the Fiske as a Department Head, Executive Officer and Commanding Officer

Addenda

During the course of her thirty-five year career with the U. S. Navy the *Fiske* received seven awards that have been verified. They are, in order of precedence, the following:

Navy Expeditionary - Caribbean Patrol – '61-'62
(Second award – Dominican Republic 1965)

Navy Occupation - Mediterranean - '46 – '48

National Defense - Service after December 1960

Korean Service (with 2 Battle stars) - Korean waters
Feb-May'51

Armed Forces Expeditionary- Cuban Quarantine 1962

Vietnam Service - Vietnamese waters 1966.

Vietnamese Gallantry Cross 1966

Anyone that served onboard during the periods above should have on their DD-214 the appropriate award(s) enumerated. Recent directives from the Veterans Administration encourage all veterans to proudly wear their ribbons at Memorial Day, 4th of July and Veterans Day events. The VA website has links where DD-214's can be corrected and/or verified; lost awards replaced; and other services for veterans in resolving many other questions.

About the Author

Gilbert E Beyer is a retired Navy veteran having served on active duty from October 1959 until June 1980. Serving aboard 2 Destroyers – USS Fiske (DDR 842) and USS Sampson (DDG 10), the Submarine Tenders USS Holland (AS 32), USS Canopus (AS 34), ComSubRon 16 Staff, USS Coronado [Plank Owner] (LPD 11), Naval Radio Station (T) Cutler, ME and Naval Auxiliary Air Station, South Weymouth, MA

While at NRT Cutler, ME he completed his BS in Education at the University of Maine-Machias with a double major – Science and History – graduating magna cum laude while serving as the Station Maintenance Chief.

He is the father of three daughters – Cyndi, Danielle and Jana – whose mother, his wife Karen, died in 2003.

After his Navy retirement in 1980 he moved his wife and family to North Idaho and has lived there ever since. Often remarking that after almost 40 years in Idaho he is close to making up his mind if he will stay in Idaho.

Since moving to Idaho he worked as a substitute teacher, Rural Route Mail substitute delivery driver, two-way communications repair tech, Eligibility Examiner for Food Stamps with Idaho Health & Welfare [which he claims is the worst job he ever held], sold lumber & building materials and repaired audio amplifiers for local musicians until his second retirement in 2003.

He is an active volunteer within the community, having served as a Library Trustee almost without a break from the mid-90s until 2019.

He remarried in 2010 to Sherry, who he attended high school with. They spend winters in the Yucatan of Mexico. In his spare time he reads historical fiction/non-fiction and thrillers, restored a 1960 Austin Healey Sprite and is currently working on a 1972 MGB Roadster and is a member of the USS Fiske (DD/DDR 842) Association and the Naval Order of the United States-NW chapter.